A Realist Philosophy of Soc

This introduction to the philosophy of social science provides an original conception of the task and nature of social inquiry. Peter Manicas discusses the role of causality seen in the physical sciences and offers a reassessment of the problem of explanation from a realist perspective. He argues that the fundamental goal of theory in both the natural and social sciences is not, contrary to widespread opinion, prediction and control, or the explanation of events (including behavior). Instead, theory aims to provide an understanding of the processes which, together, produce the contingent outcomes of experience. Offering a host of concrete illustrations and examples of critical ideas and issues, this accessible book will be of interest to students of the philosophy of social science, and social scientists from a range of disciplines.

PETER T. MANICAS is Director of Interdisciplinary Studies at the University of Hawai'i at Mānoa.

A Realist Philosophy of Social Science

Explanation and Understanding

Peter T. Manicas

CAMBRIDGE
UNIVERSITY PRESS

CAMBRIDGE UNIVERSITY PRESS
Cambridge, New York, Melbourne, Madrid, Cape Town, Singapore, São Paulo

Cambridge University Press
The Edinburgh Building, Cambridge CB2 2RU, UK

Published in the United States of America by Cambridge University Press, New York

www.cambridge.org
Information on this title: www.cambridge.org/9780521678582

© Peter T. Manicas 2006

First published 2006

Printed in the United Kingdom at the University Press, Cambridge

A catalogue record for this book is available from the British Library

ISBN-13 978-0-521-86140-3 hardback
ISBN-10 0-521-86140-3 hardback

ISBN-13 978-0-521-67858-2 paperback
ISBN-10 0-521-67858-7 paperback

To my wife

Contents

Acknowledgements

The ideas in this volume have been germinating for some time. In that time, I have accrued many debts. My education in the social sciences began perhaps with my PhD mentor at Buffalo, Marvin Farber, who, along with Bill Parry, started me on the path I pursue in this book. Farber also let me write a dissertation in the Philosophy Department which would not have been possible at most universities. My instruction in history and the social sciences was advanced when I became Director of the Program in Contemporary Civilization at Queens, a genuinely inter-disciplinary program required of all students. While Farber and Parry had convinced me that an understanding of social science was essential – we read Dewey's *Logic* along with Schütz and standard works in the philosophy of science – Rom Harré and Paul Secord, authors of the important (if for me, mis-titled) volume, *The Explanation of Social Behavior* (1973) were critical in disabusing me of my lingering and unacknowledged logical empiricism. Paul and I team-taught when we were both members of the Queens College faculty, but I remember well my failure to see the connection between the main messages of their book and what I had brought from Buffalo. Some of these ideas were tried out at Queens College at the Monday lunch group, a remarkable assembly of social scientists – too many to list here – who met regularly, lunched, heard papers and had marvelous discussions. I also regularly team-taught with many of this group in an undergraduate social science honors course – a luxury of inefficiency not much tolerated these days. The furious debates between the members of that floating group – Tito Gerassi, Ray Franklin, Carl Riskin, Mike Harrington, Bill Tabb, Paul Avrich, Mike Wreszin, Saul Resnick, Mike Brown, Burton Zweibach and Lenny Markowitz to name only a few – were remarkable learning experiences, even if we sometimes terrified the undergraduates with our passion. The *Journal for the Theory of Social Behavior*, initiated by Harré and Secord, but edited with style and insight for the past twenty years by Charles Smith, not only provided opportunity for me to test some of these ideas but was where I was introduced to the work of Roy Bhaskar. His presence, along with that of Rom

Harré, was large in my *History and Philosophy of the Social Sciences,* my first major attempt to set out what was amiss in our understanding of the social sciences.

I have been lucky also to have held two posts at the University of Hawai'i at Mānoa. After taking an early retirement at Queens, I became a member of the Sociology Department and Director of Interdisciplinary Studies at Hawai'i. My two long-standing colleagues in that wonderful unit, Jaishree Odin and Emanuel Drechsel, both powerful interdisciplinary thinkers, have been a constant source of knowledge and support. Prior to that I had taught off and on in the Department of Political Science, where I picked up some further debts, but especially to my good friend Manfred Henningsen. Each of these roles has been a delight. They certainly enabled me to continue my interdisciplinary interests. My large lecture section in sociology 100 was meant to enlarge the idea of introductory social science. While everyone talks about cultivating "the sociological imagination," it is hard to see how one can do this with the awful standard disciplinary textbooks and multiple choice exams. Teaching the sequence of required courses in sociological theory to both graduates and undergraduates forced me to re-think ideas that once seemed clear to me. I am indebted also to my close colleague and friend in the Sociology Department, Herb Barringer.

Most of my debts remain unacknowledged, but I must mention, at least, those who have read and made suggestions on the present work. In addition to some of those already mentioned, these include: Sam Pooley, Gregory Maskarinec and Manfred Steger.

Introduction

This volume reassesses the problem of explanation in social science from what remains a marginalized, realist perspective. Because the problem of explanation is central to inquiry in social science, the volume also provides a systematic philosophy of social science. It begins with the idea that the fundamental goal of theory in both the natural and social sciences is not, contrary to widespread opinion, prediction and control, or the explanation of events (including "behavior"). Rather, more modestly, theory (at least in one of its clear senses) aims to provide an understanding of the processes which jointly produce the contingent outcomes of experience. We understand why the planets move in ellipses, why materials burn, and why salt dissolves in water (if and when it does) when we have a physical theory that provides a causal mechanism. By providing the principles detailing the nature of molecules, the atomic structure of salt and water, the principles of their action, and so on, we can understand combustion and solubility – and other chemical processes. Indeed, while the theoretical work of physical scientists often begins with the effort to understand patterns, they are not interested in, nor generally capable of, providing either "explanations" or "predictions" of particular events. For example, the trajectory of a boulder splintering as it rolls down a hill is fully understood in terms of physical principles, but neither the trajectory nor the final positions of the splintered parts can be explained or predicted. But an adequate understanding of the outcome is easily available. The foregoing does not seem either surprising or novel. But, for good historical reasons, reigning assumptions both in the philosophy of social science and in much current social scientific practice violate what thus seems commonsensical.

It seems hardly deniable that understanding such natural processes as splintering, oxidizing, dissolving, fertilizing and dying requires one to understand the causal mechanisms at work – physical, chemical and biological, some available in direct experience, some not. No one will ever see a photon but they are among the important non-observables posited in a physical theory that enables us to understand a range of phenomena.

1

The argument thus joins "realist" criticisms of empiricist conceptions of theory and Humean notions of causality. Once this is in place, it is easy to see why fairly long-standing objections to both the dominant view of theory and the still dominant covering law model of explanation are fatal.

But by developing the ideas of agents as causes and of social mechanisms as agent-generated causal mechanisms, the book extends, in a novel way, the argument to the social sciences. Here we join old debates over so-called "methodological individualism," and the critical role of hermeneutics, and recent debates in the philosophy of social science regarding the ontology of society as provoked by Giddens, Bhaskar, Bourdieu and others. Thus, the ontological status of "social structure" is clarified and resolved. Understanding in social science is achieved when, as in the physical sciences, we have a causal mechanism, but unlike the physical sciences, minded persons working with materials at hand will be constitutive of social causal mechanisms.

Because these themes are interconnected, the volume introduces a philosophy, or meta-theory, for social science. Uncritically influenced by long outdated doctrines in the philosophy of science, the volume argues that, among both philosophers and social scientists, there remains a widespread set of misconceptions about the tasks and limits of social science. We need to understand that there are important differences between the scientific study of nature and the scientific study of society, but we need first to be clear about the nature and goals of science more generally. By drawing on and integrating recent developments in the philosophy of science, this volume aims to do this.

The structure of the argument is as follows: Chapter 1, "Explanation and understanding," begins with a close examination of the so-called "Deductive-Nomological" (D-N) or "covering law" model of explanation. It is of considerable interest to note that while the critical literature of this model is now of long standing, and that while many writers, both in philosophy and the social sciences, have rejected the *epistemology* of empiricist ("positivist") theory of science, many of these same writers fail to see that a powerful alternative to the D-N model of explanation is available. Once it is shown that understanding is the primary goal of the sciences, the whole edifice of science's empiricist philosophy crumbles – from its metaphysically implausible event ontology, including its contra-empirical constant conjunction conception of causality, to its conception of theory. We show then that understanding requires appeal to causal mechanisms properly conceived as productive powers. The chapter provides both illustration and argument for these ideas.

Chapter 2, "Theory, experiment and the metaphysics of Laplace," argues against what is sometimes termed "deductivism," the idea that theories in the physical sciences can be fully expressed as a deductive system, with axioms and deductions therefrom. Rather, following the too often neglected work of Rom Harré (1970), it is argued that theories identify how "things" – molecules and atoms, for example – are structured, and how they interact. Theories, of course, are representations, but they are meant to represent reality, as it is in-itself. We look then at anti-realist criticisms of this view of theory, provide an account of experiment as it actually functions in science, and offer a post-positivist (post-Kuhnian) account of theory acceptance. The chapter concludes with a criticism of the Laplacean metaphysics assumed by empiricist theories of science. In our world, most events – birth, growth, rain, fires, earthquakes, depressions, revolutions – are the products of a complex nexus of *causes of many different kinds*, conjunctively at work. Indeed, it is for this reason that the natural sciences, instead of seeking to explain concrete events, more modestly seek to understand the mechanisms and processes of nature. This means that while everything is caused, there is radical contingency in both natural and human history. The implications of this are critical for a human science, as Chapter 3 shows.

On the basis of the foregoing account of science, Chapter 3, "Explanation and understanding in the social sciences," offers a philosophy of social science, making clear the critical points of difference in the subject matter of the natural and social world and the implications for inquiry. After setting out and rejecting, by way of summary, the key prevailing assumptions regarding science, an account of "persons" is developed. The view of causality already set out is critical here. Once we notice that a host of causal mechanisms, biological, psychological and social, are epigenetically implicated in the constitution of a human being – and of their concrete actions – we can see that "nature" and "nurture" are inextricably involved and that, in consequence, there is no reason to believe that any one science, psychological or social, could improve on the way we ordinarily explain and predict behavior. As with the natural sciences, the task of the social sciences is understanding how social mechanisms "structure," but do not determine, outcomes. We turn then to an account of how this is to be conceived, drawing on the key distinction between "brute facts," or facts about features of the world that exist independently of us, and "institutional facts," or facts about features of the world which require human institutions for their existence (Searle, 1995). The usual "subjective / objective" dichotomy is fruitfully undermined. Following Giddens (1984), then, social structure is conceptualized as "real," incarnate in the activities of persons, but, accordingly, having no independent existence. If so, versus stronger forms of the idea of social structure, it cannot, like a magnetic field, for example, be causal.

Chapter 4, "Agents and generative social mechanisms," applies the causal mechanism analogy to physical science. In the physical sciences, regression to more fundamental mechanisms is sometimes possible. So quantum theory offers a generative mechanism of processes in molecular chemistry. But in social science, since persons are the critical causes of everything that occurs in the social world, the generative mechanisms are the actions of persons "working with materials at hand," and no further reduction is either possible or necessary. Drawing on the argument of agent / structure duality, a systematic account of the construction of models of social mechanisms is offered. The chapter offers a range of illustrative examples drawn from writers including Marx, Willis, Goffman, Tilly, Ogbu, Burawoy and others. For example, following Willis, a social mechanism can be theorized which gives us an understanding of why working-class kids get working-class jobs. Typically this involves identifying their place in society, their beliefs about their "world" – some true and some false – typical behavior predicated on these beliefs, and the mostly unintended consequences of this behavior. The argument shows that an ethnographic (and hermeneutic) moment is essential to grasping a social mechanism, but as Weber had long since noted, it was but the first step in social scientific inquiry. That is, while we need to understand the social world as its members understand it, we need to go beyond this and to consider the adequacy of their understanding of their world. Since social process is the product of our activity, and since members may well *mis*understand their world, social science is potentially emancipatory.

Chapter 5, "Social science and history," is very much influenced by the work of Max Weber. It looks critically at the question of history and its relation to sociology, beginning with the century-old debate over the distinction between two kinds of science, "nomothetic" and "idiographic," and the attending argument that explanation in the nomothetic sciences proceeds by appeal to "general laws," while explanation in the human sciences requires *verstehen* and a narrative rhetorical form. The idea of a historical sociology gives us direct access to current versions of the pertinent issues, including the role of comparative analysis in identifying causes. Disagreements over the nature of a historical sociology can be resolved with a proper understanding of the nature and goals of social science. Briefly, if the goal is understanding, for example, why working-class kids get working-class jobs (Willis) or why in "total institutions" (Goffman) outcomes are inconsistent with their explicit goals, one does not require history, even if, as Weber insisted, our interest remains the historically concrete. That is, unlike the natural sciences where there are "general theories" of generative mechanisms, in the social sciences, the generative social mechanisms are always historically situated. Thus, while the generative mechanisms of, for example, oxidization are the same everywhere, the mechanisms that explain why working-class kids get working-class jobs need to be concretely theorized. Social science very often goes beyond the effort to understand a social process. Unlike the "abstract" natural sciences, it seeks to explain concrete events and episodes, for example, the collapse of a regime, a depression, a dramatic rise in divorces. To achieve this goal, in addition to an understanding of the pertinent concrete generative mechanisms, one *also* needs history – as Weber rightly contended. In these cases, explanation takes the form of a narrative that identifies the critical social mechanisms and links them sequentially with the contingent but causally pertinent acts of persons.

Chapter 6 looks critically at one of the most influential and thoroughly theorized social mechanisms in the social scientific literature: the market model of neo-classical economics. This tradition was quite correct in what it sought to do, and its difficulties do not stem from its attempt to offer explanations in terms of actors. The problem is not that markets are not social mechanisms which can give us an understanding of outcomes by appeal to the actions of persons – the bogey of methodological individualism – but that the basic model makes assumptions about explanation, and very strong assumptions about the actors, their conditions and their behavior, which simply are not sustained, except perhaps in the remotest of cases. Mainstream neo-classical theory accepts the covering law model of explanation and a deductivist conception of theory. If this idea of science is misconceived, however, then these models are, on their face, poor grounds for thinking that economics is an advanced social science. Moreover, in order to carry out its deductivist program, the assumptions of the theory bear little relation to reality. Put succinctly, on the mainstream view, persons are conceived as atomized, and as historically indifferent "rational beings" with approximately similar motivations. Even more importantly, they are conceived as having approximately equal powers and capacities. But CEOs of corporations, mom and pop Chinese restaurateurs, heart surgeons, immigrant farm workers, non-unionized plumbers, unionized auto workers, part-time female sales clerks, public school teachers and drug dealers – one could go on – do not have similar beliefs *or* capacities, either as producers or consumers. Drawing on familiar criticisms, the chapter examines critically the neo-classical model and argues that it has been burdened by a spurious (positivist) theory of social science. Markets are important social mechanisms, but, drawing on the account of the preceding chapters, a sociologically richer model is shown to be both possible and necessary.

There are four appendices. They are included as appendices because they address the critical literature and provide supplementary materials not essential to the central argument of the volume. Appendix A treats the limits of multiple regression and similar techniques, given a proper understanding of causality and explanation. Appendices B and C pick up on arguments in the current literature that are highly relevant to the arguments of the volume. Appendix B considers the dispute between Theda Skocpol and William Sewell regarding narrative and causal analysis. A very recent defense of the use of Mill's methods in historical sociology is examined critically. The goal of comparative work is further clarified. Appendix C considers the lively debate in *The American Journal of Sociology* over the pertinence of rational choice theory in historical sociology. The effort is made to clarify the argument and to resolve it. Finally, appendix D offers some additional explication and criticism of neo-classical theory.

1 Explanation and understanding

Introduction

Despite some contentiousness between both working social scientists and many philosophers, ideas about explanation in social science are remarkably taken for granted. Worse, when examined in the clear light of day, there is good reason to say that these taken-for-granted ideas are downright wrong. Most social scientists have been socialized to carry on inquiry as defined by their disciplines, they have well-defined research projects and, perhaps quite reasonably, they are content to leave the philosophical problems to the philosophers. No one presses them to wonder whether, indeed, key assumptions unreflexively absorbed are problematic. Some very good work is done that cannot be squared with their implicit or, sometimes, explicit background assumptions. Not only is it not always easy to tell others exactly what we are doing, but we can be mistaken about what we *are* doing. In his 1933 Herbert Spencer lecture at Oxford, Einstein, often ahead of most people, offered pertinent advice: "If you want to find out anything from the theoretical physicists about the methods they use, I advise you to stick to one principle: Don't listen to their words, fix your attention on their deeds."[1]

A good deal of the responsibility for the taken-for-granted ideas about explanation among social scientists owes directly to philosophers in the latter half of the twentieth century, although the antecedents are found as early as Comte in the early nineteenth century. Comte, inventor of the term "positivism," had argued that "the explanation of facts is simply the establishment of a connection between single phenomena and some general facts," or in other words, a scientific explanation was a deduction from general laws. His reasons for this are also pertinent. He was much concerned to put science on a secure empirical foundation, to expunge "fictitious ideas," both metaphysical and religious, from scientific explanation. These concerns and ideas were powerfully reinforced by a host

---

[1] Quoted from Holton 1970 in Manicas, 1987: 242.

of philosopher / physicists in the later quarter of the nineteenth century. The list is impressive and included G. R. Kirchoff, Wilhelm Ostwald, Ernst Mach, Ludwig Boltzman, Karl Pearson, Henri Poincaré, Pierre Duhem and William Thompson (Lord Kelvin).[2] The philosophers of the so-called "Vienna Circle" picked up on these ideas in the 1920s and developed what came to be the dominating theory of science, "logical positivism" (or "logical empiricism"). Central to these doctrines was what came to be called the "Deductive-Nomological" (D-N) or "covering law" model of explanation.[3]

The majority of social scientists working today are not particularly aware of this history or of their indebtedness to these ideas. But they appear in seemingly innocent phrases like "the search for laws is the goal of science," "science aims at prediction and control," "a theory is a deductively organized set of propositions and law-like statements," "a good theory predicts." The relatively few methodologically oriented discussions by social scientists paying special attention to the social sciences have taken the D-N account for their point of departure, either to show its pertinence to their domain,[4] or to argue that if this is the correct model of scientific explanations, then the human sciences cannot provide them.[5]

The covering law model of explanation

While in some quarters at least, the critique of the covering law model will be old news, if we are to make sense of explanation, both in the natural and social sciences, we need to be clear about the model and its failings. Consider first the classic formulation as put forth by Carl Hempel.[6] For

---

[2] See Manicas, 1987 and for an excellent fuller treatment, John Passmore, 1957: chapter 14.

[3] An excellent history of views of causality and explanation from the Greeks to the logical empiricists and their critics is found in Wallace, 1974. While the covering law model is a defining attribute of "empiricist" (positivist, neo-positivist) understandings of science, there is now a substantial critical literature which has subjected this assumption to fatal criticisms. See, among others, Scriven, 1959, 1962; Harré, 1970, 1986; Dretske, 1977; Bhaskar, 1975; Salmon, 1978, 1984; Achinstein, 1981; Aronson, 1984; Woodward, 1984; Lewis, 1987; Kim, 1987; Manicas, 1987, 1989a. In what follows, I draw on some of the main lines of such criticism.

[4] Outstanding examples include Friedman, 1968 and Merton, 1957. More recently, see Turner, 1987 and Alexander, 1987. While Turner defends a neo-positivist theory of science, Alexander is explicitly "post positivist," endorsing the developments following Kuhn's *The Structure of Scientific Revolution*. But as with many others who would consider themselves "post-positivist," Alexander remains committed to the covering law model and thus to the idea that it is the goal of social science to "search for laws."

[5] This is the route of so-called "interpretative sociology." See below and chapter 3.

[6] His important papers are gathered together in the volume, *Aspects of Scientific Explanation* (1965).

him a scientific explanation takes the form of a deductive argument, with premises and a conclusion:

$$\frac{C_1, C_2, \ldots C_k}{L_1, L_2, \ldots L_T}$$
$$E$$

The "explanans," C_1, C_2, . . . C_k, are statements describing the particular facts invoked, sometimes called "the initial conditions," and L_1, L_2, . . . L_r are general laws. The event to be explained (the "explanandum"), E, is a logical consequence of the premise set. As he said: "The kind of explanation thus characterized I will call *deductive-nomological*; for it amounts to a deductive subsumption of the explanandum under principles which have the character of general laws." This is helpfully termed an *epistemic* conception of explanation since the relation between explanans and explanandum is logical.[7] The simplest case takes the form of a syllogism:

$$\frac{\text{If } a, \text{ then } b \text{ (the form of a general law)}}{\underline{a \text{ (the relevant ``conditions'')}}}$$
$$b \text{ (the event to be explained)}$$

Of course, this will count as an explanation only if the premises are true.

Hempel subsequently enlarged his model to include "probabilistic explanation" or "inductive-statistical" (I-S), where the "laws" are not strictly universal, as in the deductive model. Instead of the premises entailing the explanadum, the event to be explained is but probable on the strength of the premises. So roughly,

$$\frac{\text{The probability of } b, \text{ given } a, \text{ is very high.}}{\underline{a}}$$
$$\text{probably } b.$$

Moreover, Hempel went on to argue that nomological explanations, deductive and inductive, could be found in historical writing, where the "relevant generalizations" are sometimes suppressed, and in two special cases of explanation in history, what he termed "genetic explanations" and "explanation by motivating reasons." It was assumed, to be sure, that the models applied also to all explanation in the social sciences.

In the 1950s, a hardly noticed critical literature of what came to be called "the standard view" began to develop. By now there are a number

---

[7] Epistemology is inquiry into the grounds of knowledge (Greek: *episteme*, Latin: *scientia*) and thus includes, critically, logical analysis. Our alternative account is termed "ontic." Ontology is inquiry into the nature of the "real," which, after Kant, became scientifically suspect.

of fatal objections to the model, but before we get to these, notice first that there is currently no consensus among philosophers of science for an alternative account. This chapter attempts to provide at least the sketch of an alternative. Secondly, and as important, the critique of the covering law model has not yet filtered into the disciplines of the social sciences.[8] Hempel's overall conclusion is also important. He insisted that his claims did not

imply a mechanistic view of man, of society, and of historical processes; nor, of course, do they deny the importance of ideas and ideals for human decision and action. What the preceding considerations do suggest is, rather, that the nature of understanding, in the sense in which explanation is meant to give us an understanding of empirical phenomena is basically the same in all areas of scientific inquiry. (1965: 41)

For most inquirers, this was reassuring, which contributed to the account becoming conventional wisdom. To be sure, not everyone agreed with Hempel on these matters, often dubbed "naturalism" in the philosophy of the human sciences. A variety of writers, called "anti-naturalists," could not see how, given any of Hempel's models, one could escape a "mechanistic view of man, society, and historical process." This was usually joined to the claim that getting an understanding of human action in society and history was not at all "basically the same" as getting an understanding of nature, that a very different idea of explanation was required. On this view, any sort of *causal* explanation in the human sciences was wrongheaded. The alternative, then, was the idea that human action could only be explained in terms of the meanings of actors; hence the appeal to *verstehen* (understanding) or what is sometimes called "interpretative sociology." Weber, of course, had insisted, rightly on the present view, that there was no opposition between *verstehen* and causal explanation (*erklären*) and that, indeed, both were required in the human sciences.[9]

In chapter 3, we need to consider carefully these objections. In some ways they go to the heart of the problem of a human science. But the problem we need to address first is not whether there are important analogies

---

[8] Some evidence for this assertion may be found in chapter 6 and appendix C below. See also Tilly, 2001: 25. See also, of course, the standard textbooks for the entry-level courses in the social sciences.

[9] Originally, "hermeneutics" referred to the effort to understand and interpret religious texts. In opposition to the Comtean view that there were laws of history, Droysen argued that we needed to understand mind (*Geist*) differently than nature. Thus, *verstehen* gives humans access to meanings. Dilthey developed this idea. His work motivated Weber's effort to resolve the opposition between understanding, understood as *verstehen*, and causal explanation. This became part of the important *Methodenstreit*. See below, chapter 5.

in achieving explanations in the physical and human sciences. That is to say, it is not merely that the D-N model does not work as regards explanation in the human sciences; rather, the problem is that *it does not work at all*. Much of what follows in this chapter demonstrates this.

Notice first that Hempel's account took the explanation of events as the primary task. Events can be conveniently understood as being space / time locatable, concrete and particular. There are those which typically figure as conclusions in exemplary covering law explanations, for example (referring to a robin's egg in my hand now), "This egg is a robin's egg: that is why it is greenish blue," or "At time T, the body in free fall fell sixteen feet," or "At time T, the salt dissolved in water" or "At time T, the moon was at coordinates x, y, z." They may be more earthy and refer to "happenings": "Kilauea erupted on July 5, 1978"; "Tornados hit Nebraska in June of 2003." Or they involve the actions of persons: "On January 11, 1998, Sam robbed the convenience store at 16th Street and Broadway," or more dramatically: "The two towers of the World Trade Center collapsed on September 11, 2001." They may also involve complexes which are sufficiently related to allow us an adequate term of denotation, such as the expiration of the woolly mammoth, the passing of the Paleolithic era, the French Revolution, the Great Crash of 1929. More might be said here regarding the idea of an event, but for present purposes this will suffice.

Perhaps surprisingly, in most of the well-established natural sciences, attempts to explain particular events are rare. Where they occur, they occur almost entirely in those natural sciences that are historical, such as meteorology or geology, or where, as in astronomy, for some purposes at least, time is irrelevant, for example, in giving an account of the position of the earth's moon on any given day. There are good reasons for both their absence in what Max Weber usefully called "the abstract sciences," physics, chemistry, biochemistry and general biology, and for their presence where they do occur, as we shall see.[10] In what follows, we argue that, following both common usage and the practices of philosophers, the idea of explanation is most at home in contexts where the explanation of an event is what is aimed at, and that, by contrast, physicists, chemists and biochemists aim at *understanding* – a notion not at all easy to clarify, but certainly not to be confused with understanding in the sense of *verstehen* as that is generally understood.

But the foregoing suggests another observation: on the covering law model, *explanation and prediction are symmetrical*. If you are in a position to explain some event *b*, then *b* could have been predicted – and conversely.

---

[10] See his seldom studied *Roscher und Kneis* (1975) and Manicas, 1987: 127–140.

The logic is the same. If we have a law of the form "If a, then b," then given that a has occurred, we explain b. Similarly, by means of the law, we can predict b, if and when a occurs. This has some *prima facie* plausibility especially if we have as our paradigms those events which are typically instances of laws in the D-N model: if you put salt into water, it dissolves. But if we consider events like the collapse of the Twin Towers, the devastation of hurricane Iniki to Kaua'i in the Hawaiian Islands in 1992 or the Great Depression of 1929, which seem, at least, to involve a battery of laws, and in which sequences seem critical, the covering law model seems far less plausible. Once something happens, we can begin the search for an adequate explanation. But could these events have been predicted? How one answers this question depends on one's ontology, as we shall see.

The view that explanation and prediction are symmetrical leads to the idea that the goal of science is prediction, indeed, that an explanation is not scientific if it does not enable prediction. As Hobbs (1993: 177) writes: "Ex post facto explanations, those which are given only after the event to be explained has occurred, have long been considered epistemologically suspect, along with the theories that sanction them." I do not know if Hobbs is correct in saying that the symmetry thesis is no longer assumed by most philosophers, but the idea remains pervasive (and pernicious) in the social sciences where, paradoxically, the failure to provide "good predictions" is taken to be the major fault of the social sciences. This, too, we need to challenge. We can begin with an effort to clarify the idea of explanation and look also at its important relative, understanding, an idea much used when writing about science, but almost never considered by philosophers of science.

Clarifying "understanding" and "explanation"

Both "understanding" and "explanation" have many uses and, indeed, in some contexts at least, are interchangeable. Our interest here is *scientific* explanation and in the understanding offered by science. We consider first "understanding." R. L. Franklin has rightly noted:

"Understand" is a word we understand as well as any, but we do not understand philosophically what it is to understand. The word catches some notion important enough to appear in many of our book titles, yet in an age of linguistic analysis it has virtually escaped investigation in English-speaking philosophy. (1983: 307)

This is perhaps paradoxical. But defenders of the D-N model, like most philosophers of science, suggest that the problem is not theirs, since concepts like understanding and intelligibility are psychological and pragmatic. Michael Friedman is an important exception. He notes, rightly, that "the entailment relation puts a constraint on the explanation relation, but it does not by itself tell us what it is about the explanation relation that gives us understanding of the explained phenomenon, that makes the world more intelligible" (1974: 7). This is indeed the problem: how do we go about achieving an understanding of the phenomena? What makes the world "more intelligible"?

We need, of course, to be wary of an account of understanding which is subjective in the sense of it being entirely arbitrary what will count as generating understanding. If we are interested in the understanding that *science* can provide, then not just any process of generating understanding will do. While we aim for an account that is objective, the account will necessarily be pragmatic and psychological in that it will involve examining both our aims and interests, and the contexts in which scientific understanding is demanded and achieved.

Nobody has so far provided a rigorous and satisfactory account of understanding and you should not suppose that you will get one here.[11] Nevertheless, it is fairly easy to understand how scientific understanding is achieved. This requires some radical revision of conventional wisdom in the philosophy of science, especially regarding the critical concept of causality, central on the present view to both understanding and explanation.

Friedman, who noticed that explanations of events were rare in the physical sciences, offered instead what he rightly took to be typical questions for science and the typical answers to these questions. These included the following questions: Why does water turn to steam when heated? Why do the planets obey Kepler's laws? Why is light refracted by a prism? The answer to the first question is:

Water is made of tiny molecules in a state of constant motion. Between these molecules are intermolecular forces, which, at normal temperatures, are sufficient to hold them together. If the water is heated, however, the energy, and consequently, the motion, of the molecules acquire enough energy to overcome the intermolecular forces – they fly apart and escape into the atmosphere. Thus, the water gives off steam. (Friedman, 1974: 5)

This account, while informal, does give us understanding; it does make the world more intelligible. It is not an explanation of an event, but may be construed (as by Friedman), as the explanation of a pattern, or regularity – or, very loosely, a "law." The understanding comes from seeing that water – like everything else – is composed of molecules and that

---

[11] See Friedman, 1974, and the responses it generated: Kitcher, 1976, 1981; Gemes, 1994; Hintikka and Halonen, 1995. All of these are more or less efforts at "rigor" and all confess that they leave much unanswered. On the present view, all omit consideration of causality and fail to offer an appropriate analysis of the ontology of science.

there is a great deal that can be said about how they behave. Indeed, this story gives us an understanding of not only the changing of water to steam, but of an extraordinary list of experienced phenomena: the dissolving of salt in water, the rusting of iron, the nutritional capacities of broccoli . . . the list is nearly endless.[12] Indeed, as Peter Atkins (2003: 135) notes in his lovely book, *Galileo's Finger*, "chemistry is the bridge between the perceived world of substances and the imagined world of atoms." While patterns are the material for questions and questions demand answers which, in science at least, call for theory, the real goal of science is neither the explanation of events nor the explanation of patterns, though this idea catches some of the truth of the matter. *Rather, it has as its goal an understanding of the fundamental processes of nature* (Harré 1970: 260–266; Bhaskar 1975: 17, 66). Once these are understood, all sorts of phenomena can be made intelligible, comprehensible, unsurprising.[13]

Friedman's example, of course, employs critical terms in the theoretical discourse of science: molecule, intermolecular forces, energy. The depth of understanding attained depends on the knowledge of the audience. What after all is a molecule? What are molecular forces? What is energy? Most of us, perhaps sadly, lack any sort of understanding of these ideas – a regrettable failure of science education in the USA (and elsewhere). This is doubly sad since not only does this ignorance contribute to reinforcing misunderstandings about science – for example, that its goal is prediction and control, or that theory is a deductive system – but these ideas can be made available without extensive socialization in a science or an extensive background in sophisticated mathematics.

By examining how energy is dispersed in a steam engine, Atkins gives a highly informative, non-mathematical account of still more

[12] Friedman says that "scientific explanations do not confer intelligibility on individual phenomena" by showing them to be somehow "natural, necessary, familiar, or inevitable," and that we need to pay heed to the "global features of explanation," the idea that "our total picture of nature is simplified via a reduction in the number of independent phenomena that we have to accept as ultimate" (1974: 18). This is "unification" in one clear enough and important sense, even if it is not easy to provide a rigorous formal account of the notion. As Aronson, 1984 argues, the unification missed by Friedman regards showing that otherwise disparate phenomena have a common ontology. There is a sense, contra Friedman, that "natural," "necessary" and "inevitable" – though not "familiar" – are involved in understanding. See below.

[13] Including, perhaps especially, patterns which are anomalous. Two characteristics of black-body radiation which were identified in the nineteenth century and became known as Wien's and Stefan's laws could not be explained in terms of classical physics. The problem provoked Lord Kelvin and then Max Planck to propose what came to be quantum theory; providing an enormously improved understanding of "the deep structure of reality" (Atkins, 2003: 204).

fundamental processes involved in the changing of water to steam. He writes:

Let's suppose that the fuel is oil, a mixture of hydrocarbons (compounds built up from carbon and hydrogen only) . . . [A hexadecane molecule is easily represented in a graphic model, fig. 4.11 in his book, as a chain of sixteen carbon atoms to which are attached thirty-four hydrogen atoms.] This is the molecule typical of fuel oil and diesel fuel; it is also closely related to the molecules of fat that are present in meat and which help to lubricate the muscle fibers as well as acting as an insulating layer and a reserve of fuel. That we eat foodstuffs closely related to diesel fuel, some more than others, is no accident, but the thought is a little sobering.

When the oil burns, molecules like the one in the illustration are attacked by oxygen molecules of the air. Under the onslaught of the attack, the carbon chain breaks up and the hydrogen molecules are stripped from it. The carbon atoms are carried away as carbon dioxide molecules and the hydrogen molecules are carried away as water molecules. A great deal of heat is produced because the new formed bonds between the atoms are stronger than the original bonds in the fuel and in the oxygen, so energy is released when the weak old bonds are replaced by strong new ones and the atoms settle into energetically more favorable arrangements. And why does the hydrocarbon burn? Because in doing so there is a huge decrease in disorder and therefore in entropy. There are two principal contributions to this increase in entropy. One is the release of energy, which disperses into the surroundings and raises their entropy. The other is the dispersion of matter, as long, orderly chains of atoms broken up and the individual atoms spread away from the site of combustion as little gaseous molecules. The combustion is portraying the content of the Second Law [of Thermodynamics]. (Atkins 2003: 128–129)

This account, unlike the example of the boiling water, deepens our understanding by showing how molecules break up and recombine into new molecules. Combined with oxygen, the hexadecane molecule becomes carbon dioxide and water; and entropy explains the release of energy in this process. Now, of course, we need an account of the forces which explain the "bonds," we need an account of energy – an absolutely pervasive feature of all processes in the universe – and we need to understand entropy, "the spring of all change." As Atkins writes, with an understanding of entropy at hand, "we shall come to understand the simple events of everyday life, such as the cooling of hot coffee, and we shall see at least the ankle of the explanation of the most complex events of everyday life, such as birth, growth and death" (Atkins 2003: 109).

Atkins's way of putting the situation is just right. "We get an understanding but only an ankle of an explanation of the most complex events of everyday life." The explanation of events *presupposes* understanding, and we get only "an ankle of explanation" because we need a good deal more than an understanding of entropy. But the foregoing account does not even touch on questions of the forces which explain inter- and intra-molecular processes, nor have we mentioned the level below atoms, the world of electrons, s- and p-orbitals, quarks, waves and particles: essential for a still deeper understanding of not only all chemical processes, but of matter itself.

Reaching an adequate understanding at this level will not be easy – but it need not be that demanding either. Questions asked are pragmatic and aim at serving some purpose; hence also the answer given. A small child asking why the egg in my hand is greenish-blue may be satisfied to be told that it is a robin's egg and that all robins' eggs are greenish-blue. Indeed, even that answer offers some understanding in that it offers an order to the experience. But most of us will want more. And surely a *scientific* answer to this question would require a good deal more. This requires an account of causality and how it functions in science.

Understanding and causality

Such examples give a general picture of how understanding proceeds in physical science, but we need now to connect these examples to an account of causality including, critically, the idea of a causal mechanism, which is an important feature of both understanding and the explanation of events. On the present view, the aim of science is to provide an understanding of the fundamental processes of nature and this requires identifying the causal mechanisms which are, willy nilly, at work in the world.[14]

---

[14] My account is influenced by the writings of Harré, 1970 and Bhaskar, 1975. But see also Cartwright, 1989 and, more recently, the accounts of Glennan, 1996; Machamer, Darden and Craver, 2000, and Bunge, 2003. There are differences, terminological and substantive, between these writers, which are not developed here. One critical difference regards the understanding and pertinence of "laws." The account of Machamer *et al.* (2000: 3) seems closest to the present account. They define mechanisms as "entities and activities organized such that they are productive of regular changes from start or set-up to finish or termination conditions." Bunge objects, insisting that this definition is incomplete and "misses the concept of a concrete system – one of the categories sadly absent from mainstream ontology, along with those of matter, energy, state and emergence" (Machamer *et al.*, 2000: 3). But the reference to a "concrete system" may raise more problems than it solves. See chapter 4, below. Machamer *et al.* may be correct in saying that "there is no adequate analysis of what mechanisms are and how they work in science" (2000: 2). Of course, "adequate" is a pragmatic term. But all these writers would seem to agree that causal mechanisms are critical to understanding and that this is the goal of science. As Machamer *et al.* put the matter: "In many fields of science what is taken to be a satisfactory explanation requires providing a description of a mechanism" (2000: 1). Bunge notes, using "understanding" in the sense of the account in this chapter, that "the relevance of mechanism to understanding is such that it is not uncommon to find in the scientific literature apologies of the form, 'Unfortunately, no mechanism is known to underlay the fact [or equation] in question'" (Bunge 2003: 186). We noted earlier the often interchangeable uses of the terms "explanation" and "understanding."

As before, let us begin with the dominating, though mistaken, view of causality. This view comes from David Hume (1711–76), who argued that all we can know of a causal relation is that there is an observable constant conjunction between two events. Thus "*a* is the cause of *b*" means nothing more than "if *a*, then *b*." The idea that a cause is a *productive power* was dismissed as a metaphysical idea since, on this view, there is nothing in experience which says that *a produces b*. The Humean view of the matter is not the common-sense view of the matter – nor is it empirical, if that means known by experience. On this view, when we push a door open, our action was the cause, and it produced the outcome. Indeed, as Harré and Madden write: "Can anyone seriously deny that we sometimes veridically perceive the waves eating away the shore, the axe splitting the wood, and the avalanche destroying the countryside" (1975: 49). Terms like "eating away," "splitting" and "destroying" are clearly causal concepts, and it is likely that our ordinary understanding of causality comes directly from our experience, especially the experience of our own actions as causes in contexts like pushing open a door.

Nor, according to the Humean conception, can we impute necessity to the relation: as empirically established, the connection of *a* to *b* is purely contingent. As Hume put the matter: "If we have really no idea of a power or efficacy in any object, or of any real connection betwixt causes and effects, it will be to little purpose that an efficacy is necessary in all operations" (Hume, 2000: Part III, Section xiv). But as shown by the active verbs (above), which function as causal terms, there is no problem in seeing a "real connection," even if we will need to say more about "power and efficacy" in the scientific application of causality. The presumed absurdity that one explains the drowsiness which comes from taking opium by saying that it has a "soporific power" (*virtus dormitiva*), is the pertinent example here. Avoiding such "absurdity" powerfully motivated the Humean idea that causal laws had to be analyzed as invariant, if contingent, relations, as Comte put it, "of association and resemblance." On this view, according to the dominating strand in philosophy of science, to say that opium is a "soporific power" is to say only, "if one takes opium, one becomes sleepy," where, as above, this is an invariable relation of association.

There were many reasons why the Humean view became conventional wisdom. But foremost were the empiricist prohibitions which motivated Hume and Comte. "Science" had to fight off the metaphysical philosophers and the theologians if it was to establish its independent authority, and that meant that experience and experiment would be the anchors of its claims. Indeed, Pierre Duhem (1861–1916) went even further and insisted that since we could not disconnect explanation from causality, *science does not seek to explain.* He wrote: "A physical theory is not an explanation. It is a system of mathematical principles, which aim to represent as simply, as completely, and as exactly as possible a set of experimental laws" (1954: 19). Bertrand Russell (1872–1970), explicitly rejecting the common-sense idea as pertinent to modern science, noted that causality was "a product of a bygone age" and suggested that it be expunged as unnecessary to science. As this also suggests, part of the reason for abandoning the commonsensical notice of causality was the capacity to employ mathematics to express relations and make deductions from these. Newton's systemization of celestial mechanics was very much the background to this. Thus, at the end of the nineteenth century, Ernst Mach (1838–1916) argued that mathematical functions of theory were "abridged descriptions." The compendious representation of the actual, necessarily involves as a consequence "the elimination of all superfluous assumptions that are metaphysical in Kant's sense" (1959: 210), that is, as exceeding the bounds of experience.[15]

This, then, takes us back to the covering law model. Indeed, it was the assumed Humean notion of causality which gave it much, if not all, of its power. To anticipate, if causal necessity had to be expunged from science, then *logical necessity* might well serve in its place. This involved, more fundamentally, an *epistemic* conception of explanation instead of the commonsensical *ontological* conception – which, presumably, had no place in metaphysically cleansed science. That is, instead of construing explanation in terms of causes as productive powers, it was construed in terms of rational argument.

Thus in a much used and highly regarded textbook, *Research Methods in the Social Sciences*, Frankfort-Nachmias and Nachmias (1992: 10) write: "Ever since David Hume . . . an application of the term explanation has been considered a matter of relating the phenomenon to be explained with other phenomena by means of general laws."

Let us go back to the simplest form of the D-N model and see both how the Humean conception fit neatly into the by then well-conscribed logical analysis of science, how it avoided the pragmatics and psychology

---

[15] An important nineteenth-century exception was Hermann Helmholz. In the twentieth century the exceptions include Albert Einstein, Max Planck and David Bohm. In a letter to Schlick, Einstein pertinently insisted: "In general your presentation fails to correspond to my conceptual style insofar as I find your whole orientation so to speak too positivistic . . . I tell you straight out: Physics is the attempt at the conceptual reconstruction of a model of the real world and its lawful structure . . In short, I suffer under the unsharp separation of Reality of Experience and Reality of Being . . . You will be astonished about the 'metaphysicist' Einstein. But every four- and two-legged animal is de facto in this sense a metaphysicist" (quoted by Holton, 1970: 188).

of understanding and how, by illicit conflation, it pretended to do what was needed.

> If salt is put in water, then it dissolves.
> <u>The salt was put in water.</u>
> Therefore, the salt dissolved.

As a deduction, the explanandum follows logically. If P, then *necessarily* Q. If the premises are true, we have provided sufficient grounds for believing that the explanandum is true. So, presumably, this fact is explained. But it is easy to construct counter-examples of D-N explanations with true premises which are just plain silly. They not only do not explain, but they do not even provide grounds for believing that the explanandum is true:

> Anyone who takes birth control pills regularly will not become pregnant.
> <u>John took his wife's pills regularly.</u>
> Hence, John did not become pregnant.

When a woman takes a birth control pill, there is a causal mechanism at work which prevents pregnancy. This would explain why *Joan* did not get pregnant. But this is plainly not what is at issue as regards John. Given that he is male, it is biologically impossible for him to become pregnant. (For a Humean, the *only* impossibility is logical.)

It is easy to construct D-N "explanations" with true premises in which there is not even the suggestion of causality. Suppose, for the sake of argument, that there is perfect correlation between the price of eggs in China and the behavior of Microsoft stock the next day on the New York Stock Exchange. We can construct a D-N explanation which explains the price movement of Microsoft by appealing to the price movements of eggs in China! As I argue subsequently, strong correlations are most useful for prediction though not, symmetrically, for explanation – as nearly everyone would agree.[16] That is, if it is true that there is a strong correlation between these two variables, I can act profitably on the NYSE by knowing the price of eggs in China today, whatever is the correct explanation for price movements on the stock exchange tomorrow.

The point here is that even *logical necessity* between premise set and conclusion does not make the argument an explanation. This is the wrong relation. We need necessity but not logical necessity. Laws (like the

---

[16] Both Wien's and Stefan's laws (above, note 9) offered perfect correlations which, functioning as D-N explanations, manifestly fail. Indeed, while every textbook in quantitative methods warns students not to confuse correlation and causation, it is usually left mysterious how it does this. Indeed, it is left to one's common sense and intuition. That is, one must suspect that there is or is not a mechanism at work. See appendix A.

foregoing) which subsume instances (still less mere generalizations) cannot explain since "entails" is the wrong relationship. As Dretske (1977) writes: "The fact that *every* F is G fails to explain why *any* F is G."

Consider again our salt example. This is plausibly an explanation – even if the understanding conveyed is minimal. It is surely pre-scientific; the "law-like" major premise is a generalization – and there are thousands like it, familiar for centuries, and indispensable to ordinary life.

We can certainly acknowledge that this particular salt would not have dissolved in that particular water unless someone put it in the water. So, on the common-sense way of thinking, this was also the cause that brought about the outcome. Indeed, the "if . . . then" statement even looks like a causal law, as analyzed by a Humean. This perhaps explains some of the confusion. If putting salt in water is necessary for the outcome, we think we have an explanation and in some contexts, at least, perhaps this will suffice. But if it does, it is also because we take for granted that there is something about both salt and water such that when one puts salt in water, it dissolves. Salt is water-soluble. This is surely causal, but it is not part of the explanation that was offered.

Worse, as stated, the law-like major premise, "if salt is put in water, it dissolves," is not even true: when it is put in water, salt doesn't always dissolve, for a variety of reasons. One might patch this up, of course, and say that it usually does, so we have here not a D-N explanation but an "inductive statistical" explanation. Consider what this does.

While at least a true universal maintains the hold on the individual case, anything less loses all sense of explanation. Perhaps 67 percent of people exposed to herpes contract it; Sam and Harry were both exposed, but why did Sam contract the disease and why didn't Harry? Similarly, suppose we contend that most Texans are Republicans and that Jones is a Texan. It follows that probably Jones is a Republican. But suppose that most philosophers are not Republicans and that Jones is a philosopher. It follows that he is probably not a Republican. Or consider the explanation that people who have colds will probably get over them in a week if they drink plenty of Coca Cola. Jones did this, and he got over his cold. But not only do most colds last about a week, but we know of no mechanism which would link this behavior with this outcome. In these sorts of cases, there is no explanation because there is no "real connection" between drinking Coke and getting over the cold in one week. In the D-N case, we could be more easily misled because at least there is *logical* necessity between the explanans and the explanandum. Explanation, like understanding, requires that there is a "real connection," a generative mechanism or causal nexus that produced or brought about the event (or pattern) to be explained.

A causal relation presupposes a *nomic* and *necessary* connection. We need not balk at this. Indeed, Jaegwon Kim is prepared to say that "most philosophers will now agree that an idea of causation devoid of some notion of necessitation is not *our* idea of causation – perhaps not an idea of causation at all" (1987: 234). The basic idea is clear enough. Causes bring about their effects, either as events which initiate a change in circumstances, e.g., the match which lights the fire, or as mechanisms with causal powers, the combustible material which burns (and doesn't evaporate or become vinegar).

We alluded earlier to "causal powers" and to "causal (or generative) mechanisms" – the core of an alternative realist account of causality. Consider the following improved explanation.

> If salt is put in water, then because salt is water-soluble, it dissolves.
> <u>The salt was put in water.</u>
> Therefore, the salt dissolved.

On the Humean reading, the clause, "because salt is water-soluble" is redundant since it can only mean, "If salt is put in water, it dissolves." While this empiricist analysis of dispositional concepts has won considerable favor in contemporary accounts – especially in the social sciences – solubility cannot be unpacked in terms of if-then clauses. If salt is water-soluble then *there is something about it such that* if it is put in water, it dissolves. "Water soluble" is a *promissory note* to be filled in by providing a causal mechanism. The same is true regarding the appeal to *virtus dormitiva* ascribed to opium. This attribution is hardly satisfying, but it does give us the promise of better explanation because it directs us to look for the relevant generative mechanism. Still, as Harré notes, even having only the promise is an improvement, simply because the explanation no longer supposes that the outcome results merely from the fact that it was put in water. Nor will we understand the outcome better if we repeat the experiment a hundred times. Rather, we now are directed to consider what it is about salt and water – or opium – such that salt dissolves in water, and opium induces sleep. This shifts the question from the presumption that *any* law-like regularity from which one can deduce the event to be explained counts as a scientific explanation. Critically, it also shifts the problem of explanation to the question of the nature of salt and of water – a theoretical question for science, and as we have noted, the answer to which can provide genuine understanding.

The physicist David Bohm wrote: "Clearly . . . the concept of a causal relationship implies more than just regular association, in which one set of events precedes another in time. What is implied in addition is that (abstracted from contingencies of course) the future effects come out of past cause through a process satisfying necessary relationships" (1984: 5f.). Moreover, the concept that is needed and overlooked entirely by concentrating on events as causes, is the idea that *things have causal properties by virtue of their nature*. It is here that necessity can be located. Bohm writes:

> Thus, the qualitative causal relationship that water becomes ice when cooled and steam when heated is a basic part of the essential properties of the liquid without which it could not be water. Similarly, the chemical law that hydrogen and oxygen combine to form water is a basic property of the gases hydrogen and oxygen . . . Likewise, the general mathematical laws of motion satisfied by bodies moving through empty space (or under other conditions) are essential properties of such bodies, without which they could be bodies as we have known them. Examples of this kind could be multiplied without limit. (1984: 14)

We need some new language to get at what is going on here. We can think of a causal property of a thing as an ascription of a power or tendency, true of it because of what it is.[17] Accordingly, causal laws are not universal conditionals of the form, "if X, then Y." Rather, causal laws look more like: "By virtue of its intrinsic structure S, C *phi's* when C is triggered," where *phi-ing* refers to the activity of the mechanism C. It is important to notice here that the outcome of C's *phi-ing* will be a function of what other causal mechanisms are also at work. If salt is put in water, it dissolves; if iron is put in water, it will rust.

Moreover, salt usually dissolves in water, but if it does not, then while the causal mechanism that explains this may be triggered, there are other causes at work. Something has happened, but not what we expected to happen. Finally, ordinary, concrete salt is what we experience. *NaCl is a theoretical object arrived at by abstraction from the concrete*. It exists, but perhaps only or usually in a less than pure form. While if our theory is true, NaCl must dissolve in H_2O, if on some occasion, the salt did not dissolve when put in water, we would almost certainly assume that what we put in water was not salt or that there was something about either the salt or the water which prevented it dissolving. If sufficiently sophisticated, we might suggest that the solution was super-saturated, perhaps because it was too cold. Indeed, in our world there is contingency, but in a world where there was only contingency, there would be no stability. Salt does not explode when one puts it in water; nor does it change the water into gin, etc. In

---

[17] The concept of powers does not figure in the discourse of science. Nor need there be reference to causes in this discourse, even if it is replete with terms which imply causality. But indeed, there is frequent reference to "mechanisms." "Powers" and causality are terms employed by philosophers of science in the effort to get a better understanding of how science proceeds.

our world, there is both necessity *and* contingency, the upshot of which is, to use John Dewey's language, both stability *and* precariousness.

Thus to add to Bohm's potentially limitless examples, consider the apparently non-causal concept, "copper." Scientists think of copper as having a host of properties, including malleability, fusibility, ductility and electric conductivity. These properties assign powers and liabilities – what copper will do or undergo given certain conditions. They are promissory notes, which may be analyzed as dispositions understood as permanent (or relatively permanent) capacities or liabilities which exist whether or not they are exercised and whether or not, when exercised, they are ful-filled. Science does not simply ascribe causal properties to things: it fulfills the promissory note by explaining them in the sense of offering an account of the causal mechanisms which give them these properties. To be sure, the components and modes of operation of such causal mechanisms will differ depending upon the phenomena they explain. More importantly, they will not, in general, be like the "mechanisms" typical of the inner workings of an old-fashioned clock. The "mechanism" of electron trans-fer is different from the "mechanism" by which, according to the second law of thermodynamics, waste heat is discarded.[18]

Thus, theory tells us that water and salt molecules are composed of atoms, which in turn are composed of electrons, neutrons, and below that, of quarks and photons. At each level, the theory provides an account of the generative mechanisms that account for the causal properties at the next level, why in other words, they have the powers they have. As Harré notes, "explanatory mechanisms become a new subject for scientific study and the explanation of their principles of operation calls for the hypothesis of further explanatory mechanisms, new model building and so on" (1970: 262). The theory provides an understanding not only of why water turns to steam, and why salt dissolves in it, but an understanding of all the *possible behaviors* of these molecules in interaction.

As Atkins says, for chemists, the periodic table is "their single most important concept. It summarizes the properties of the elements – the variation in their physical properties, such as the number and type of bonds they form to other atoms . . . At a glance we can see whether an element has the properties characteristic of a metal (iron), a non-metal (sulfur), or something in between (silicon)" (Atkins, 2003: 159). Mendeleev compiled the table empirically, that is, in accordance with the observational properties of the elements. But, continues Atkins, "he knew

---

[18] The point is sufficiently important to suggest that we abandon the term "mechanism" in these contexts. But I can find no preferable alternative. Causal processes require causal mechanisms. See also Machamer, Darden and Craver, 2000; Bunge, 2003.

nothing of the structures of atoms and could have had no conception of the underlying foundation of the table. We have that understanding. The periodic table, as we now know, is a portrayal of the rhythms of the filling of the energy levels of atoms" (Atkins, 2003: 160). Thus, to round out his superb account,

> for hydrogen, with its single electron, all the orbitals of a given shell have exactly the same energy. For atoms other than hydrogen . . . each shell contains orbitals of progressively higher energy. In all cases, p-orbitals first become available in the second shell, d-orbitals become available in the third shell and f-orbitals become available in the fourth shell (Figure 5.7).
>
> With two simple ideas – that electrons organize themselves so as to achieve the lowest possible energy, and that no more than two electrons can occupy any given orbital – the pattern of matter becomes understandable. (Atkins, 2003: 161)

Obviously, armed with such a powerful understanding, it will hardly be a complicated task for the chemist to explain why salt dissolves in water – at whatever level of understanding one demands.

But if grasping the nature of salt is within the competence of anybody who knows some chemistry, there are a host of other very stable patterns which require a more complicated account. Consider our earlier example, that robins' eggs are greenish-blue. As stated, this is at best misleading, but it can easily be rewritten to be more scientifically accurate. Thus, "Under normal conditions, a robin's egg will appear greenish-blue to normal percipients." There are, plainly, a number of generative mechanisms at work here which, taken together, explain the generalization. These include the well-understood biological properties which explain the inherited traits of organisms (why robins lay eggs which produce only robins), and the chemical and optical properties of material surfaces. There are also the less well-understood neurophysiological properties of the human perceptual system. But finally, there are the not at all understood processes which give normal percipients the experience of seeing greenish-blue when looking at a robin's egg. Such generalizations presuppose the natural necessities of "things," and, indeed, it is these which make acting on our generalizations rational. If, in normal circumstances, an object which was identified as a robin's egg appeared white, we would rightly be suspicious. Perhaps, after all, it was a small chicken's egg, or a genetic fluke? Perhaps it is only that there is an unnoticed light effect? Since scientists are not, in general, interested in explaining patterns of this sort – requiring as they do an understanding of mechanisms theorized in very different disciplines – you will not find this example in any book by a biologist, a physicist or a chemist.

To round out this part of the argument: what are best termed the "abstract sciences" aim at an understanding of the fundamental processes of nature. Such inquiry may be motivated by discerning a pattern, but not all patterns will be of concern. Indeed, patterns which emerge from experimentally generated data, e.g., the results of Lavoisier's painstaking use of the chemical balance, are of high importance. Finally, their interest in concrete events is also at best marginal, pretty much restricted, as we shall subsequently suggest, to events which can provide an especially potent test of theory. This raises a new nest of problems to consider.

2 Theory, experiment and the metaphysics of Laplace

Introduction

Chapter 1 noted that understanding came when we had a well-confirmed theory about a generative mechanism. In this chapter we consider the essentials of construction and confirmation of theory, including the role of experiment in those sciences where experiment is possible. While the literature on theory is both vast and contentious, we can here be relatively brief. Our aim is to focus on what is absolutely essential for the purposes of a philosophy of the social sciences. More important for us is the effort in this chapter to undermine the bad metaphysics of what is too often taken for granted in talk about theory and the goals of science. A key theme will be to show that celestial mechanics is a very poor example for the sciences, social *and* physical.

What a theory is

Despite much talk to the contrary, no real theory in the physical sciences can be fully expressed as a deductive system, with axioms and deductions therefrom. The idea has a long legacy dating at least from Descartes, from Newton's great work, and from the still older idea that mathematics is the ideal of knowledge (Harré, 1970: 8). As Harré says:

> In fact, in actual science, deductive systems are quite rare: fragments of such systems can be found in physics, but mostly scientists come up with descriptions of structures, attributions of powers and laws of change, related by having a common object, not being then and there deducible from a common set of axioms. (Harré, 1970: 10)

For some theories – though surely not all – mathematics will play a critical role, especially in developing the abstractions of system dynamics. But expressing laws and descriptions of objects in mathematical style does not make them mathematical propositions: their meaning remains non-mathematical – even where we resist relating the mathematics to visualizable models. Indeed, Atkins concludes, reluctantly, that "any final theory, if there is one, is likely to be a purely abstract account of the fundamental structure of the world, an account that we might possess but not comprehend" (2003: 358). This is, he notes, "probably too extreme a view." He continues: "Humans are adept at interpreting mathematics, particularly the mathematics used to support physics, in homely terms, aware all the time that their interpretation is fraught with danger and incompleteness, but interpreting nonetheless" (Atkins, 2003: 358).

Harré's definition of theory acknowledges the necessity of interpretation: "A theory consists of a representation of the structure of the enduring system in which those events occur which as phenomena are its subject matter, and by which they are generated" (1970: 14). As already insisted, theories supply "an account of the constitution and behavior of those things whose interactions with each other are responsible for the manifested patterns of behavior" (Harré, 1970: 35). They identify "things" – molecules and atoms, for example, how they are structured, and how they interact. They are, of course, representations, but they are meant to represent reality – as it is in-itself.

Following Harré (1970), it is convenient to think of this representation as involving hypotheses of several types, (1) existential: "atoms exist;" (2) a model description: "molecules are in random motion;" (3) causal hypotheses: "pressure is caused by the impact of molecules;" (4) modal transforms: "temperature is another way of conceiving of mean kinetic energy." The examples taken from Atkins (above) were meant to give a hint of this (see also Machamer *et al.*, 2000).

Realist versus instrumentalist conceptions of theoretical terms

As a consequence of empiricist commitments, beginning at least with Mach but extending through the heyday of logical empiricism, there has been much debate among philosophers about the function of theoretical terms. For the dominating empiricist view, in contrast to the realist view briefly summarized above, theoretical terms can function without making "existential" commitments. Thus, the meaning and application of terms like "electron" are fully given by means of "reduction sentences," of which "operational definitions" are a key variety, or by means of "correspondence rules," which more indirectly link the theoretical term (T-term) to terms in the observation language (O-terms). Thus:

"X has theoretical property T," means "if X is placed under test conditions C, then the test yields observable results O."[1]

There is hardly a textbook in quantitative methods in the social sciences that does not repeat some version of this. Compare the example in the previous chapter from Frankfort-Nachmias and Nachmias (1992). They write:

> Often the empirical attributes or events that are represented by concepts cannot be observed directly . . . In such cases, the empirical existence of a concept (sic) has to be inferred. Inferences of this kind are made with operational definitions. (1992: 31)

When we refer to T, we mean: "If C, then O." So "T" has been "reduced": for all practical purposes, it has been eliminated. By 1958, Hempel saw that there was a serious problem with an account of theory in which no existential commitments were made. He remarked: "The use of theoretical terms in science gives rise to a perplexing problem: Why should science resort to the assumption of hypothetical entities when it is interested in establishing predictive and explanatory connections among observables" (Hempel 1965: 179). Indeed, if this is their purpose, the problem can be expressed as a dilemma:

1. Either theoretical terms serve their purpose or they do not.
2. If they serve their purpose, since they establish predictive and explanatory connections among observables, they are unnecessary.
3. If they do not serve this purpose, they are surely unnecessary.
4. Hence, theoretical terms are unnecessary.

Indeed, if their meaning and application can be given by sentences in the O-language, they are but handy place-markers for organizing experimental data. Hence 2. But perhaps this is not at all their purpose? Hempel came to see that theoretical terms serve another and more critical purpose. As he said:

> When a scientist introduces theoretical entities such as electric currents, magnetic fields, chemical valences, or subconscious mechanisms, he intends them to serve as explanatory factors which have an existence independent of the observable symptoms by which they manifest themselves. (Hempel 1965: 205)

Indeed! As argued in chapter 1, appeal to these ideas can explain exactly because they are taken to represent the generative mechanisms which

---

[1] As in chapter 1, this is also the standard empiricist explication of dispositional terms, like water-soluble. So "X is water-soluble" means "if X is put in water, X dissolves." For the realist, roughly, "X is water- soluble" means "there is something about X and water, such that if X is put in water, it dissolves." For the realist, water-soluble refers to the powers and tendencies of X and of water. And theory provides an account of these.

produce the pertinent observables. All useful theories make inescapable ontological commitments. But doesn't this introduce metaphysical speculation into science? How does it remain empirical?

Post-Kuhnian grounds for establishing scientific consensus

Thomas S. Kuhn's *The Structure of Scientific Revolutions* (1962) caused an enormous stir. Many came to the conclusion that science was not the rational enterprise it was thought to be. But this was the wrong conclusion to be drawn from his work. Rather, along with several others,[2] he showed that it was not rational in the sense that the logical empiricists had held it to be rational. Today, there would be agreement that there is no "theory-neutral" observation language that could serve as a foundation for truth claims, that the logic of confirmation or of falsification fails, and the historical and social environment of scientific practice is the key to understanding scientific success. It was in terms of these factors that at some point a consensus regarding a theory emerged in the scientific community. To be sure, this opened the door for the idea that science was no more rational than any other practice, for it raised the question of what brings the scientific community to this consensus – of agreeing that hypotheses, existential, descriptive and causal, are true? It is safe to say, perhaps, that while few writers remain holdouts to what is sometimes termed empiricist "foundationalism,"[3] few writers would now argue that science is just another practice that gives us no special access to knowledge about the world. In what follows, a third alternative is sketched.

The problem begins by acknowledging that all we can do as human inquirers is to represent the world. As would now also be generally acknowledged, since there is no "theory-" or "concept-neutral" way to do this, we can never be sure that our representations truly represent the world the way it is in-itself.[4] The problem begins with our ordinary experience and runs straight through to sophisticated scientific theory. Put in

---

[2] Included here are Quine, 1961; Hanson, 1958; Toulmin, 1953, 1961; Sellars, 1963; Feyerabend, 1975. For an excellent collection of essays, see Suppe, 1977. A still very useful account is Brown, 1977.

[3] Empiricist foundationalism assumes a "theory neutral" observation language which anchors all theory. It is in terms of it that theory is tested, confirmed or falsified. See below.

[4] In its modern form, this is the problem raised by the philosopher Immanuel Kant who distinguished between "things as experienced" (phenomena) and "things-in-themselves." Kant argued that the latter were unknowable, but rescued scientific objectivity by holding that the categories of mind were universal, the same in all "rational beings." For a perceptive view of the history of modern epistemology, see Rorty, 1981.

other terms, we cannot step out of our history and have a God's-eye view of the world.[5]

This entails an intractable fallibilism: no truth claim is certain and all are revisable in the light of new experience and new theories. But we need not abandon the idea of truth. The products of scientific practice vindicate the physical sciences as the preferred means of fixing belief about the world.[6] Like juries, scientific communities come to agreement, but each member of the community is constrained by historically generated values, goals and practices which, as a community, they accept. Let us not forget, the world, as it is in-itself, remains the most critical constraint. No set of beliefs will allow humans to fly like birds, to stay healthy on an exclusive diet of cheeseburgers, to build a perpetual motion machine, to pollute the air and the earth, and maintain, indefinitely, an environment suitable for human life.

Consider a parable. It is possible that a society could come to believe that women should be forbidden from eating bananas because they believe that doing so will undermine their reproductive capacities. It also may be that this belief is well supported by convictions arising from their creation story and other ongoing practices in their everyday life. We say that bananas will not have ill-effects on female reproduction. Indeed, we say that they are quite nutritious. Who is right? Or perhaps both are right?

In our culture we accept the idea of science – even if we are not always clear why we should. We might say to our new-found friend that he should allow females to eat bananas and see who is right. Likely, he will not, but even if he did and the female who consumed bananas continued to be fertile, he could, we can be sure, explain this outcome in terms of intervention by one of his well-respected gods. And he could insist, consistent

---

[5] Kuhn's concern was wholly the representations of scientific theory, but his line of argument conjoined with other so-called, post-modern epistemologies. Thus it is now argued that, for example, women, the colonized or indigenous people have a distinct perspective or framework of meaning and experience, and that these are privileged, or at least that some scientific perspective is not privileged. We will return to this idea in chapter 3.

[6] The expression, "scientific practice" – like "scientific method" – is both highly abstract and crude. Both are learned from those skilled in the practice of the sciences, as apprentices, neither may be articulated in any sort of clear fashion and, as the text from Einstein quoted when we began says, when articulated – especially by philosophers and textbook authors – they are all too often distortions of real practice. Since Kuhn's book, a host of literature shows this to be the case. See, for example, Latour *et al.*, 1979, 1987; Pickering (ed.), 1992; Knorr-Cetina, 1981, 1999; Hacking, 1983, 1992, 2000. For a defense of the so-called "strong programme" in the sociology of knowledge against the charge that it is guilty of vicious epistemological relativism, see Manicas and Rosenberg, 1985, 1988. It is also the case that when good scientific practice is violated we get "shoddy science", "reckless science" and "dirty science." The best account remains Jerome Ravetz, 1971. Indeed, given the development of "big science," it has been increasingly difficult to sustain "good scientific practice." See, for example, Richard Lewontin's review (2004) of two pertinent recent accounts.

with our logic, that there remain scores of yet untested cases. How do we know what will happen in these? We feel confident that bananas are nutritious and good for both females and males, in part because we think that his beliefs about creation and all the *kapus* which are legitimated by it are wrong – interesting perhaps, but not plausible. Moreover, and much more important epistemologically, although our human practices are socially constructed, bananas are not – even if the meanings attached to them in social interaction are. Bananas exist and they exist independently of our beliefs about them. We know that they are wrong about them because we understand why bananas are nutritious. We can produce well-established theories about reproduction, health and the bio-chemical properties of bananas.

Of course, our kinsmen may not be convinced. Moreover, one might argue that their belief system is to be preferred. Perhaps it has allowed them to reproduce a pleasant and just life. (Their women might not agree!) So we might not wish to interfere with our "scientific" ideas and we may hope that they might be able to preserve the way of life that they prefer. Indeed, it is a huge error to suppose that just because we believe that some claim is true, coercive intervention can be justified.[7] This is all quite consistent with saying that they are wrong about bananas. Indeed, we can now offer technologies based on this knowledge which can prevent ill-health, extend mortality and increase fertility. This is, of course, the second obvious argument in favor of believing the claims of science. We are today surrounded by technologies made possible only through the understanding provided by the physical sciences – for good or for ill.

In the foregoing, the idea that we could test the hypothesis that bananas were good for females as well as for males was appealed to uncritically. We need, straightaway, to reject two claims about scientific method that are dead ends. One is the inductivist assumption that one confirms a hypothesis by piling up cases. This has plausibility as regards hypotheses like the one in our example – even if, as we noted, our kinsman has our logic on his side. Not only is it the case that for any finite number of instances, there will always be more instances not yet tested, but we need to be confident that the sample is apt – an enormous problem which should not be underestimated. For example, inferring ancestry from gene markers of sampled populations is fraught with difficulty (chapter 3). The other error, promoted by Karl Popper, is the idea that (versus the inductivists), since we cannot positively confirm hypotheses, we can falsify them. No

---

[7] Which is not to say either that coercive intervention is never justified. For some discussion of a very large and difficult topic, see, for example, essays by Seyla Benhabib, Martha Nussbaum and Jonathan Glover in Nussbaum and Glover, 1995.

fallacy will be committed here. Hypotheses which resist falsification then are accepted.

Popper was interested in demarcating science from non-science and his main interest was in showing that some hypotheses resist falsification in principle, for example, that God is good, and hence, that they cannot be scientific. This remains a viable way to distinguish science from non-science. But the idea that one can escape fallacy by seeking to falsify hypotheses will not do either: the effort to falsify any hypotheses always involves auxiliary hypotheses and thus, as a matter of formal logic, the test is no more conclusive when it is negative then when it is positive. If T is the theory, A are auxiliary hypotheses needed to make the test, and O are observations, this is the logic of the situation: The argument on the

Confirmation	*Falsification*
If T (and A) then O_1	If T (and A), then O_2
O_1	*Not-O_2*
Therefore T	Therefore Not-T *or* Not-A

left commits the formal fallacy of affirming the consequent and is invalid. Which is to say that the premises may both be true and the conclusion false. The argument on the right is valid (which was Popper's point), but it shows that T need not be rejected – on the evidence. More generally, the idea, so critical to the empiricist understanding of science, that it was possible to develop a logic of confirmation which had the power of mathematical logic, seems now to have been abandoned.[8]

Plainly theories need to be judged by their fit with observed and experimental data – even while we acknowledge the always present problem of assessing the significance of evidence and the ever present possibility of a fudge factor – but a third overlooked factor relevant to theory acceptance is the explanatory role of the theory. That is, it is a critical feature of good theory that the representation be a convincing description of real, but perhaps unobservable processes which would explain not merely observations that are readily available, but observations made available by controlled experiment – where this is possible. As Hempel ultimately came to see, versus instrumentalist (anti-realist) conceptions of theoretical terms, theories function to provide explanations – or better understanding in the sense that chapter 1 argued. But in addition to this, as Michael Friedman and others have insisted, *a fundamental criterion for building a consensus in the scientific community is explanatory unification.* The kinetic theory of gases, for example, gives us an understanding of

---

[8] Some of the early key papers in this now largely forgotten debate may be found in Manicas, 1977: section VI, "Induction."

the pattern given in the Boyle-Charles law, but other phenomena, for example, that gases obey Graham's law of diffusion, are made intelligible as well.

Even if the foregoing is granted, it is very often said that the real test of theory is its predictive capacity. There is a sense in which this is true, but another in which it is not. It is true as regards the typical experiment, but despite much mythology to the contrary, predictions are not, in general, a reliable test of theory. To clarify this, we need first to introduce the concept of closure. This discussion leads to a sketch of the implications of the fact that in the real world, all the countless generative mechanisms are operating open-systemically. The upshot is radical contingency and, with it, critical limits on our ability to make predictions.

Experiment and the concept of closure

Following Harré (1970), and more recently, Bhaskar (1975), the key feature of experiments is that the experimenter actively intervenes in the course of nature. She makes things happen which otherwise would not have happened. Putting aside what might be called "exploratory experiments," such as anatomical dissection, the aim of an experiment is to isolate or make constant all those properties except those one wants to study. Put roughly, the experimenter has a theory about some generative mechanism / causal process which, once initiated, has a predictable (in theory) outcome. Her aim, accordingly, is to trigger the mechanism, but to preclude anything which would have an effect on the outcome so predicted. The idea is to show that since no other potential causes are at work in the experimental situation, only the one being manipulated accounts for the outcome. This is an extraordinarily difficult thing to bring off and what needs to be done varies with the problem being addressed: from the attempt to test the mean-speed theorem by having a ball roll down an inclined plane so that it was easy to measure distances and times accurately, to Michaelson and Morley's idea to float their apparatus on a bath of mercury in order to isolate it from vibrations and other disturbances which would have affected what they expected to occur, to the hurling of nuclei of one element against the nuclei of another expecting that they form the nucleus of as yet unknown elements. To use other language here, *the experimenter seeks closure.*

We have closure when (1) we are able to identify all the pertinent initial conditions; (2) we can either isolate the generative mechanisms that theory says are implicated in the outcome, or serially keep them constant; (3) we can be assured that there is constancy of extrinsic conditions. In this situation, the system is not only deterministic, which entails that whatever happens is caused, but that contingency has altogether been eliminated. *The intrinsic structures (the generative mechanisms) of the system ensure that for each set of antecedent conditions only one result is possible.*

Experiment presupposes our ability artificially to establish closure or to take advantage of partial closures where we can find them (Conley 2001). A successful experiment is a highly potent test of a theory exactly because if conditions of closure are even approximately satisfied, the predictions of the theory are tested. It is in this sense that it is said that a good theory can predict. As before, logically, if the experiment fails to produce the predicted outcome, it may be because some assumptions of the theory are false, or because some other factor has entered, unnoticed, into producing the actual outcome.

This situation is very different from predicting outcomes in open systems. In nature, there are no closed systems – even if, as in astronomy one has, without experiment, what amounts to closure. Indeed, it is this fact which makes plausible the idea that theory can be formalized mathematically and that outcomes, accordingly, will be explained as simply the product of mathematical calculations.

This is easily illustrated. In analyzing the dynamics of the solar system, we assume, not unreasonably, that we have identified all the masses, that all the relevant causal mechanisms governing the movement of all the masses which have been identified are known (there are really only two), and that no large masses, not already identified, will subsequently become part of the system. Our dynamical description is, as it were, unchanging. Indeed, linear equations effectively model the system. The problem of identifying the location of any body anytime then becomes strictly computational. Thus, we can predict the exact location of the moon at any instant into the infinite future. But to do this we assume, not unreasonably, that no huge mass will come flying into our solar system. If it were to do so, all our predictions would fail. The system, closed to that point, would be opened. All our calculations would be wrong.

Alternatively, when we think of classical physics, perhaps we think of a projectile whose path is beautifully described by the formula for a parabola, $y = ax^2 + bx + y$. But we don't think of a falling leaf or a boulder crashing down a mountain, splintering and leaving its parts strewn down the side of the mountain. Yet these phenomena are also, in principle, describable by the same physics. We can predict the positions of planets and projectiles with considerable exactitude; we cannot do this with leaves and boulders. Why not?

The falling leaf is still subject to the laws of motion, but it might go anywhere exactly because we cannot specify the initial conditions and there are all kinds of things in the system – the erratic air mass through which it falls, a bicycle rider speeding by – which will affect its downward trajectory. The system remains open. (We can construct an experiment, however: we can create a vacuum in a closed chamber, and so on.)

Getting ahead of ourselves, we can here contrast the behavior of clockwork soldiers and real people whose behavior is manifestly open-systemic. As Bhaskar says:

Clockwork soldiers and robots do not more nearly observe the laws of mechanics than real people. Rather, their peculiarity stems from the fact that if wound up and left alone their intrinsic structure ensures that for each set of antecedent conditions only one result is possible. But outside the domain of closure the laws of mechanics are, as Anscombe has put it, 'rather like the rules of chess; the play is seldom determined, though nobody breaks the rules'. (1975: 110)

In our world, most events – birth, growth, rain, fires, earthquakes, depressions, revolutions – are produced by a complex nexus of causes of many different kinds, conjunctively at work. Thus, as Bhaskar notes, "the predicates 'natural,' 'social,' 'human,' 'physical,' 'chemical,' 'aerodynamical,' 'biological,' 'economic,' etc. ought not to be regarded as differentiating different kinds of events, but as differentiating different kinds of mechanisms" (1975: 119). Indeed, a good measure of the extraordinary success of the disciplines of the abstract physical sciences is due to the fact that inquirers have been able to ignore concrete complexity and, via abstraction from the real concrete, they have been able to theorize physical, chemical and bio-chemical mechanisms as if they were operating without interference. This involves a reductionist strategy in the sense that as Atkins puts it: "they prefer to disentangle the awesome complexity of the world, examining it piece by piece, and build it up again, with deeper understanding" (2003: 2). Here not only is experiment critical but the capacity to deal with the real concrete in terms of strata – the physical, chemical and biological – has been a critical feature of the successes of the physical sciences.

To go back to our earlier example, we can think of the periodic table as abstractly summarizing the chemical possibilities for all the elements, what causal properties they have, what molecules are possible (and impossible) and what causal properties they must have qua chemical, even when they are functioning as they normally are, in open systems. Similarly, one can understand mechanical outcomes in terms of the generative mechanisms of physics, and so for biology, which provides us with theories of biological mechanisms. But since in the world, they are operating open-systemically, this knowledge, powerful as it is, is not sufficient to either explain or predict any concrete outcome – even the dissolving of a particular spoonful of salt in the water glass in my hand. Pertinently, if lacking in interest, *the salt has to get into the water and the condition of the water must be appropriate.*

The foregoing has enormous implication for a human science, to be considered in the chapters that follow. Here we can only notice the consequences regarding experiment in the human sciences, for not only is there no way to seek even relative closures, but intervening to make things happen which would not have happened otherwise will likely be immoral. But there is one piece of unfinished business.

Explanation and prediction are not symmetrical

Of considerable pertinence to the problem of understanding and explanation in the human sciences is the idea that explanation and prediction are symmetrical. This idea must be heartily rejected. As already noted, one often encounters the idea that a good theory makes good predictions. But where this idea is appropriate, it does not mean that some naturally occurring event is thereby predicted. Rather, it concerns the powerful idea, important to accepting a theory as true, that on the basis of the theory, we are able to test our theory and sometimes make new discoveries. There are many instances of this. An easy one to describe is the filling in of the periodic table. We noted that lacking any knowledge of the structure of atoms and their dynamics, Mendeleev had to compile his table empirically. Still, by interpolating between known properties of neighboring elements in his table, he was able to fill in some of the gaps in that table. (Atkins notes that he also "predicted elements that do not in fact exist.") But the powerful quantum theory developed by Neils Bohr and Erwin Schrödinger allowed chemists to infer the existence of elements which experiment then proved to exist. Mendeleev began with 61 known elements. We now know that there are some 110 elements.

But this is very different to arguing that we can judge a theory by its ability to predict events in open systems. Thus, as Milton Friedman argued: "theory is to be judged by the predictive power for the class of phenomena which it is intended to 'explain'" (1968: 512). As he says:

the relevant question to ask about the 'assumptions' of a theory is not whether they are descriptively 'realistic', for they never are, but whether they are sufficiently good approximations for the purpose at hand. And this question can be answered only by seeing whether the theory works, which means whether or not it yields sufficiently accurate predictions. (Friedman, 1968: 517)

Again, if prediction means that given our knowledge of chemical mechanisms, there should be an unknown element between two already identified elements, then proof of its existence is a powerful test of the theory.

But if it means that theory will allow us to predict any and all chemical outcomes in the world, then while theory gives us an understanding of powerful constraints on what can happen, there are nonetheless limitless possibilities regarding what *will* happen. The salt in my hand may never dissolve, or be a party to the rusting of the can, to the seasoning of my steak, and so on.

There is indeed a paradox here: we don't need current theory to make very good predictions regarding many chemical outcomes. We noted earlier that to explain that a particular quantity of salt dissolves in water, we need to understand that salt is water-soluble (but we need not understand the mechanism which explains this) and (non-trivially) we need to know that it was put in water. That is, we often can and do offer conditional predictions: if X, then Y will occur. These are, indeed, the bread and butter of ordinary life, and as long as we are speaking of the countless generalizations available to us – all known independently of the discoveries of science – we are *generally* not disappointed. But not only is this hardly the prediction and control so often taken to be the test of scientific theory, but as noted, we are also very often disappointed, either because in an open-systemic world, the conditions of the antecedent were not satisfied, or they did not constitute a set of sufficient conditions. Were it otherwise, of course, we would all get rich on the stock market and there would be no divorces.

The world is not Laplacean

Pierre Simon Laplace (1749–1827) was a brilliant mathematician who left us with the powerful idea that a theory of n-variables with n-equations would make all science computational. Indeed, we can think of the universe as one gigantic closed system. Remarkably, it is just this assumption which lingers in the background of what has been called "regularity determinism," the idea that "the world is so constituted that there are descriptions such that for every event the simple formula, 'whenever this, then that' applies" (Bhaskar 1975: 69). And of course, it is just this assumption which is promoted by the empiricist "search for laws" as the goal of explanatory science.

But if what happens in the universe is the product of the particular conjunction of initiated generative mechanisms, and the configurations of these changes with time, there will be no such description – and there will be contingency and plenty of it. This means that after something has happened, we are often able to explain it – it was caused, but we could not have predicted it – sometimes without even a modest measure of probability. This is typical of many of the events which interest us most: a war; the fall of the Berlin Wall; a powerful upswing in the economy; an extended drought; an earthquake; a hotel fire; a fatal stroke; the emergence of a new virus.

The assumption of regularity determinism encourages two counter-productive regressions. If the predicted outcome fails to occur, one searches for "the missing variable," either to continue to enlarge the system to include new "factors," or to reduce elements to their presumed atomistic components. There is no rational limit to how far one might go. In the first, perhaps more typical case, the system continues to include variables until it includes everything. In the second case, since there are no conditions intrinsic to the system, the reduction proceeds until it includes nothing. The aspirations of Wilfredo Pareto, economist-cum-sociologist, illustrate this beautifully. For him:

In order thoroughly to grasp the form of a society in every detail, it would be necessary first to know what all the very numerous elements are, and then to know how they function – and that in quantitative terms . . . The number of equations would have to be equal to the number of unknowns and would determine them exclusively. (1935: vol. 4, paragraph 2072)

For Pareto, working before the age of the supercomputer, the problem was wholly the practical difficulty of solving the linear equations.[9] Thus, the economic system was but "a small fraction of the social system," but even then, "in the case of 100 individuals and 700 goods there would be 70,699 conditions . . . We would have to solve a system of 70,699 equations."

Perhaps unsurprisingly, Pareto's vision was not ignored by social scientists. For example, Talcott Parsons insisted that "not only do theoretical propositions stand in logical interrelations to each other so that they may be said to constitute 'systems' but it is in the nature of the case that theoretical systems should attempt to become 'logically closed.' That is, a system starts with a group of interrelated propositions which involve reference to empirical observations within the logical framework of the propositions in question." And indeed, "the simplest way to see the

[9] We can employ linear equations when the variables represent a stable, closed dynamical system. General equilibrium theory is a perfect example; see chapter 6. Non-linear equations are used to model "chaotic systems." Edward Lorenz (1996) developed three non-linear equations for the analysis of weather. He programmed these and ran the sequence. On another run, he stopped the sequence mid-point, but rather than go back to the start, he typed the mid-point values into the computer and ran the sequence from there. The two sequences diverged, at first by a small amount, then increasingly. The computer stored six digits, but the printout only three. When he began the sequence from the mid-point, there was a very small difference in the input values of the variable and these were amplified as the sequence ran. See the discussion of meteorology, below.

meaning of the concept of a closed system in this sense is to consider the example of a system of simultaneous equations. Such a system is determinate, i.e., closed, when there are as many independent equations as there are independent variables" (1937: 9–10). Parsons's commitment to positivist principles is clear enough here. But, as noted, the world is not Laplacean and celestial mechanics is a poor model for science.

It is clear why we can often explain when we could not have predicted: time makes the difference. Since the universe is not a closed system, what happens has consequences regarding what will happen next. These ideas are best illustrated, perhaps, by considering two historical sciences: evolutionary biology and meteorology.

Darwin gives us a notion of a science radically unlike the ideal bequeathed (mistakenly) by classical physics. The key difference is this: Darwin showed us that, at least with respect to living things, history matters a great deal (Manicas, 1989c; Rosenberg, 2005). Roughly, he offered us a way to understand the taxonomic order of living things in terms of "historical pathway, pure and simple." That is, species and their characteristics are explained as adaptations, where, importantly, adaptation is a response to the historical sequence of selective demands of the environment (including other organisms). Darwin thus showed that there was absolutely no requirement for us to impute some form of design or intrinsic purpose or meaning to what exists nor, as importantly, that there was any sort of necessity or inevitability about which species have perished and which have come to exist. It is important to be clear about this.

Darwin did not explain the evolution of the species. He provided one powerful mechanism for explaining this: natural selection. Explaining the outcomes of natural selection presupposes that we have detailed information regarding organisms and the relations of organisms to their environment. If we had this information from the beginnings of life, we would have a start in reconstructing the course of evolution. Unfortunately, such information is not and will not become available. As Richard Burian writes, "the course of evolution, even on a fairly large scale, is fraught with the consequences of historical accidents and contingencies" (1989: 160). This does not mean that biological phenomena are either wholly or partly uncaused. It means rather that, as with any concrete event, the evolution of a species, like the onslaught of a drought, is the outcome of a multiplicity of causes in a continually changing configuration. To call something a historical accident is but to say, as above, that it could not have been predicted, that there was an "incalculability" as regards what in fact happened. To speak of contingencies is to say only that there is no reason to believe that the world is like the solar system as described by classical physics, a world where all the masses and their relations are accounted for and nothing new will happen.

Meteorology, like evolutionary biology, is a historical science and, like geology, it draws on non-geological laws pertaining to the mechanical and thermodynamical properties of gases, solids and liquids. Its problems with predictions are well known, but we can now see clearly why. Weather is a wonderful example of a chaotic system. Such systems are "mixing in finite time." That is, "what is initially known about the system becomes probabilistically irrelevant to its future" (Hobbs, 1993: 124). This depends upon noticing that the system is sensitive to initial conditions, which means that as a function of the accuracy of our knowledge of these conditions, even under conditions of relative closure, there will be a range of degrees of freedom as regards the subsequent states.

This is best illustrated with the example of successive tennis balls hit into a forest. Two successive balls, hit at nearly identical velocities, can hit a tree at nearly identical locations. But each time they are deflected, their trajectory changes. The very small initial difference results in a difference in all the subsequent hits. Accordingly, the two balls may end up in two very different locations. Indeed, as Max Weber long ago pointed out using a boulder rolling down a rough hill as his example, even if we assume "ideal conditions of antecedent observation," while we could calculate "the occurrence and perhaps general angle of the splintering," we could not calculate "the number or shape of fragments, the patterns they formed when they come to rest or a veritable infinity of other aspects" (1975: 122). Even putting aside the lay of the mountain, at each instance in the downward trajectory, the splintering is itself altering the conditions of future falling and splintering. Because what is happening has consequences on what then happens, there is, he rightly insisted, an eradicable "incalculability." Mathematically, this is a non-linear system. For such systems, there is in principle unpredictability. Jesse Hobbs applies the idea to weather.

For example, meteorologists use parameters such as temperature, humidity, pressure, wind direction, and wind velocity to make predictions. This yields systems with five or six degrees of freedom multiplied by the number of distinct locations for which these values are measured or represented – a level of computational complexity that already demands the largest supercomputers to manage. Even so, the resulting "Accu-weather" predictions might as well be called "Unaccu-weather" predictions because of meteorological chaos . . . But suppose undaunted meteorologists take the plunge into ever greater levels of precision. Should they otherwise succeed, they will run up against what Edward Lorenz calls the "but-terfly effect" – the unanticipated flapping of a butterfly's wings in a chaotic air mass would perturb it enough to throw off all long-range weather predictions (1993: 124–125).[10]

While we need not pursue the point here, putting aside the unanticipated flapping of the wings of the butterfly and the computational problems that greater precision would bring, Hobbs doubts that taking "the plunge" to greater levels of precision will improve our predictive abilities. The limit of precision, as with all chaotic systems, is literally infinite. Hence, while we have determinism – outcomes are causal products – there is also in-principle unpredictability.

These considerations entail that we cannot say that an event had to happen. To be sure, once something happens, we can always go back in time, identify the relevant generative mechanisms and causal contingen-cies and provide an account which explains the event. This will generally take the form of a narrative which identifies the particular collocation of causes as they developed in time. As Harré says:

Temporal concepts allow us to order the influences as causes and effects. Each cause is an influence exerted on some mechanism from without, and so itself produced by some other mechanism; that is, is itself an effect. The stimulus or stimuli which brought it into being are causes, and to come into existence in a world of enduring mechanisms must themselves be effects. Effects become causes of further effects, and causes are the effects of antecedent causes. (1970: 262)

All our explanations of events will be incomplete. The effort to find the causes will cease when we have satisfied the demand that called for the explanation.[11]

In the chapters that follow, we can draw on the account of the foregoing to examine the problem of explanation and understanding in the human sciences, and hopefully to generate some useful strategies for responding to their distinct tasks.

[10] The weather forecaster is but minimally interested in explanation, but the meteorologist is in a position to provide a good understanding of meteorological phenomena, both before and after the fact. That is, like the physicist, she can offer an account of the critical generative mechanisms at work in producing meteorological phenomena, for example, the thermodynamical properties of ocean cooling.

[11] This temporal regress of causal explanation has a parallel as regards understanding where we have a regress of micro-explanation, from "salt is water-soluble," to an account in terms of molecules, to atoms to quarks. See Harré 1970: chapter 10.

3 Explanation and understanding in the social sciences

Introduction

It is often supposed that because the social sciences must deal with people, social science is either quite impossible, or at best, inevitably incompetent. Unfortunately, this view is promoted, in quite unintended ways, by many writers who have a mistaken view of the natural sciences. These writers suppose that:

1. If science is to be empirical, it must be experimental.
2. The main task of science is prediction.
3. The successful sciences can both explain and predict events (including, then, the acts of individuals).
4. Nature is uniform in the sense that scientific laws are regularities of the form, "whenever this, then that."
5. Theories are "deductive systems."
6. Scientific observation is theory-neutral.

If we measure the social sciences on any of these grounds, they look very bad – even hopeless. But things are not as bad as they seem, since none of the foregoing propositions is true. In the previous chapters, we tried to show why. The alternative offered shows that:

1. There are very successful non-experimental sciences.
2. A main task of any science is description and understanding; prediction plays a minor role.
3. Explaining concrete events is generally neither the interest, nor often within the competence, of a science.
4. Nature is uniform not in the sense that there are "invariant relations of resemblance and succession" (regularity determinism), but in the sense that things have causal powers that allow us to generalize and have expectations.
5. Theories are almost never deductive systems; rather, they offer a representation of causal mechanisms and processes, both observable and non-observable.

6. Finally, it is quite impossible to "observe" anything independently of some conceptual frame of reference, but this does not undermine the quest for a true representation of reality.

We will put some of these ideas to work in the present chapter. We shall not argue, however, that there are *no* important differences between inquiry in the human sciences and inquiry in the natural sciences. Unfortunately, these differences are not, in general, properly understood. These misunderstandings are, usually, part of the more general misunderstanding about science generally.

There are two very large differences to be considered. The first is the obvious one that studying people is not the same as studying "things." The second follows on this. Unlike the objects of study in natural science, the objects of study in social science – institutions, social structures, social relations – do not exist independently of us. They are, as we shall explain, real but concept- and activity-dependent. We begin with an account of persons.

Explaining human powers

Persons are organisms, but they are also social beings. We need to see what this means, and we need to be careful here. Both in ordinary conversation and in social science, we tend to speak not of persons, but of individuals. We do this because by "individuals" we tend to mean persons – individuals with a host of capacities which they employ in interaction. These are, in the jargon, "socialized" individuals. Understanding these capacities is a necessary first step. We can then draw what are some important conclusions bearing on explaining the actions of persons.

The view of causality that we have sketched helps enormously in clarifying what is at issue and we think also to dispel an illusory problem: the bearing of biology on human action. We can begin with the fact that (excepting for identical twins) no two human genotypes are the same and that from the moment of conception the developmental process is epigenetic. That is, everything that happens is a complex transactional interplay of causes and processes through time.

It may be useful here to have a workable definition of "genotype," "phenotype" and "epigenesis." The genotype is the "internally coded, inheritable information" carried by all living organisms. The phenotype is the observable physical features of an organism and includes anything that is part of the observable structure, function or behavior of a living organism. Another way to speak of epigenesis is to say that the phenotype is the non-additive causal product of gene–gene transactions, gene–environment transactions and environment–environment transactions. As regards phenotypical outcomes, including even most genetic disorders, nearly all are epigenetic causal products, a point of considerable importance.

Each of us begins (at conception) as but two cells – the genome which establishes the genotype. It is often said, wrongly, that the "genetic code" is a "program," as if whatever we come to be was fully "determined" by the string of DNA. But as the biologist Paul Weiss says, in the first place, the genome "is, and always has been a captive of an *ordered* environment," and "while the genome contributes to the specific properties of that environment in mutual interactions with it . . . it is only by virtue of the primordial frame of organization of the cytoplasm of an egg that an individual can maintain . . . the unity of overall design."[1] For the overall design, for example, *Felix catus* or *Homo sapiens*, not any DNA chain will do, of course, but an immensely complex – and contingent – interplay of causal processes determines the specific character of the organism. That is, DNA contains all the information necessary to build and sustain an organism, but it needs a living organism in an environment. And the building and sustaining of it involves a marvelously complex causal nexus.

From the point of view of biology, an organism is an ordered complex of orderly complex systems. Biochemistry starts from the level of atoms and molecules and works upward through the larger and more complex molecules to complicated systems, organelles, cells, tissues, organs, systems and finally to the organism itself. Activities within systems may have, as the outcome of their causal transactions, properties at higher levels. These are properly termed emergent properties. For example, proteins are capable of at least eight major activities of which the amino acids from which they are polymerized are not capable. Complete information about all the atomic positions of an unknown protein does not allow us to infer even that the protein is an enzyme, still less, what in a specific system its particular causal properties or functions might be. What it does is a consequence of its relations in the system. This holds true at every level, including the psychological.

Moreover, higher level properties have bearings on lower level functions and properties. The coordinated movements of an organism are paradigmatic. The cat reaches for the ball of string. In achieving his goal, fantastic constraints are imposed in coordinating the array of systems, perceptual, muscular, anatomical and so on, which are involved.

The organism is not a closed system. That is, the effects of microprocesses at the molecular level are mediated not only at that level but

---

[1] The following owes much to the various writings of Paul A. Weiss (1968, 1971, 1972). See also Hull, 1974; Wimsatt, 1976a, 1976b; Craver, 2001.

by mediations in a wider environment, an environment which, strictly speaking, extends to the far reaches of the universe. For example, exposure to radiation, alcohol, drugs, poor nutrition and so on is devastating to the organism's course of development. As Weiss writes, "in this incessant interplay, the latitude for epigenetic vagaries of the component elements on all levels . . . is immense."

The epigenetic "vagaries," of course, are not unlimited: they are, if you will, restricted by our "biologically determined" human nature. It may be useful here to give a restricted meaning to a term used widely but vaguely (and usually wrongly). We can say that some trait, capacity or difference is a feature of our (biologically determined) "human nature" only if, in realizing that trait, the developing conceptus undergoes a "characteristic" human development such that it is substantially irrelevant where and when that process takes place. To be sure, there is no characteristic human development since development is consistent with a fantastic range of very different environments. Nevertheless, the idea is clear enough. We want here to rule out (at least for the moment), such genetic and environmental accidents as Down's syndrome and thalidomide babies. Most crucially, while we must acknowledge that humans need a human environment to realize their distinctive human capacities, we want to put aside (for the moment) the social and cultural differences encountered in all human development.

Given this restricted sense, there are some obvious biologically determined traits: our human anatomy and physiology is one. This makes some capacities possible and others impossible. Humans cannot fly and, lacking gills, they cannot breathe in water. Biology determines sex and manifest physical traits that mark family resemblance, such as facial features, body type and skin color. But race is not biologically determined since on all the evidence there are no biological grounds for grouping people into distinct races.[2] In other terms, there is no non-arbitrary statistically significant difference between populations which we would like to call "races" and neighboring populations. Indeed, "each population is a microcosm that recapitulates the entire human macrocosm, even if the precise genetic composition varies slightly" (Cavelli-Sforza, 2000: 25, 29). Gould concludes with a wonderful illustration from Lewontin: "If the holocaust comes and a small tribe in the New Guinea forests are the only survivors, almost all the genetic variation now expressed among the innumerable groups of our four billion [1980] people will be preserved' (Gould, 1981: 323).

---

[2] For a review and summary of the evidence, see in addition to Gould (1981), Lewontin, 1982; Drechsel, 1991; Cavelli-Sforza, 2000; and the special issue of *Nature Genetics* 36 (2004).

Race (like ethnicity) is a social construction: we simply employ a socially agreed-upon difference as the criterion for the grouping. Of course, there are historical reasons which explain why the cluster of differences associated with physiognomy became the criterion for distinguishing "races," but this important issue cannot be pursued here.[3] Since, however, the idea of race as a biological notion has been reinvigorated by some recent work, and because much is at stake, a brief diversion on the topic of race is warranted. This will also provide a useful example of problems in explaining and predicting phenotypical outcomes, including here the best cases for study – the range of diseases which include sickle cell anemia, type 2 diabetes and multiple sclerosis.

Biology, race and disease

This new vigor, along with some old problems, comes with the widely disseminated idea that gene studies have transformed forensics, with its use in understanding and predicting the probabilities of diseases, and with the construction of so-called "ethnic drugs," for example, BiDil, used for the treatment of heart disease among African-Americans. All of these have made an impact on the popular imagination, too often in a misleading or downright mistaken form.[4] Accordingly, it is critical to be clear on the central issues.

First, there remains agreement that there are no gene variants present in all individuals of any demographic group and absent in individuals in any other such group. Indeed, there is considerably more genetic variation within populations as between them (Bonham et al., 2005: 12). Second,

---

[3] See Hanaford, 1996; Voegelin, 2000; Henningsen, 2004. See especially Lentin, 2004, who argues that racism was not an aberration in the modern democratic state: "On the contrary, 'race' and racism, following central authors such as Bauman, Arendt, Voegelin and many others is shown, not only to be a particularity of modernity, and specifically of the mid-nineteenth century on, but also to be grounded in what Gilroy (2000: 59) calls a 'statecraft' which at a particular historical moment requires a notion of racial hierarchy as the legitimating framework of its actions" (Lentin, 2004: 11).

[4] A particularly egregious case was the misreporting of the efforts of the National Human Genome Center of the College of Medicine at Howard University. A headline in the *New York Times* (May 27, 2003) read: "DNA of Blacks To Be Gathered To Fight Illness." The article reported that "samples would be used to find genes involved in diseases with particularly high rates among blacks like hypertension and diabetes." But, indeed, its goals were hardly so narrow and misconceived. Rather, its aim is "to study the complex interplay between environmental and genetic factors." See Rotimi, 2004. Another example is the Op Ed essay in the *New York Times* (March 14, 2005) by Armand Marie LeRoi, "A Family Tree in Every Gene." LeRoi seems to think that correlations are sufficient to establish distinct racial groups. He seems also to confuse "race" and "ancestry." See below. See also Jerry A. Coyne's review of Vincent Sarich and Frank Miele, *Race: The Reality of Human Differences*, in the *Times Literary Supplement* (February 25, 2005).

there is no argument that there are correlations between phenotypical outcomes and genetic variation. Third, as already insisted, the problem is not that genes are not causally critical to phenotypical outcomes, but that the explanation of these outcomes cannot, in general, be reduced to genetic mechanisms.

What then is the problem? It stems from the fact that while as Cavalli-Sforza says, "each population is a microcosm that recapitulates the entire human macrocosm" (2000: 28) it is also true that "frequencies of genetic variation and haplotypes differ across the world" (Bonham *et al.*, 2005: 12). Critical here are so-called SNPs, a special sort of genetic "marker."[5] Enormous ingenuity and energy have been devoted to identifying SNPs. These also are critical to the idea that there are "ethnic drugs," or drugs specifically pertinent to "ethnic estimation based upon allele frequency variation" (Duster, 2004: 7).

The route to misunderstanding is easily identified. One begins by noting a statistical difference in the incidence of some disease, for example, sickle cell anemia, between African-Americans and European-Americans. One then identifies a correlation between these differences and differences in genetic variation in the two groups: an association is established between being a member of a phenotypically defined "race" and sharing in the particular genetic variation. Since genes are surely causal, we conclude, mistakenly, that racial differences explain differences in phenotypical outcomes. The fallacy is plain: these are all correlations and not particularly strong ones at that. Thus, socially constructed categories of race and ethnicity in use are reasonably correlated with ancestry,[6] but given that the individuals may have membership in several bio-geographical clusters, that the borders of these are not distinct and are influenced by sampling strategies, ancestry is not race. While it has

---

[5] Some further critical terms may be introduced here: an allele is a form of a gene which codes for one possible outcome of a phenotype. For example, Mendel found that there were two forms of gene which determined the color of a pea pod. Accordingly, alleles are causal. SNPs (single nucleotide polymorphisms) are alleles whose sequence has only a single changed nucleotide. For example, in the genetic code, GGG becomes GGC. "Genetic variants that are near each other tend to be inherited together. For example, all of the people who have an A rather than a G at a particular location in a chromosome can have identical genetic variants at other SNPs in the chromosomal region surrounding the A. These regions of linked variants are called haplotypes." "The number of tag SNPs that contain most of the information about the patterns of genetic variation is estimated to be about 300,000 to 600,000, which is far fewer than the 10 million common SNPs." Haplotypes, then, may be correlated with diseases (see www.hapmap.org). It is generally recognized that while convenient, there are obvious dangers in this approach, of which some are noted below.

[6] In contrast to SNP studies, inferring ancestry from DNA requires a very large number of loci. Inferring ancestry from such data remains probabilistic. See Jorde and Woodling, 2004: 531–532. See also Cavalli-Sforza, 2000: 31.

better predictive value than race, ancestry, then, is a weak correlate for variation across the genome.[7] An example makes the case: "the town of Orchomenos in central Greece has a rate of sickle cell anemia twice that of African-Americans and . . . black South Africans do not carry the sickle cell trait" (Rotimi, 2004: 545). That is, since one can be phenotypically "black" and lack the variation and one can be "white" and have it, race (comprehended as biologically meaningful) explains nothing.[8]

Indeed, the epigenetic character of outcomes shows that even if the probability of an African-American having heart disease is higher than for European-Americans, this need not be explained in terms of genes, still less in terms of race or ancestry. Again, an example makes the point. As Duster pointed out, a classic epidemiological study (using the same quantitative methods as used in gene / disease studies: see appendix A) concluded that hypertension among African-Americans need not be the direct result of genes; rather "darker skin color in the United States is associated with less access to scarce and valued resources in society. There is a complex feedback loop and interaction affect between phenotype and social practices related to this phenotype" (Duster, 2005: 1050).

Finally, and morally critical, employing racial surrogates for SNPs not only risks reinscribing race as an explanatory biological category, but risks denying appropriate therapy to persons who could benefit. For example, as regards hypertension, despite the correlated patterns, "many African-Americans would respond better to ACE inhibitors than would many European Americans" (Jorde and Woodling, 2004: 528).[9]

Similarly, Duster also rightly argues that there are appropriate and inappropriate forensic uses of these new capacities. Since the genotype is unique, a match (or the absence of one) may be decisive as regards the guilt or innocence of a suspect or of someone already wrongly imprisoned. Problems arise with "the dangerous intersection of 'allele frequencies in special populations' and 'police profiling via phenotypes'" (Duster, 2004: 10). The problem is that having identified some person by a "racial category," the criminal behavior is "explained" and "predicted" by appeal to allele frequencies. Nor is sampling bias altogether overcome by having

---

[7] This may be generous given that the standard technique examines only a few selected loci in the DNA. As Duster notes, "what is being assessed is the frequency of genetic variation at a particular spot in the DNA of each population" (2004: 8).

[8] Put in other terms, the database problems are huge and are a consequence of the fact (already noted) that "not only do all people have the same set of genes, but all groups of people also share the major variants of those genes" (Rotimi, 2004: 544, quoting Steve Olsen). Thus, inferences drawn from one or two African populations will likely be different than a sample of 100 African populations drawn from very different geographical locations.

[9] For discussion of the BilDil case. see Rotimi, 2004 and Duster, 2004, 2005.

a universal DNA database, since if the police are not stopping white cocaine users, it does not matter if their DNA is in the database. And, of course, "DNA is only as reliable as the humans testing it" (*New York Times*, May 16, 2005).

Chapter 1 argued that causes are not merely correlations and chapter 2 insisted that explanation and prediction are not symmetrical. Both ideas were in the background of the foregoing discussion of race and biology. In this section we argued that while genes certainly figure in explanation, properly understood, race as a biological category does not. Phenotypical outcomes, whether they are diseases or behaviors, are causally complex products. We must resist the easy assumption that any single mechanism or event from among the ensemble of events and mechanisms, physical, chemical, biochemical, biological and social, is sufficient to explain some outcome, whether it be schizophrenia or measured competence in an IQ test. But once we put aside "the 800 pound gorilla which is race" (Duster) – and this may be harder than we think, and we fully acknowledge the complexity involved – there can be little doubt that current work in genetics can give us a better understanding of the role of genetic mechanisms in phenotypical outcomes. By recognizing database problems and the limits of exploiting correlation, many researchers are now aspiring to the situation where in medical decision-making, disease-related genetic variation is directly assessed.[10]

Consciousness and collective intentionality

To complete the account of human powers, and indeed, to understand distinctly human actions and outcomes, we need to take another giant step which lays the foundations for social mechanisms (chapter 4). This requires that we identify a critical emergent causal product of our species-specific brain and central nervous system. It is consciousness and the capacity of mind to represent objects and situations outside itself – technically what is termed intentionality (Searle, 1983, 1992). While it is next to impossible to deny that humans have this capacity, we still lack any sort of adequate understanding of it. Included in this is a capacity

[10] The Haplotype Map Project (HapMap) assumes, contestably, the "common disease – common variant hypothesis" which further assumes that complex diseases are influenced by SNPs that "are relatively common in human populations" (Rotimi, 2004: 543). The HapMap project has tended also to encourage the reification of racial categories. But until direct assessment of disease-related genetic variation becomes feasible, there remains disagreement regarding trade-offs in the use of current techniques for predictive, diagnostic and therapeutic uses. See especially Duster, 2004, 2005; Jorde and Wooding, 2004: 532 and Rotimi, 2004.

for collective intentionality, usually unnoticed, and, a capacity for language that is always noticed – and is almost certainly an essential feature of human society. Following Searle, collective intentionality means not only that persons have the capacity to engage in cooperative behavior and use a language, but that they can "share intentional states such as beliefs, desires and intentions."[11]

There is no good reason to be squeamish about the idea of a collective intentionality. To be sure, there are those who have supposed that it requires an untenable ontological commitment, an independently existing Hegelian spirit or a Durkheimian "collective conscious." Of course, all consciousnesses are individual, in someone's brain. As powerfully argued by George Herbert Mead and John Dewey, mind is necessarily social. Accordingly, if humans everywhere and anytime, abstractly have these capacities, given that societies differ, they will be concretely realized in a wide variety of ways.

It will be useful to distinguish realized capacities, e.g., the ability to speak (say) Dutch, from capacities as potentialities, the ability to acquire language. Capacities as potentialities are biologically determined but in actual development (contrary to our mind experiment), realized capacities are not. That is, social mechanisms (like genetic mechanisms) are necessary causes. *Homo sapiens* everywhere and anytime has the potential to be "minded" and linguistically competent, and more generally, to function in society. But of course, depending upon the time and place, children acquire some very different languages. That is, in the actual world, the potential is concretely realized in differing societies.[12] There

---

[11] Searle (1995: 23–26) gives a linguistic argument. Mead's "social behaviorism" is certainly the best explanation we have of the fact that we can share intentions, cooperate – indeed communicate. In arguing against both Wundt and Watson, his problem was precisely to explain mind and meaning in terms consistent with Darwin. In sum, "self" presupposed "communication" which presupposed "meaning" which presupposed "significant symbols" which presupposed "vocal gestures" which presupposed the "conversation of gestures" already available to lower animals. "Acts" were "social" in exactly the sense that "the human animal has the ability over and above the adjustment which belongs to the lower animal to pick out and isolate the stimulus. Mentality consists in indicating those others and to one's self so that one can control one's response" (Mead, 1967: 132). See also Gillespie, 2005. Of course, this still leaves many questions unanswered. Bickerton (1990) provides a powerful account of the origins of language which draws on evolutionary theory, biology and linguistics.

[12] As we might expect from our evolutionary history, there are important correlations between populations defined in terms of ancestry and languages. Cavalli-Sforza asks: "How is it possible for these two very different systems to follow parallel evolutionary trajectories, to 'co-evolve'? The explanation is quite simple: two isolated populations differentiate both genetically and linguistically. Isolation, which could result from geographic, ecological, or social barriers, reduces the likelihood of marriages between populations, as a result, reciprocally, isolated populations will evolve independently and

are probably biologically grounded propensities or tendencies of other sorts, for example, toward cancer and schizophrenia and perhaps also traits of personality, for example, temperament, and musical or mathematical pre-dispositions. Some people have a tin ear; some cannot hit the curve ball; others seem especially apt with numbers or things mechanical. Many potentialities of persons are either not realized at all or are barely realized. There are many reasons for this. One obvious reason: other conditions necessary to realize the capacity were absent: insufficient protein; no violin; no teacher. Another obvious reason is that realizing some capacities often requires work, often at a sacrifice of other goals and interests.

From birth onward, then, in order to realize their distinct human capacities, humans need to interact with other humans. This is also a complicated epigenetic causal story requiring contributions both from the developing child who is an active participant and from the wider social environment: the immediate nurturer, family, friends, consociates, then teachers and so on.[13] Since the process is in time, everything that happens can have effects on what will then happen. At some point – and evidently quite early on – a person with a personality – a distinct ensemble of habits, attitudes and beliefs – emerges.

Three fundamental theses would seem to follow:

1. Except for humanness, *nothing is programmed*. But we can have a better understanding of the relevant mechanisms, biological, psychological and social which, taken together, produce "personalities," and, based on this knowledge, it will be possible to offer some very useful generalizations, for example, that regarding persons experiencing crisis situations in their lives, the probability of depression is less among persons with two copies of a long allele of the gene known as 5-HTT.[14]

---

gradually become different" (2000: 15). Not only is isolation a highly relative matter (contact is continuous and reveals itself both linguistically and genetically), but because the microcosm recapitulates the macrocosm (notes 2 and 7 above), populations, best defined on the basis of endogamous behavior (a tendency to marry and reproduce within the group), are not races.

[13] In a powerful but not widely acknowledged account, Harris (1998) offers an explanation of "why children turn out as they do." For her, "parents matter less than you think and peers matter more." From the present point of view, while she uses the evidence of behavioral genetics to refute standard psychological misconceptions, especially in undermining assumptions of correlations, she seems a bit insensitive to the transactional or epigenetic character of all development.

[14] This is a conclusion of a British and New Zealand longitudinal study as reported in the *New York Times*, July 18, 2003. The mechanism is also identified. 5-HTT "contains the code to produce a protein that escorts the chemical messenger serotonin across the spaces between brain cells, or synapses, and then clears away the leftover serotonin. Drugs like Prozac, Paxil, Zoloft and Celexa, which are widely effective in treating depression, work by acting on the serotonin system."

2. The causal complexity of human development assures that, even as regards identical genotypes, concrete persons will be idiosyncratic individuals.

3. While there remains considerable contention regarding the importance of biology in human behavior, nobody denies that both nature and nurture are inextricably involved in all development (Ridley, 2003). But there is also an emerging consensus that deciding how much of either is a question that cannot be answered. Because development is epigenetic and causes are not additive, there is no reasonable way to discriminate the causal importance of any of the countless factors, neither the enormous range of implicated mechanisms nor the probably not identifiable contingent events involved in outcomes (see appendix A).

4. Given the complicated idiosyncratic biography of particular persons, there is no reason to believe that any science could offer much improvement over our ordinary ways of explaining the concrete behavior of a person.[15] Assuming that our character is causally linked to our behavior, what we do in any particular circumstance also depends upon highly variable concrete circumstances, how we understand these, what particular judgements we make, and how we assess aims and alternatives. Physics cannot explain or predict the final landing place of a falling leaf. Behavior is caused, but once we grasp the complexity of the causal nexus involved, it hardly seems plausible that any science should enable us to improve on our ability to explain and predict the concrete acts of individuals. We turn directly to this question.

Science and the explanation of the actions of persons

It is very often held that it is the task of a social science to explain behavior. It is further assumed that what a person does has natural causes and that

---

[15] Despite persistent assertions that "the explanation of behavior" is a goal, this includes psychology as a science – for all the same reasons. The task of psychology, as of other sciences, is understanding, in particular the understanding of human powers: perception, cognition, motivation, learning, imagination, language, etc. See Manicas and Secord, 1984; Margolis et al., 1986. Although developing this would call for another book, the idea is not new. See, for example, Campbell and Misanin (1969: 77): "Few, if any psychologists now believe that those conditions once labelled basic drives, such as hunger, thirst, sex, and material behavior, are predominantly governed by some common underlying generalized drive state, even if there is some activating or energizing state common to many basic drives, it is clear that the specific behaviors elicited by those drives are controlled by a complex of inter-actions among environmental stimuli, hormonal states, physiological imbalance, previous experience, etc. and that the basic drive concept is of little value in unravelling these complexities."

explaining behavior, accordingly, requires their identification. If so, even if we think we have free will, our acts are determined.

In this view, determined means caused; but in the context of the dichotomy, free will versus determinism, it implies, critically, that a person "could not have done otherwise." That is, it denies the agency of persons. It insists that even if we think that we always could have done other than what we did, we are, in fact, automata, programmed by causes to do just what we do. Our failures to explain and to predict behavior, then, are merely functions of our ignorance: if we had all the pertinent laws, and a precise description of all the initial conditions, predicting behavior would be like predicting the positions of planets. Indeed, despite the fallaciousness of this idea of science, it is usually believed that we must presuppose this if a human science is to be possible. This idea has historically been at the bottom of a debate which began with the philosopher Immanuel Kant. So-called naturalists take the position that we must bite the bullet and deny free will. Anti-naturalists take the common-sense position that since we could have done otherwise, we need to reject altogether the causal model of explanation. The alternative model on this view is that of the historian: thus, Collingwood (1969:12):

The historian need not and cannot (without ceasing to be an historian) emulate the scientist in searching for the causes or laws of events. For science, the event is discovered by perceiving it, and the further search of its cause is conducted by assigning it to its class and determining the relation between that class and others. For history, the object to be discovered is not the mere event, but the thought that expressed it. To discover that thought is already to understand it. After the historian has ascertained the facts, there is no further process of inquiring into their causes. When he knows what happened, he already knows why it happened.

Collingwood's idea can be generalized. Understanding Roman history requires that we understand why Brutus stabbed Caesar. We need to grasp his reasons and beliefs. Similarly, as regards explaining why Sam robbed the convenience store. (Both could have done otherwise.) And surely this seems right. But Collingwood's main conclusion is mistaken since his image of causality (and of science) is mistaken. And because he assumes that reasons are not causes.

As we argued in chapter 1, causal laws are not of the form, "whenever this, then that," and since the universe is not Laplacean, contingency is the constant feature of all events in the world, including the acts of persons. We can predict the position of a planet because there are only two pertinent causes (inertia and gravitation) and three pertinent variables (mass, velocity and position). Most critically, there is no "butterfly effect": for all practical purposes, the system is closed. Remember that we could not explain or predict the final pattern of splintered pieces of rock from a boulder rolling down a hill, that even in this very simple case involving nothing human, there was an inherent incalculability resulting from the fact that what happens at each instant has effects on what happens in the next instant. Given that this is true of humans and that persons are immensely complex open systems, it is hardly surprising that we cannot predict (or explain) with the ease and certainty of celestial mechanics. Indeed, suppose that just as I am about to start this sentence, an errant throw of a baseball shatters the window in my office. The sentence I started to write does not get written.

Indeed, as noted in the account of prediction in the previous chapter, there is a paradox in explaining and predicting the acts of persons. We are, in fact, quite good at both explaining and predicting the acts of persons, quite independently of knowledge provided by the human sciences. Indeed, as ordinary socialized human beings we are better at explaining and predicting human acts than sophisticated science is at explaining and predicting the final outcome of falling leaf. *And, indeed, there is no reasonable hope that the human sciences could do better in explaining and predicting the acts of persons than we do in our own very pre-scientific way.*

Our ordinary explanations of action, of course, are not scientific. They take the form of providing reasons for what people do – just as Collingwood suggests. Although this topic remains contentious in some quarters, there is no good reason to say that reasons are not causes; and there are good reasons to say that they are. To say that Sam did A because he believes B seems unavoidably to mean that Sam's belief that B is the cause of Sam's doing A, otherwise, there is no real connection between the reason and the act. As Bhaskar writes: "If and whenever they explain . . . reasons must be interpreted as causes, on pain of ceasing to explain at all" (1979: 115). One can assent here that my reason to do so-and-so was itself caused, but surely this hardly matters since it is my reason. Had I chosen otherwise, that too would have been my reason.

Moreover, like other sorts of causes, the possession of a reason can be a state or disposition: being honest gives one a reason to tell the truth. Being a liberal gives one a reason for voting for a Democrat. Like other causes which must be analyzed as dispositions, reasons may be possessed even when not exercised, and even when exercised they may not explain the act: in that case they would not be the reason for the action. On the other hand, without thought, when appropriate conditions are present, we act. Indeed, the overwhelming percentage of our actions fall into this category: they do not, in general, require that we recognize, articulate or acknowledge the reasons for our action. Of course, we may be asked retrospectively to give an account, which we are generally in a position to do. This is, of course, a powerful insight of the ethnomethodological literature.

The point is of considerable importance. As Searle has suggested, in the social science literature, there are two dominating sorts of theories which aim at explaining action. One is "mental causation, according to which the agent is operating consciously or unconsciously, with a set of rational procedures over more or less well-defined sets of intentional states, such as preference schedules or internalized rules" (1995: 141). This model is now termed "rational choice theory," but in various forms, it has been around a long time.[16] The other model "does not appeal to intentional states but to brute physical causation." Most powerfully associated with behaviorism, it affirms causality, but caught in the mode of regularity determinism – "whenever this, then that" – it denies agency altogether. Searle is quite correct that what we need here is a causal account "that will explain the intricacy, the complexity, and the sensitivity of behavior, as well as explaining its spontaneity, creativity, and originality" (1995: 141).

Beginning with the idea that people have reasons for what they do, rational choice theory is an effort at spelling out what makes a decision to act rational. To be sure, this model may sometimes seem appropriate. We sometimes make a careful assessment of our situation, clarify our goals and try to assess the pluses and minuses of alternatives according to some rational ordering. But, first, this is not generally what happens. Moreover, even when it does, we are not logic-machines. By the standards of modern logic, we often do very foolish things – even if we have our reasons. Thus, according to the theory, it is irrational not to prefer a to c, if one prefers a to b and b to c. On this theory, if you value two things, such as your life and your nickel, there must be some odds at which you would bet your life against the nickel. Decision theory says, if you say "no" to any such odds, you are irrational. But, indeed, who is irrational?

A third model rejects both of these models and begins by extending the idea, already noted, that the possession of a reason must be analyzed dispositionally. More generally, as noticed by Aristotle, George Herbert Mead, John Dewey, C. W. Mills and, more recently, Pierre Bourdieu, our character and the habits we have developed, figure hugely in what we do, and they do so because they give us capacities, or powers, and these dispose us to act in certain ways. Like the powers of the theoretical things of science, these are tendencies which, although causally critical, do not,

---

[16] Hempel offered that what he called "explanation by reasons" satisfied the D-N model (1965: 463–487). RCT is well-ensconced in modern micro-economics and has become prominent in sociology and political science. See below, chapter 5 and appendix B.

in open systems, generate invariances. Knowing that Sam dislikes rock, when asked whether he likes a recently released Jimi Hendrix album, we may expect him to be critical, but what he says is not "determined." Indeed, he may well surprise us and tell us that he was pleasantly surprised by several of the cuts. Similarly, if he is honest, the answer will likely be an honest answer, but it may not be, if there are good reasons not to tell the truth: for example, if he is disposed also to try to please you. In the next chapter, this idea is complicated further to include the constraining and enabling of action by one's place in social relations. We can expect that these will be causally related to who we are.

Because we know that there is connection between what a person does and the reasons for doing it, we have a store of generalizations which give us considerable predictive ability. Thus, we can predict (or explain) that Sam will shortly go to lunch by knowing that he usually gets hungry at such and such a time, that he dislikes being hungry, that nothing prevented him from satisfying his desire to eat. As with any event, a host of causal mechanisms are at work here, physical, chemical, biological, psychological and social, and at least the first three are quite well understood. Indeed, on the present point of view, a good deal of our ignorance of the pertinent psychological and social mechanisms results from misconceiving the goals of the human sciences, but in particular, the assumption that their aim is the explanation of behavior. In any case, we do very well in explaining and predicting Sam's behavior even without an adequate scientific understanding of any of these mechanisms. Social life preceded modern science by several millennia, but it is very hard to imagine social life in the absence of such competence. This knowledge is reflected in human languages, whose concepts and distinctions regarding action are the product of long historical experience. Max Weber correctly insisted that as humans we have been "schooled in the world of own everyday experience."

Here we might consider the problem of a Martian social scientist. He lacks a human historical experience – and perhaps also a different natural history. If so, perhaps his perceptual system, not to mention his social system, is radically unlike our own. Our actions would be utterly unintelligible to him. He would first need to identify the patterns of human everyday life, and then seek an understanding of these in terms of the causal mechanisms at work. He may well have an understanding superior to ours of the physical, chemical and bio-chemical mechanisms, but he would need to put this to work to understand humans, after which he would need to do some very serious human ethnography. Harré and Secord (1973) were absolutely correct to insist that the social scientific problems of our Martian would not be at all like our social scientific problems, yet a good deal of our social science acts as if our ordinary human understandings were utterly irrelevant.

There is a paradox, ignored in the preceding, that needs to be confronted. There are no persons without society and no society without persons. But society, unlike nature, does not exist independently of our activities. We turn next to these problems.

Society

In our effort to provide a meta-theory for inquiry in the social sciences, we turn to the second huge difference between the natural sciences and the social sciences: nature exists independently of us; society does not. Searle has rightly argued that more fundamental than the distinction between "nature" and "culture," or "mind" and "body" is the distinction between those features of the world that exist independently of us and those that are dependent on us for their existence. Trees and molecules exist independently of us. Were the human race suddenly to perish, they would still exist – even if our representations of them would disappear. Money and science, by contrast, would perish along with us. Of course, the paper which for us represents a dollar bill would still exist. It would still be an ensemble of molecules with specific causal powers. For example, it would still burn. But it would not be money, since there would be no one to use it to buy anything.

Searle (1995: 27) offers a distinction between "brute facts," facts about features of the world that exist independently of us, and "institutional facts," or facts about features of the world which require special human institutions for their existence. Institutional facts necessarily require collective intentionality: we share in believing that the paper is a dollar bill which allows me to purchase the ice-cream cone from you. That H_2O is water is a brute fact. That an ice-cream cone costs one dollar is an institutional fact. There are other critical features of institutional facts:

- Brute facts are logically prior to institutional facts. The "natural" (independently existing) material world is the stuff out of which institutional facts are made (and sustained). But these need not be physical objects (as is the case with old-fashioned money) but may be magnetic traces on a tape, or in the case of conversation, sounds coming from our mouths.
- Institutional facts are interconnected with other institutional facts. As Searle writes: "In order that anybody in society could have money, that society must have a system of exchanging goods and services for money. But in order that it can have a system of exchange, it must

have a system of property and property ownership" (1995: 35). This in turn requires a system of law. This also suggests that institutional facts may presuppose other institutional facts, suggesting different degrees of depth or generality. But it does not follow from this, that the ensemble of institutional facts comprise an integrated totality.

But if we now think of society as an ensemble of interconnected institutions, we must face the troubling consequence that society's existence depends wholly on us. If so, then it would seem to be all in our heads, and hence, it is hard to see how it could function causally. On the usual reading, Durkheim was the first to see this problem. On the usual reading of Durkheim, social facts are external to us and have a coercive power. This then easily explains the stability and regularities of action. Indeed, it almost seems commonsensical to say that society influences our behavior. Especially since the influential work of Talcott Parsons, social scientists have been more or less committed to some version of Durkheim, often without noticing. Symptomatically, appeals are made to social forces, or to explanations of action in terms of social structure. Something external, real and causal, like the forces of nature, seems essential for explanation. But the account with which we began offers what seems to be an "idealist" ontology of social reality. It has continued to trouble contemporary writers for whom Anthony Giddens's "structuration theory" has often been a point of departure. The critical concept in this regard is the concept of "social structure" or simply "structure."[17]

The concept of social structure

Giddens (1984) distinguished between "system," "structure" and "structuration."

• *System*: "The reproduced relations between actors or collectivities, organized as regular social practices." As relatively bounded ensembles of practices more or less having a pattern, these are observable. System in this sense is often referred to as "society." But one needs to be careful here. We don't see society. We see parents teaching their children; workers engaged in work, supervised by bosses; legislatures making laws which are obeyed by citizens and so on. Second, the term "system" in wide use is often taken to mean that its parts are functionally and coherently integrated. But as with institutional facts (above),

---

[17] As Sewell notes, "'structure' is one of the most important and most elusive terms in the vocabulary of current social science," but for better or worse, "any attempt to legislate its abolition would be futile" (1992: 3).

Giddens makes no such assumption.[18] The observable patterns are the empirical point of departure for inquiry.

- *Structure*: "Rules and resources, organized as properties of social systems." Structure is not the patterned practices, but the principles that give pattern to the practices. Structure is thus a theoretical term, and a highly abstract one at that. The observable patterns (system) are concrete, while structures are abstracted from them. Rules and resources are interconnected.

  Rules "imply methodical procedures of social interaction," and are "generalized procedures" applicable over a range of contexts and occasions. They have two aspects: the constitution of *meaning* and the *sanctioning* of modes of conduct. Finally, and critically, "rules cannot be conceptualized apart from *resources*, which refer to the modes whereby transformative relations are actually incorporated into the production and reproduction of social practices. Structural properties thus express forms of *domination* and *power*." (Giddens, 1984: 18)

- *Structuration*: "The conditions governing the continuity or transformation of structures." To anticipate: if patterns are observable, and structures are abstracted, then structuration refers to the mechanisms which produce the patterns. For Giddens, structure has but a "virtual existence." As he writes, "structure enters simultaneously into the constitution of the agent and social practices and 'exists' in the generating moments of this constitution." This is certainly the central idea in Giddens's formulation.

Structuration involves the idea of "duality of structure," that social life is fundamentally "recursive," that is, agent and structure presuppose one another: there is no action without structure and no structure without action. Accordingly (as Mead had insisted), there was no time when there were agents and no society, and conversely. We should, accordingly, avoid saying that persons create society. Instead, since all individuals are born into actually existing societies, social structures pre-exist for them, incarnate in the ongoing activities of members. Hence, they

[18] Although Giddens has written most perceptively in rejection of functionalism in social theory, his own use of "system" is undertheorized and perhaps even dispensable. His best statement may be: "The connotation of 'visible pattern' which the term 'social structure' ordinarily has, as employed in Anglo-American sociology, is carried on in my terminology by the notion of a system: with the crucial proviso that social systems are patterned in time as well as space, through continuities of social reproduction" (Giddens 1979: 64). Following this, he also says: "A social system is thus 'a structured totality.'" But this is wildly misleading at best. William Sewell makes some very useful suggestions regarding the "multiple, contingent, and fractured" character of society and of structure. We return to this.

become persons in society, and by their actions they reproduce and transform it.

We want to preserve the Durkheimian insight that society influences
behavior. We can see more clearly what this must mean. We can think
of society as an ensemble of practices. There is, first, the social process
of becoming a person. A baby is born into a world of adults acting with
materials at hand. Their activity is thus structured, both enabled and
constrained. That is, there are materials being employed in particular
ways by people. Some of these individuals rear that child, passing on a
fantastic range of tacit knowledge about activities in their society. The
child creatively appropriates this, becoming an active participant. A battery of dispositions are formed giving that person a personality. For every
generation there are given materials, materials given by the activities of
previous generations going back into time. This is one of the facts that
makes history important to any human science.

But society (as incarnate in the activities of persons) influences behavior also in the sense that structures make available the range of choices
available in society to the socialized person and this point runs from the
obvious to the not so obvious. You may know Hindi but if you are living in a society with no Hindi speakers, you will not speak Hindi. If you
lack the language of that society, you will likely make the effort to learn
it. Less obvious, different societies make different kinds of alternatives
available to different kinds of people. Here is where theories of race, gender, class and status enter the picture. For example, in some concrete
social system, "class" can refer to objective social relations between people. "Class" is a theoretical term which, by abstraction, might well be a
principle which explains, against the background of a host of institutional
facts, a structured pattern of practices, for example, the mechanism of
labor markets.

Thus, structure is both medium and product of conscious activity.
Structure is a medium in the sense that it is material used, both enabling
and constraining. For example, a person knows a language and thus can
speak. She creates her sentences with the materials of the language; she
uses it to describe, protest, explain and so on. On the other hand, she
is also constrained by her language. To be understood, she must conform, more or less, to the rules of that language (even though these rules
are mainly tacit, unacknowledged by speakers). Some sentences make
no sense. Sometimes, she strains to communicate her meaning, perhaps
by creatively employing a metaphor. And some things simply cannot be
said!

These features are fully generalizable. Everything we do involves
socially available materials, what are often called institutions. When we

work, we work with materials, language and all the particular rules, relations and tools which make up that work activity. Thus there are tasks expected of us and ways to accomplish these, we have a boss who can fire us, and we work with a computer, files, telephones and so on. So, too, when we play, marry, worship, engage in politics and so forth. When we play a game, chess for example, the movement of pieces is prescribed, but within these rules, we are free to decide what moves to make. When we marry, both partners accept roles and responsibilities, acquire some rights and lose others. And so with all the things we do.

On the other hand, social structures are products in the sense that, since language is embodied in concrete utterances, as an unintended consequence, when we speak and write, collectively and cumulatively, we reproduce and transform it. And similarly with all other activities: our work activity realizes the rules and relations which are incarnate in that sort of work activity; our interactions with a mate realize family life and so on.

Since structures are virtual and exist only as incarnate in ongoing practices, social science is inevitably historical and concrete. If we want to understand present practices we must acknowledge that they are historical products. But different historical experiences will make otherwise similar societies concretely different. One can speak abstractly of France, South Korea, El Salvador and Canada as capitalist societies, but their very different histories make them, today, very different in many important ways.

The historical and concrete character of social science generates special problems for theory. While theorizing is never finished in any science, in the social sciences, theory is continually revisable not merely in the sense that new theories replace or amend older theories, but in the sense that reality is changing. Given the immense changes in American society since, for example the 1950s, theories developed to understand the American family then will likely not be suitable today.

Understanding social change is, indeed, a critical feature of the social sciences and there are all sorts of possible explanations for social change, depending upon concrete material and historical conditions. But it remains true that aside from natural events, hurricanes and the like, everything that happens in society is produced by persons working with materials at hand, sometimes as the intended, but usually as the unintended consequences of their activities. Understanding social change, then, requires specific hypotheses of existing social mechanisms which detail, concretely, the capacities that agents have and the constraints to which they are subject, what they know and understand and, finally, the uses to which they put their capacities and knowledge (chapter 4). To merely hint at what is at issue here, compare the recent past of the former USSR and the United States during its recent national elections. Fantastic differences in the structure of the two economies, their political arrangements and so on, made for enormous differences in the capacities and constraints of persons, from leaders, such as Putin or Bush, to ordinary workers and citizens.

The historical and concrete character of the social also raises a danger about generalizations. Since social phenomena are historical and concrete, generalizations that are meant to apply to many or all societies may easily lead to triviality or distortion. It is, for example, almost surely true that "an organization is more likely to be strongly centralized during external crises than during normal periods" or that "economic / demographic resources of contending states determine capacities for military domination." But these would be extremely unhelpful in understanding the behavior of France during the Napoleonic wars or the very different situation of (say) the USSR in the 1950s. Similarly, one needs to distort the ordinary understanding of "entrepreneur" to hold that "in all societies, entrepreneurs have been the catalyst for change." This is not to deny the importance of generalization in social science as potentially descriptive and thus illuminating. We might remind ourselves here that, as argued in chapter 1, it is an important task of science to provide explanations of significant patterns and generalizations. This will be true also of the social sciences. Just as we can understand oxidization and understand why iron rusts, we need to understand sexism and why, despite efforts to the contrary, there is still a glass ceiling (chapter 4).

The double hermeneutic

Because social structures do not exist independently of human activity, there is a critical epistemological implication regarding inquiry into society. In all sciences, since scientists must communicate with one another regarding their claims about the world and, hopefully, come to a shared understanding, they are engaged in hermeneutics – "the art of interpretation."[19]

In order to build a consensus about claims made, all scientists must continually seek mutual understanding about such claims, the standards and methods employed, the evidence adduced and so on. For the natural scientist, nature stands independently of us. Brute facts are whatever

[19] Originally, hermeneutics was the theory and method of interpreting the Bible, extended by Dilthey to human acts and products.

they are irrespective of our human interests or of the meanings we might impose on them. The social scientist must also build a consensus about claims and theories about society; so social scientists are, with one another, similarly engaged in a hermeneutic process.

But for the social scientist, there is a "double hermeneutic" (Giddens, 1984). The world that the social scientist is describing, communicating and seeking consensus about is itself a meaningful world, a world having meaning for the members of the society under study. As argued, activity is meaningful in that human action involves concepts, rules, norms and beliefs that are shared by members. This datum is the point of departure of inquiry in the social sciences. Social scientists must come to an agreement about what are already ongoing interpretations by members whose activities constitute their world. We must understand it if we, as scientists, are to communicate and confirm claims about what is going on in that world. We need to grasp their motivations and the norms they live by. We need to know what, for members, counts as marriage or filial piety, what is immoral, criminal, democratic, just and unjust. This is as much true of our own society – and its subcultures – as it is of so-called "exotic" societies, even if we often – and disastrously – think that we can understand or explain outcomes without considering what activities mean for members. Indeed, this was precisely Schütz's criticism of positivist social science: the positivist thinks of himself as a natural scientist making claims about an "objective" world to which he gives meaning. In his criticism of the work of Talcott Parsons, Schütz rightly insisted:

Professor Parsons has the right insight that a theory of action would be meaningless without the application of the subjective point of view. But he does not follow this principle to its roots. He replaces subjective events in the mind of the actor by a scheme of interpretation of such events, accessible only to the observer, thus confusing objective schemes for interpreting subjective phenomena with these subjective phenomena themselves. (Grathoff, 1978: 36)

But, the answering of our question, "What does the social world mean for me, the observer?" has as a prerequisite the answering of the quite different questions, "What does this social world mean for observed actors within this world, and what did he mean by his acting within it?" With these questions, we no longer naively accept the world and its current idealizations and formalizations as ready-made and meaningful beyond all doubt, but undertake to study the process of idealizing and formalizing as such, the genesis of the meaning which social phenomena have for us as well as for the actors, the mechanism of the activity by which human beings understand one another and themselves. (Wagner, 1983: 48)

This plainly is the strong suit not only of ethnography, but of symbolic interactionist orientations, ethnomethodology, Goffman's work and other forms of what is called qualitative research.[20] But, indeed, this "ethnographic moment" is essential to any explanatory effort in the social sciences – and for that matter, in history (see chapter 5).

This raises two difficult questions. First, is it possible for the social scientist (historian or linguist) as outsider to come to grasp the meanings of action in the society under study? Perhaps only natives, insiders, really understand what is going on. Second, and more problematically perhaps, can we ask whether the natives' understanding of their world is adequate? Do they really understand what is going on?

Ethnographic skepticism?

Ethnographic skepticism is healthy, but one need not turn a problem into an impossibility.[21] Consider again our taken-for-granted ability to understand one another in our everyday lives. As Weber pointed out, this involved what he called *verstehen*, the human capacity to grasp the meaning of another's actions. We must not think of *verstehen* as some sort of special, intuitive, sympathetic understanding, a reliving of the experience of others. *Verstehen* is something we all do all the time. We are engaged in *verstehen* in judging that a person on a ladder is painting the house, in judging that the expression on another's face is distress produced by our careless remark, and so forth. We learned to do this, indeed, when we learned to use language. There is nothing dubious about such judgements since, as with any judgement, they require evidence and may, subsequently, be rejected.

Second, our ethnographer is not a Martian, but a human being. Even if the culture she studies is very different to her own, it remains a human culture: *verstehen* will still be critical.[22] In the worst case, accordingly, the researcher has available the same evidence that the members have – the actions and products (for example, texts and artifacts) of members. Some actions will be immediately understood: they are seeking food or building a shelter. Moreover, as the philosopher W. V. Quine argued, hypotheses about meaning are tested and either seem to work or they don't. Eventually (following what Mead had to say on the subject) interactions succeed,

[20] There are various forms of qualitative research, including participant observation, interviews, analysis of texts and documents, focus groups and so on, that offer ways to grasp members' understanding of their world, some better than others. Quantitative work that often appeals to surveys is not among the better ways. But discussion of these issues must be forgone here. As noted, in appendix A, quantitative work may still be descriptively and evidentially important. See, for example, C. Wright Mills, 1959.

[21] For examples and discussion, see Clifford and Marcus, 1986; Rosaldo, 1989.

[22] Sahlins (2004: 5) suggests the ethnographer must be a cultural animal if he is to make any headway, but surely to be a human (cultural) being is a very big advantage.

expectations are realized, there is communication and understanding. Of course, this will take some time, and of course, our ethnographer might be wrong – perhaps in detail, perhaps in some fundamental way.

Moreover, the idea that the native has a privileged or unique understanding that is inaccessible to the other, runs into a logical difficulty. We are all situated and there is no God's-eye view of the world. Consider, then, other possible privileged viewpoints: the colonized, women, black women, women of color, upper-class women of color, urban lower-class women of color and so on. The issue is not whether these voices have been suppressed in white male dominated positivist social science: they have. Nor is it argued that much qualitative work is poorly done, distorted in this way or that. The issue rather is epistemological: because each of us, logically, has a unique biography and position in society, each person's viewpoint is unique. We seem driven beyond relativism to a radical subjectivism. I cannot be a native but I cannot be you either. That is, the problem of understanding the other begins at home. In everyday life, we do not turn a problem into an impossibility. Indeed, as Mead and Schütz insisted, if I am to communicate with you at all, I must in some measure take your position.[23]

Any viewpoint, accordingly, will leave much out. The social scientist is obliged to take care that other voices are heard, that the account is as objective as is humanly possible. Granting that such objectivity is situated and not absolute, a situated objectivity will require reflexivity in Bourdieu's sense. In addition to the obvious potential positional biases, there is the question of "the objective space of possible intellectual positions offered to him or her at a given moment . . ." and finally, there is the intellectualist bias (rejected firmly by Dewey long ago) of construing the world as "a spectacle" (Bourdieu and Wacquant, 1992: 39). On the present view, knowing is not a reflection of reality, nor a mere construction, but is "disciplined by the otherness with which it engages" (Pickering, 1992: 412).[24] Sahlins pertinently quotes Bahktin:

There is an enduring image, that is partial, and therefore false, according to which to better understand a foreign culture one should live in it, and forgetting one's own look at the world through the eyes of this culture . . . To be sure, to enter in some measure into an alien culture and look at the world through its eyes, is a necessary moment in the process of understanding . . . [but] *creative understanding* does not renounce its self, its place in time, its culture; it does not

---

[23] Here again, the Mead / Dewey theory of meaning which rejects, at the outset, a Cartesian point of departure gives us the philosophical ground that we need.

[24] I perhaps here extend Pickering's sense which speaks of the "mangle of practice," and "the dialectic of resistance and accommodation" (1992: 412). See also Fabian, 1991; Williams, 2005.

forget anything. The chief matter of understanding is *exotopy* of the one who does the understanding – in time, space, and culture – in relation to that which he wants to understand creatively . . .

In the realm of culture, exotopy is the most powerful lever of understanding. It is only to the eyes of an *other* culture that the alien culture reveals itself more completely and more deeply (but never exhaustively, because there will come other cultures, that will see and understand even more).[25]

In what follows, we offer that there will be no paradox in holding that the social scientist could have a better understanding of the society than a member – otherwise, indeed, it would be hard to see the point of doing social science. There are two reasons for this. First, the ethnographer may be obliged to make an effort at articulating that which is not articulated by members. Competent members must know enough to carry on activities – they have practical knowledge even if they would often be unable to offer this discursively. We can think of qualitative research as aiming at getting clear about what actors do know, both discursively and non-discursively. Thus, an ethnographer may, after inquiry, know more than members do exactly because she has uncovered the implicit rules, recipes, and norms that are implicated in everyday activity. This is also one of the virtues of a comparative approach.

Getting a handle on members' beliefs and understandings of their world is but a necessary first step for both understanding and explanation in social science. Because she can take a second step and provide an understanding of the social mechanisms that explain typical activities in that society, her understanding is still greater.[26]

This last observation, to be developed in the next chapter, suggests an opportunity not available to natural science. Improving our understanding of the natural world can certainly help us to better adjust, even to better influence the outcomes of its processes. But we cannot change the processes of the natural world; we cannot make gravity cease to exert its effects, even if we can build powerful engines that propel rockets into space. But improving our understanding of the social world does give us

---

[25] Quoted from Sahlins (2004: 5). Sahlins is quoting Bakhtin from Tzvetan Todorov, *Mikahil Bakhtin: The Dialogical Principle* (Minneapolis: University of Minnesota Press, 1984). See also, Patricia Hill Collins, who writes: "Each group speaks from its own standpoint and shares in its own partial, situated knowledge. But because each group perceives its own truth as partial, its knowledge is unfinished. Each group becomes better able to consider other groups' standpoints without relinquishing the uniqueness of its own standpoint or suppressing other groups' partial standpoints" (2000: 330).

[26] Bourdieu and Giddens share in arguing that the work of symbolic anthropology (e.g., Geertz), symbolic interactionists, and those influenced by Schütz, for example, Garfinkel, provide incomplete accounts, stopping at what is termed here, "the first step." For Bourdieu and Giddens, there is a need, as here, to try to explain why the social world is the way it is. Foucauldian genealogy may well fit in here as well.

the chance to change social reality in ways more congenial to our values and interests.

Social science as emancipating

While activity requires that the members have practical knowledge, it does not require that they have a grasp of the mechanisms that produce and sustain the beliefs of members. Thus, what role does mass media play in forming belief? How is this related to mechanisms of the political economy? To voting behavior? Nor does action require that all the beliefs that sustain these mechanisms be true. Indeed, the reproduction of a practice may require that members have false beliefs about the practice that their activity sustains. If it can be shown that some of the beliefs essential to the reproduction of practices are false, distorted or otherwise inadequate, that conditions are not what they seem and that consequences were unexpected, agents will have grounds for changing their practices. Consider the belief that males are superior. Is this belief essential for the practices that define the traditional patriarchal family? But if (as people increasingly appreciate) this belief is false, people have good reason for changing their behavior and thereby altering the inherited roles and relations. It is not that the social scientist has inserted his (or her) values into the inquiry. It is rather that there are inherent practical implications that follow from seeing how beliefs enter into the constitution of a practice and then asking whether these beliefs are true or false. Establishing the truth or falsity of our beliefs about the world is, it must be agreed, the task of any science. For the social sciences, this has an added emancipatory potential (Giddens, 1984; Bhaskar, 1979).

Problems and objections

What are the problems with the foregoing theory of society? It will be profitable to focus on typical criticisms of structuration theory. Remarkably, perhaps, Giddens has been read both as a structuralist determinist who effectively denies agency, and as a voluntarist who "emphasizes the control we exercise over our worlds."

Thus, Richard Ashley (1989), influenced by post-structuralist criticism, sees Giddens as lapsing into structuralist determinism. He argues that Giddens makes two moves. First, his narrative dichotomizes "the utter arbitrariness of history" and "the structures of social totality whose form theory represents and whose continuity theory narrates." Second, "knowing agents" are located "at the frontier of this *already established* opposition; as beings who, behind their backs, are constituted in reflection of the structure of the social totality and who, looking forward, find narrative significance only insofar as they administer historical contingency and bend it to the reproduction of the structure that constitutes them" (Ashley, 1989: 277). Thus, the dependence of structure on practice is a mere supplement – "a way of rendering the structuralist escape in the face of contingent events that threaten to undo a structure's supposed hegemony in the determination of what history means" (Ashley, 1989: 277). According to Ashley, then, Giddens effectively subordinates "the dependence of structure on practice" to the "dependence of practice on structure." Putting aside the darkness of the prose, Ashley sees Giddens as obliterating agency and seems to have managed this by giving structure a reading characteristic of much deterministic social science: as both oversocializing the individual and by giving structure the sole causal role in action.

But far more of his critics have read Giddens as a voluntarist (and subjectivist).[27] On this view, because structure is but virtual, there are no objective constraints on action. This line of argument, like the previous one, trades on giving structure a critical causal role and we need to say more about this. But two points regarding constraints on action may quickly be re-emphasized.

First, there are the objective material constraints which severely limit us because we are organic beings in a physical environment. These are both powerful and usually underestimated (or ignored). They provide the background causes of everything we do – and suffer.

Second, there are the objective constraints imposed by history. Agents reproduce and transform structure in acting: they do not create it; they do not, as state of nature theory typically assumes, agree to form a society *ex nihilo*, nor do they *ex nihilo* create the structures in terms of which they will act. Since they can create only with the materials at hand, the legacy inherited is profoundly constraining. But, for structuration theory, in contrast to a determinist understanding of structure, actors reproduce and / or transform structure by acting. Hence, there is always both change, often unintended, and stability. Nor for structuration theory, echoing C. Wright Mills, is there a general theory of social change. Constraints on action, like the capacities for transforming structure, are historically variable, both in relation to the material conditions and inherited institutional circumstances but also in relation "to the forms of knowledgeability that

---

[27] A very good recent example of the latter is the work of Michael Burawoy (1998: 15), who, while valuing reflexivity and ethnographic depth, holds that for Giddens, "in the end, intuitive notions of structure evaporate and we are left with a voluntarist vision that emphasizes the control we exercise over our worlds."

agents possess about these circumstances" (Giddens, 1984: 179). The charge of structural determinism and of voluntarism denies this.

Third, as regards members of societies, there are the constraints (and enablements) imposed by the lottery of life. We do not choose our parents; nor, accordingly, do we choose our time and place in history and society. Both these generate objective constraints, best understood as "placing limits upon the range of options open to an actor, or plurality of actors, in a given circumstance or type of circumstance" (Giddens, 1984: 177). Moreover, as Durkheim noted, these appear as "facticities," or as Marx said, as "natural." But this is not inconsistent with the idea, argued here, that " 'society' is manifestly not external to individual actors in exactly the same sense as the surrounding [natural] environment is external to them" (Giddens, 1984: 172).

A further range of criticisms regards the relation and ontological status of rules and resources, the two elements that, according to Giddens, constitute structure. It is unfortunate that the idea of rules, which has been so important in the philosophical literature, has misled some otherwise careful readers of Giddens. Sewell (1992), for example, offers that the "cultural schemas" would be a far more preferable term, since it provides opportunities not available to the usual meanings of rules. Cultural schemas are the meat of cultural anthropology (and, one should add, work by ethnomethodologists and others, for example, Goffman) and opens a richness which includes an array of "various conventions, recipes, scenarios, principles of actions, and habits of speech and gesture," in addition, then, to "the sorts of things spelled out in statutes, proverbs, liturgies, constitutions and contracts" (Sewell, 1992: 8). We can welcome this suggestion (whether or not we take it as a clarification or an extension of Giddens's idea). But critically, for Sewell, these latter "more formally stated prescriptions" should be considered "resources" not rules. And for him, resources are not virtual, but actual.

Giddens's view that resources are virtual has troubled a host of writers who, like Sewell, agree that rules (schemas) are properly understood as but virtual. For these writers, resources, unlike rules, have an objectivity. Of course, statutes, constitutions and so forth, actually exist. But this misses the point. The marks on the paper, like the paper, exist independently of us, but they are statutes only because of our beliefs, beliefs that we act on. These are, in Searle's terminology, institutional facts, concept- and activity-dependent. Moreover, none of these more formally stated prescriptions is self-interpreting – as would be admitted. That is, writing down the rules of grammar does not make them less virtual in Giddens's sense: they are actualized concretely only in action.

Sewell suggests another argument for making resources actual rather than virtual. "To say that schemas [but not resources] are virtual is to say that they cannot be reduced to their existence in any particular practice or any particular location in space and time: they can be actualized in a potentially broad and unpredetermined range of situations" (1992: 8). But it is hard to see why this is not true of resources which also empower agents "in a potentially broad and unpredetermined range of situations."

Sewell rightly notes that for Giddens, "resources can be anything that can serve as a source of power in social interactions" (1992: 9). In an effort to extend and clarify this, Sewell offers that such sources of power may be human or non-human. Non-human resources are independently existing objects, for example factories owned by capitalists; human resources are strength, knowledge, etc. Remarkably, he omits one's place in social relations, for Giddens surely the most critical resource of power (Giddens, 1984: 25–26, 83–86, 89). But as above, a building is a factory owned by capitalists only because of an array of institutional facts, only because members have an array of concepts and beliefs in terms of which they act. Indeed, it is just these which make a person who owns a factory a capitalist and which, accordingly, gives him power lacked by the workers.

A more plausible version of this criticism has been made by some interpreters of Bhaskar's very similar "Transformational Model of Social Activity" (TMSA). While Giddens has noted that his view assumes a realist ontology, he has been less specific than Bhaskar on what this entails for social science.

In agreement with Giddens, Bhaskar holds that structures are continually reproduced (transformed) and "exist only in virtue of and exercised only in human agency (in short they require active 'functionaries')" (1979: 51). "Such a point, linking action to structure, must both endure and be immediately occupied by individuals . . . [T]he mediating system we need is that of positions (places, functions, rules, tasks, duties, rights, etc.) occupied (filled, assumed, enacted) by individuals, and of the practices (activities, etc.) in which, in virtue of their occupancy of these positions (and vice versa), they engage" (Bhaskar, 1979: 51).

Plainly, Bhaskar's emphasis is on social relations as sources of power, but unlike Giddens, for him, what Giddens calls rules and resources are collapsed – perhaps wisely. These differences have been thought to be inconsequential.[28] But some of his interpreters, at least, have insisted

---

[28] I am one of those who thought so. More lately, I have been convinced that there is an unresolved tension in Bhaskar's work on this issue. For an excellent account, see Varela and Harré, 1996.

that, unlike Giddens, Bhaskar is firmly materialist and maintains a strong objectivist view of social relations.

Thus, Porpora insists on a "difference between a materialist and idealist approach to reality" turning on a difference between "a concept of social structure as an objective reality and a concept of structure as an intersubjective reality" (1989: 202). Thus, "what Giddens means by structure are cultural rather than material conditions." Porpora illustrates his point with the argument about poverty. One side attributes poverty to "cultural factors, to the resocialization of each new generation of poor people into rules and norms and ways of thinking that perpetuate poverty" (Porpora, 1989: 202). This seems very much like Giddens. On the other side are those who find the causes of poverty to be "objective circumstances of the social position the poor find themselves in," a feature of which is the absence of cultural capital, which, says Porpora, Giddens can also acknowledge. But "another feature of the objective circumstances . . . relates to the distribution of jobs or social positions in society . . . [W]hat we are talking about here are relational properties of a social system . . . [and] the causal effects of those relationships on the life chances of the poor." He concludes: "Ultimately, we are talking about those relationships as precisely the sort of external constraints on action, the existence of which, as we have seen, Giddens wishes to deny" (Porpora, 1989: 207).

This very typical response probably resonates with many structuralist writers, but it is quite plain that, typically, it bifurcates structure and culture, subjective and objective. Institutional facts are as objective as brute facts. The present level of unemployment is an objective fact even while it depends upon features of the world that require special human institutions for their reality, and even if, as noted, these depend upon collective intentionality – otherwise intersubjectivity.[29] As regards external constraints on action, what is intended is safe enough. There are no jobs, so one cannot get one. But that fact is not external to the activities of persons; it is not a brute fact but an institutional fact.

It was part of Giddens's project to transcend the now familiar culture / structure dichotomy. Rules are cultural, but as he insisted, they "cannot be conceptualized apart from resources." Resources generate capacities, powers, including relational power, or power over others and these are sustained by rules which provide both meaning and sanctions to activity. Plainly, the capitalist / wage labor relationship distributes resources unequally, but that the capitalist owns the factory and that the worker

---

[29] Contrary to Searle who speaks of "ontologically subjective features" of things it would be better to speak of "ontologically intersubjective features" of things.

works for wage, requires an extensive range of institutional facts which members sustain in their activities.

Of course, unemployment puts persons lacking cultural capital at a deep disadvantage. But the cause of employment is not social forces, market forces or social structure. It is the unintended product of the reproduction of capitalism by agents working with materials at hand – capitalists, workers, consumers, government officials and so on.

Of course, if social structure is reified – made independently real – it could be causal, but not only is this ontologically dubious, it is not a move available to the position defended by Porpora. A similar argument has been made by Margaret Archer (1995) who argues, following Bhaskar, that structure and culture are both emergent properties and as such are "bearers of causal powers." Still, quoting Bhaskar, Archer insists that "the realist is committed to maintaining that 'the causal power of social forms is mediated through social agency'" (1995: 195). The question to ask is this: why postulate the existence of structure or culture as causally relevant if, to be causally effective, these must be mediated by social actors?

This suggests another move. Paul Lewis (2000) has rightly noted that the analysis of causality developed by Harré and Madden (1975) and assumed in this volume is not an appropriate framework if one insists that social structures have causal efficacy. As Lewis says, "social structures are not efficient causes and hence are not powerful particulars (as the latter are understood by Harré and Madden)" (2000: 257). He agrees, to be sure, that persons as agents are "powerful particulars": as agents, they can make things happen. Accordingly, as he notes, to sustain a notion of causality for social structure, one needs another framework. Following suggestions by Bhaskar, Lewis offers that social structure can be thought of as a material cause of social action. Thus, following Aristotle, the slab of marble that is fashioned by the sculptor is a material cause of the finished work. On the present account of the foregoing, agents do work with materials at hand, but this is to be understood in terms of both their human capital and the actually existing social situation in which they find themselves. Both enable and constrain their actions. It is true also that the marble enables and constrains the action of the sculptor: were she working with some other materials – for example, wood – she would be enabled and constrained differently. On the analysis offered in the present account, these differences are the consequences of the causal properties of marble and of wood. But as is plain enough, the slab of marble does exist independently of persons and their actions and thus can have causal powers. As Lewis would not deny, social structure is concept- and activity-dependent. But if so, the analogy fails. Indeed, it is difficult to see how a cause can be a material cause if it is not a powerful particular.

The same problem would seem to arise with those recent arguments that advocate realist views of mechanisms, but hold that social structure is an emergent property with causal powers (Sawyer, 2003; Wight, 2003). Bunge rightly insisted that "mechanisms are processes in concrete (material) systems, whether physical, social, technical or some other kind . . . By contrast, the conceptual and semiotic systems have compositions, environments, and structures but no mechanisms" (2003: 191).

Of course, organizations have properties that cannot be ascribed to their members. Bureaucracies, for example, are difficult to dislodge, operate impersonally and are often painfully slow in getting to a conclusion. But first, these properties are not causal and second, they are explained by looking at how bureaucracies are organized and what enables and constrains individuals acting in them. Indeed, as we argue in the following chapter, we understand bureaucracies by providing the social mechanism that explains these properties.

On the other hand, one need not accept Harré's linguistic characterization of social phenomena as "generated in and through conversation and conversation-like activities" (Harré and van Langenhove, 1999: 10). Of course, these are pertinent, but unless conversations and conversation-like activities are but extended metaphors for a whole range of transactions and interactions, of which some are not self-conscious, too much is omitted (see May, 2002). Perhaps here Bunge's admonition (above) is relevant. Nor need we accept Harré's view that concepts like "class" cannot refer to objective social structures and are but taxonomic categories used to classify and label people and practices (Harré and Varela, 1996). Like brute facts, institutional facts can be theorized. As noted, "class" is a theoretical term which, by abstraction, might well explain a structured pattern of practices. More generally, skeptical of a slip toward Durkheim, Harré has been reluctant to extend his realism to institutional facts. His account, accordingly, is vulnerable to a materialist critique of the sort mounted by Porpora and Archer.

An account of institutional facts as the background of all human action, along with a firm acknowledgement of the material and historical constraints of virtually existing social structure, is quite sufficient to provide all the benefits of structuralist insights without any of the manifest disadvantages of attributing causality to a concept- and activity-dependent social structure. Indeed, much would seem to be lost. In addition to the potential incoherence of a theory of causality which allows that something that is not a powerful particular can have causal efficacy, we risk the reification of social structure and the tempting slide into determinism and the loss of agency.[30]

On the present view, agents, nature and natural happenings are causes – with profound consequences on what happens in society. "Social forces" is a misleading metaphor – and a profoundly destructive one at that. The idea that it intends to capture can easily be unpacked in terms of social processes generated by the activities of persons working with materials at hand. Indeed, it will be a critical part of our argument that the generative mechanisms of macro-outcomes must be theorized in terms of the actions and interactions of persons. The analogy of atoms to the properties of molecules is quite exact, except that the atoms of social outcomes are irreducibly social persons. This is the topic of the chapter that follows.

[30] See Sewell's treatment of this. He argues, plausibly, that "in spite of his devastating attacks on Cartesian and Lévi-Straussian 'objectivism' . . . Bourdieu's own theory has fallen victim to an impossibly objectivized and overtotalized conception of society" (1992: 15). The problem, of course, is exactly analogous in Parsonian structuralist theory.

4 Agents and generative social mechanisms

Introduction

In those sciences we termed "abstract," theory provides representations of the generative mechanisms, including hypotheses regarding ontology, for example, that there are atoms, and hypotheses regarding causal processes, for example, that atoms form molecules in accordance with principles of binding. We noted also that a regression to more fundamental elements and processes also became possible. So quantum theory offers generative mechanisms of processes in molecular chemistry. Typically, for any process, there will be at least one mechanism operating, although for such complex processes as organic growth there will be many mechanisms at work. Theories that represent generative mechanisms give us understanding. We make exactly this move as regards understanding in the social sciences, except that, of course, the mechanisms are social. As with complex natural processes, typically, there will be many mechanisms at work. As in the physical sciences, the theorizing of mechanisms in the effort to understand is not the only task of social science. As we argued, understanding presupposes good description, both quantitative and qualitative. Finally, we will need to consider the problem of explaining events and episodes. This is developed in chapter 5.

The foregoing has also argued that persons are the dominant[1] causal agents in society – even while, of course, they work with materials at hand. It follows, accordingly, that in the social sciences, the generative mechanisms of social outcomes are the actions of persons and no further reduction is either plausible or demanded. That is, for purposes of inquiry in the social sciences (excepting here experimental psychology), the fundamental unit of analysis is the person (understood as above) – the half-truth of methodological individualism.[2]

---

[1] Dominant causal agents – not exclusive causal agents, since there are also critical non-social natural causes at work in society.

[2] Experimental psychology is variously understood, but as conceived here its problem is to identify the mechanisms which produce powers of "mind," including cognition, memory,

Social mechanisms

The idea that the explanatory goals of social science require theories of social mechanisms is hardly new, even if the idea is very often an unarticulated background assumption of studies. This is fairly evident among writers we think of as doing agent-centered work, for example, symbolic interactionists, Erving Goffman, rational choice theorists and the recent work of James Coleman. But although less noticed, it is also at least in the background of many more historically oriented writers, for example, Barrington Moore, Marshall Sahlins, E. P. Thompson, Richard Sennett and Jonathan Cobb, Charles Tilly, William Sewell, Arthur Stinchcombe, Stephan Vlastos, Michael Burawoy, Mark Granoveter, Pierre Bourdieu, Anthony Giddens, Raymond Boudon, John Elster and many others.[3] More recently, it has played a central role in the provocative debate generated by Margaret Somers over the role of general theory in historical sociology[4] and the idea has recently been rearticulated by a number of very recent writers.[5] This development is most encouraging even though, to be sure, there remains considerable disagreement even among advocates of the idea of social mechanisms as to what exactly this involves. We begin with an illustration by means of a concrete study, Willis's *Learning to Labor* (1981). Willis was not self-consciously employing Giddens's metatheory,[6] nor did he offer a formal model of the key social mechanism at work in explaining why working-class kids get working-class jobs. But his account is a superb illustration of how structuration theory leads easily to the idea of explanatory social mechanisms.

---

learning, perception, emotion, etc. See Manicas and Secord, 1984. As noted, it is not engaged in "explaining behavior" and is not, strictly speaking, a social science. Learning is a psychological mechanism: what is learned is social.

[3] Thus, Bourdieu writes that the task of sociology is to "uncover the most profoundly buried structures of the various social worlds which constitute the social universe, as well as the 'mechanisms' which tend to ensure their reproduction or their transformation" (Bourdieu and Wacquant, 1992: 7).

[4] See appendix C, "Rational Choice Theory and Historical Sociology."

[5] See especially, the collection of essays in Hedstrom and Swedberg (eds.), 1998; McAdam, Tarrow and Tilly, 2001; more recently, the special issue of *Philosophy of the Social Sciences*, 34, 2, 2004 and the panels of the American Political Science Association meeting of August 2003 with papers by Bennett, Mahoney and Gerring. These are available on the Internet: http://www.asu.edu/clas/polisci/cqrm/Bennett_APSA_2003.pdf. Replace "Bennett" with "Mahoney" and "Gerring" to access the other two papers.

[6] It has been argued that Willis did not need structuration theory to produce his study, that the influence of Marx and Marxists is evident in his work. This hardly needs to be denied. But structuration theory was not born *ex nihilo*. It was, it seems, exactly the re-thinking of Marxism which led Willis, Giddens and Bhaskar to such similar conclusions. As Giddens has said, his work is an extended gloss on the famous text in Marx's 18th Brumaire, that men make history but not with materials of their own choosing.

Learning to labor: an example

Willis defines his task as follows: "The difficult thing to explain about how middle class kids get middle class jobs is why others let them. The difficult thing to explain about how working class kids get working class jobs is why they let themselves" (1981: 1). Indeed, if Willis is correct, it is "too facile" to say that they have no choice, and misleading to say that they are "socialized" for those jobs. On the contrary, those who end up taking the worse jobs are active participants in constituting a culture that effectively prepares them for those jobs. It is this mechanism that interests Willis.

In Part I of *Learning to Labor* Willis offers a very rich ethnography of a working-class school. The description focuses on "the lads" who articulate a counter-school culture which in its most basic dimension is "entrenched general and personalized opposition to 'authority'" (1981: 11). The "conformists" or "ear'oles" have "a visibly different orientation. It is not so much that they support teachers, rather they support the *idea* of teachers" (1981: 13). The teachers, finally, recognize that their authority "must be won and maintained on moral not coercive grounds."

The lads have ample resources with which to resist: "a continuous scraping of chairs, a bad tempered 'tut-tutting' at the simplest request," "comics, newspapers and nudes under half-lifted desks melt into elusive textbooks," and more. To be sure, the lads know "the rules." It is thus that they can so successfully avoid outright confrontation and manipulate them to serve their own purposes. But even more important, within the "space won from the school and its rules" the lads have created a "multi-faceted" implement of their culture. Called "having a laff," it is used to define the group, "to defeat boredom and fear, to overcome hardship and problems – as a way out of almost anything" (1981: 29). Striking in this regard is their discovery of Garfinkeling: "Let's laugh at everything he says," "Let's pretend we can't understand and say, 'How do you mean?' all the time."

The lads also define themselves against girls and ethnic minorities. Women, for the lads, are both "sexual objects and domestic comforters." Girlfriends are called "the missus." But while "mum" is the model for the girlfriend, she "is definitely accorded an inferior role: 'She's a bit thick, like, never knows what I'm on about'" (1981: 45).

Finally, since this is a working-class school, Willis provides an account of the "shopfloor culture" which is the domestic context for the students and thus a potential resource for them. He finds two critical features: first, "a massive attempt to gain informal control over the work process" and second, a disdain for theory: "The shopfloor abounds with apocryphal stories about the idiocy of purely theoretical knowledge. Practical ability always comes first and is a *condition* for other kinds of knowledge" (1981: 56). It is plain that these work against the school and provide a critical contrast to middle-class environments and schools. As Willis writes: "When the middle class child is thrown back on to his indigenous culture, instead of finding strengthening and confirming oppositional themes there, he finds the same ones" (1981: 76).

The critical difference, then, between "the lads" and the "ear'oles" is that the latter have accepted the critical principle of the teacher / pupil relation, the idea of teaching as a "fair exchange: knowledge for respect, guidance for control." Of course, this is supported and sanctioned in many ways, beautifully developed by Willis.

In Part II, then, Willis attempts to explain the key aspects of what he has described. Critical theoretical concepts are introduced. "Penetration" is defined as "impulses with a cultural form towards the penetration of the conditions of existence of its members and their position with the social whole but in a way which is not centred, essentialist or individualist" (Willis, 1981: 119). This firmly realist formulation demands a great deal. In the first place, and importantly, members are not trying to achieve penetration, however much "practical consciousness" may reveal that they have some understanding of the conditions of existence. Second – and this is a problem shared by social scientists who specifically seek such understanding – penetration is, at best, partial, since there are always limitations: "blocks, diversions and ideological effects which confuse and impede the full development and expression of these impulses" (1981: 119).

Indeed, the fact that members may lack any sort of adequate discursive knowledge of what is going on and may still have practical knowledge which, if properly understood, shows that they have achieved at least partial penetration is the basis for the failure of survey research. As Willis (1981: 122) writes, "direct and explicit consciousness" "may well reflect only the final stages of cultural processes and the mystified and contradictory forms which basic insights take as they are lived out." It is only by fully immersing oneself in extended interaction that one may discover what is really known by members. Moreover, methods which rely on verbal or written responses cannot distinguish "attempts to please the other, superficial mimicry, earnest attempts to follow abstract norms of, say, politeness, sophistication or what is taken as intelligence" from comments and responses offered in ongoing activity which "have a true cultural resonance" (1981: 122).

Willis then seeks to explain and assess the beliefs and actions of the agents in his study. On his view the lads' rejection of school and opposition to teachers is a consequence of their penetration of the "teaching paradigm." They know better than "the new vocational guidance what is the real state of the job market." Thus, they have a "deep seated scepticism about the value of the qualifications in relation to what might be sacrificed to get them" (1981: 126). More, the lads make "a real penetration of what might be called the difference between *individual* and *group* logics and the nature of their ideological confusion in modern education" (1981: 128). In the school and in the culture, "it is never admitted that not all can succeed." Finally, and even more profoundly, since the grasp of this reality leads them to assume that they will be doing the least skilled forms of labor, they make the further penetration into the fundamental features of capitalist production, that "the measure of abstract labour is . . . time" (1981: 135).

The lads' indifference to the particular form of work they enter, their assumption of the meaninglessness of work not what kind of "right attitude" they take to it, and their general sense of the similarity of all work as it faces them, is the form of a cultural penetration of their real conditions of existence as members of class. (1981: 136)

These are, however, but partial penetrations and by no means are they sufficient to make these youths into politically active radicals. Willis argues that these penetrations may be seen as a rejection of conventionally constituted individualism. But individualism is not defeated in itself, but "for its part in the school masque where mental work is associated with unjustified authority, with qualifications whose promise is illusory" (1981: 146). The upshot is the reverse polarization of the manual / mental labor distinction and the consequent rejection of all that school might offer. But, argues Willis, this re-evaluation of manual labor depends upon sexism: "Manual labor is associated with the social superiority of masculinity, and mental labor with the social inferiority of femininity" (1981: 148). Indeed, "we may say that where the principle of general abstract labor has emptied work of significance from the inside, a transformed patriarchy has filled it with significance from the outside . . . The brutality of the working situation is partially re-interpreted into a heroic exercise of manly confrontation with the *task*" (1981: 150). To be sure, this youthful re-evaluation need not be permanent. It suffices that it lasts long enough to effectively trap them forever.

Willis notes that while this goes some way toward explaining why all do not aspire to the "rewards and satisfactions of mental labour," it is easy enough to see how insights into their future in the world of work would lead people to refuse to work at all. Willis had in mind here West Indians who have inherited a culture of wagelessness and poverty, but black Americans with similar legacies might also seize this possibility.

Before concluding this section, several further features may be noted. Willis's school was working class in a fairly straightforward sense: the students were all from families of manual laborers. This fundamental structuring mechanism is critical, but largely in the background of his account. Similarly, Willis makes no effort to explain how it is that some of the youths in his study become lads and some become conformists. Differentiation, the process by which this occurs, is left largely unanalyzed. Since individuals are biographically unique and many contingencies may well enter into an individual's decision to conform or not, this is perhaps as it must be. As in any science, there are limits to explanation. Willis is clear that the answer is not in parenting: "Parents have their own complex and creative relations to class themes and in no sense press their children into a simple standard working class mold" (1981: 73). Rather, working-class values and problems – including the need for cash – are materials for differentiation. Thus, the idea of socialization as that is used in mainstream sociology played no role in Willis's account. As he was at pains to show, "social agents are not passive bearers of ideology, but active appropriators who reproduce existing structures only through struggle, contestation and partial penetration of those structures" (1981: 175).

Similarly, dominant ideology theses misidentify what is at issue. Not only is the functional neatness of such theory totally rejected, but much of the critical cultural material is not mediated downward from dominant groups, Rather, it comes from "internal cultural relationships," for example, the working-class affirmation of manual labour. On Willis's view, ideology does "naturalize" what is conventional and potentially fragile, and, crucially, it does "dislocate." Thus, in liberal culture, there is a pervasive emphasis on the differentiation of occupational possibilities for youth and on the range of opportunities these provide for individual satisfactions. But since these ideas do not convince those who doom themselves for manual labor, "the effect of its thrust is reversed and acts centripetally, not to make jobs various, but to decentre the cause of their sameness" (1981: 163).

It is . . . no one's fault that work is boring and tiring and mostly meaningless . . . Instead of a centred world of oppression from a specific and determinate social organization of thought, production and interests[,] we have the naturalistic world of a thousand timeless causes. (1981: 163)

The political consequences of this are obvious. But we should emphasize also that both the lads and the conformists tended to end up doing similar work, even if the conformists can believe that since they are especially equipped with qualifications, they should be in "better" jobs than, and to be a "different kind of person from, 'the lads'" (1981: 152). Indeed, as Willis says, "once such a division is founded in the working class . . . it massively legitimates the position of the middle class: not capitalism but their own mental capacities keep them where they are" (1981: 152). If you're so smart, why ain't you rich?

At a very high level of abstraction and simplification, the social mechanism which explains why working-class kids get working-class jobs looks something like this:

1. By virtue of their location in prevailing social relations, working-class kids believe that, despite what they are told, there is little real opportunity for them to get out of the working class.
2. Accordingly, drawing on materials available to them, they resist.
3. Accordingly, they do not succeed in school, often dropping out.
4. Accordingly, they are unqualified for anything but working-class jobs.
5. A final unintended consequence also follows: criticism of outcomes is diffused and the existing social distribution of jobs is legitimated.

The structure of social mechanisms

We can use this example to flesh out more formally the structure of social mechanisms. I here follow a groundbreaking essay by Gudmund Hernes (1998). Hernes identifies two sets of abstract elements in a social mechanism: a set of assumptions regarding the specification of the actors and a set of assumptions regarding "structure." The first set is generated by providing answers to the following questions: (a) What do they want? (b) What do they know? (c) What can they do? and (d) What are their attributes?

In our example, working-class kids and the two subgroups, the lads and the ear'oles are the key actors (but of course, there are many others, the teachers and parents among them). The first question, (a), is answered by identifying the preferences, purposes and goals of the actors. Answers to the second question, (b) What do they know? was, in the Willis study, the most difficult to answer, but this probably is typical. As we have argued, while actors have practical knowledge, not only are the conditions and consequences of action not generally available to them, but there are problems even regarding their preferences and goals. Worse, beliefs may be unacknowledged, unstable and context-bound. (We commented on this as regards the dubious benefits of conventional survey research.) The answer to question (c), What can they do?, is a question of what powers they have. In our formulation (which is hardly sacrosanct), it will be answered in terms of rules and resources, the key elements of social structure as conceived here. Again, we need to keep in mind that resources involve rules and thus rules and resources are not concretely disconnected. Resources can range, of course, from the personal capacities of the actors to the capacities they have by virtue of their positions in social relations. Identifying the actors as working-class kids is full of promissory notes regarding the latter. Finally, as regards (d), What are their attributes?, Hernes has in mind their sex or race, and in some contexts, their health, or other special attributes pertinent to the mechanism being theorized.

The second set of assumptions he terms "structure assumptions." But not surprisingly, given the idea of the duality of structure, we can expect considerable overlap between these assumptions and the assumptions attributed to actors. Indeed, it is not entirely clear that even for analytical reasons, these are usefully distinguished. Thus, Hernes asks: What are the states actors can be in? He notes that this includes "positions or roles taken." These were, of course, critical to the understanding of "what can they do" (above). Structure assumptions include "the number of other actors, the number of relations they can enter . . . the alternatives they confront, options they face, or constraints they encounter" (Hernes, 1998: 94). Some of these, he continues, as just noted, include "norms, rules and laws." He adds, importantly, that a key question "will usually be whether such states remain constant or whether they are subject to change." These are all important specific considerations for understanding but it may well be that the distinction is misleading. There are two sorts of problems here.

First, Hernes remarks that the first set of assumptions regarding actors corresponds to "methodological individualism," but plainly, his individuals are persons and are robustly social beings. There is no attempt to reduce social predicates to predicates of individual psychology. As Bhaskar has rightly said, "the real problem appears to be not so much how one could give an individualist explanation of behavior, but that of how one could even give a non-social (that is, strictly individualist) explanation of individual, at least characteristically human behavior . . . A tribesman implies a tribe, the cashing of a cheque, a banking system" (1979: 35).

Moreover, while actors are assumed to have purposes and to be rational, there is no commitment here to some version of rational choice theory. As Boudon argues (in an essay in the Hedstrom and Swedberg volume), since it cannot accommodate a host of beliefs "which are a normal and essential ingredient of many social actions" (1998a: 183), rational choice theory is fatally flawed. Keeping in mind considerations already adduced (above), his alternative "cognitivist model" – perhaps misleadingly named – is perhaps sufficient. It "supposes that actions, decisions and beliefs are meaningful to the actor in the sense that they are perceived by him as grounded on means" (1998a: 191). This is, of course, the key insight of the work of Weber, extended by Schütz, properly understood.

There is, accordingly, nothing amiss in focusing on agents and their capacities, provided we are talking about situated social beings. But there is the danger of making social structure causal. Hernes argues that some mechanisms "are based on what could be dubbed 'collapsed actors'" (1998: 94). For this model, "no specific assumptions are made about what the actors want, know or have." But it is highly doubtful that there are any outcomes in which this is possible, even if we include non-social causes as structures, for example, contagious diseases. As Hernes says, disease is a critical causal component of what happens to people. But even so, any sort of explanation will require a mechanism which includes not merely the biological causes, but the condition and actions of people who are responding to the threat of disease. That is, there are no outcomes where, as Hernes puts it, "the actors are just objects." Thus, one can apply "a standard diffusion model" in which "the infection rate is proportional to the number of haves and have-nots," but even on this model, the actors are not fully collapsed since explaining outcomes requires assumptions about the actions of persons, that at the very minimum, they are not acting to be infection-free. In arguing that we can have a mechanism in which "the structure will overwhelm the actors whatever assumptions are made about them" (1998: 94), Hernes effectively adopts a structural determinism in which agency disappears altogether. But this is never the case. For agents, there are always choices – however restricted they may be. As regards the infection rate, for example, decisions by agents will play a critical causal role in the outcomes. Thus, will they be fastidious regarding cleanliness, avoid congested areas, and so on.

It is worth pausing here to emphasize that structuralist explanations tend to be satisfying exactly because they acknowledge that the situation of actors is critical to understanding what they do. But the greatest advantage of thinking in terms of social mechanisms, as developed here, is to acknowledge that agents, nevertheless, remain the key players. Not only does this reinforce the idea that agents sustain, reproduce and transform structure, but as well, it calls attention to them in the effort to explain whether and how "structure" is changing or not changing. As will be argued in the next chapter, we need Louis XVI to explain the French Revolution, but we need also to understand the mechanisms involving the actions of peasants and nobles, of *sans culottes* and bourgeois.

Perhaps a more interesting case is an effort to explain increased divorces and extramarital affairs. We can theorize a mechanism in such a way that opportunities for extramarital affairs vary with labor force participation.

Thus, as the proportion of sexes becomes more equal, the number of potential couples increases. Here two kinds of actor are assumed. As above, we need to make some strong assumptions about their goals and beliefs if we are to reach any outcome. We need to assume that the persons are sexually motivated, that they have beliefs about how desires can be satisfied, and so on. That these may be taken for granted does not alter the logic of the mechanism. Typically, accounts omit much that is essential to explanation, but reasonably taken for granted. As Hernes rightly notes, this mechanism (like the former one) can be elaborated to make it more realistic. Thus, one might distinguish different subgroups with different beliefs and purposes, between, as he says, the Philanderers and the Purehearted.

Abstraction, representation and realism

This suggests a deeper issue that needs clarification. Consider Hernes's definition of a social mechanism:

A mechanism is an intellectual construct that is part of a phantom world which may mimic real life with abstract actors that impersonate humans and cast them in conceptual conditions that emulate actual circumstances. A mechanism like a *model* is a stripped-down picture of reality; it is an abstract representation that gives us the logic of the process that *could* have produced the initial observation . . . Mechanisms are the virtual reality of social scientists. But it is the stuff of which the world of the social scientist is made: This artificial, manmade world of mechanisms is real–real virtuality. (1998: 78)

This formulation needs careful gloss. Epistemologically speaking, all theory is a representation of a reality, an intellectual construct, and it is always abstract: it can never catch the full-bodied reality. Indeed, we would not want it to. We strip down reality to get at the bare bones exactly because faced with the complexity of concrete reality, understanding requires that we identify abstractly the pertinent causal mechanisms. The chemist is interested in concrete salt as NaCl, and the mechanism regards the movements of electrons of the theoretical entity NaCl. Assuming then that ordinary salt is mainly NaCl we can explain its dissolving in water. But if we accept the theory, we accept that the generative mechanism is real. That is, not only could it have produced the outcome, but having ruled out alternative explanations, we believe that it did produce the outcome.

Social mechanisms, like the social structures which are the product and medium of action, are real, but they are not independently real; their existence is dependent on the beliefs and actions of persons; hence they are but "virtually real." (Hernes is not interested, we may judge, in relating his account to Giddens's. Nonetheless, it is plain that it coheres neatly – as I think it must.)

Moreover, the construction of "abstract actors" – in Alfred Schütz's formulation, "homonculi" or "typical actors" – are abstractions from real persons, representations of them qua some significant attributes which they have. In our example, Willis constructed theoretical actors based on his ethnographic materials. The lads are all different in all sorts of ways, but as regards the mechanism being theorized, they share in a set of typical attributes.[7] Thus, given an abstracted representation of their condition, the concrete behavior of real flesh and blood individuals becomes intelligible. As with causal mechanisms in nature, we get understanding not predictive ability. That is, we understand the process by which working-class kids tend to get working-class jobs, but we cannot predict that Sam, for example, will identify with the lads or that he will end up in a working-class job. For reasons particular to Sam's biography, he might be a great success in business. In other words, the mechanism explains the generalization: working-class kids get working-class jobs.

But we must resist an instrumentalist interpretation of social mechanisms, typical of mainstream economics. As noted in chapter 2, on this view, the assumptions of the mechanism need not be realistic at all. That is, not only need there be no real persons with all the attributes of the construction, but the assumptions can be contrary to facts known about them. Thus, neo-classical price theory assumes that firms and consumers have complete knowledge, are consistent maximizers and so on. On this view, since prediction and explanation are thought to be symmetrical, good predictions are thought to be good explanations, it is hard to see how manifestly false assumptions about persons and their conditions can yield explanations of real concrete outcomes.[8] Of course, it may not be easy to know if the assumptions of the mechanism are true. Willis's study is convincing because he gives us good reason to believe that the attributes of the actors identified by him are true of the lads.

Using the Willis example, there are a number of other important observations which we can make regarding social mechanisms: as in the

---

[7] These are not, accordingly, ideal-types as these are usually understood. The attributes in the construction are true of "the lads," etc.

[8] Lawson (1997) rightly insists that conditions for the so-called "method of successive approximation" cannot be satisfied in the case of neo-classical theory. Also see chapter 6, below. Similarly, Weber seems to have assumed that neo-classical theory provides an ideal-type, but the same problem arises: it is not just that there are no markets satisfying these conditions, but that there never could be.

natural world, in the social world, mechanisms seldom, if ever, operate in isolation.[9] There are a host of other mechanisms at work which are either connected or partially constitutive of those which are the focus of Willis's account. This is, to be sure, a problem for theory. In the foregoing example, we can identify at least the following as plausible candidates:

(a) Mechanisms which give us an understanding of the working of capitalism and thus explain why it is quite impossible that everyone succeed. These mechanisms will be highly abstract. Willis simply assumes that not everyone can succeed, but Willis employs Marx's analysis of abstract labor in his account of the behavior of the lads.

(b) Mechanisms which (as part of the foregoing) provide an understanding of the working of labor markets, for example, how networks function, credential barriers, the role of the reserve army and so on. (Compare here, of course, important work by Collins (1979), Tilly and Tilly (1997), Granoveter and Tilly (1988) and many others.)

(c) Mechanisms which give us an understanding of schools, including mechanisms which generate neighborhoods, and accordingly, mechanisms which explain the class distribution in the school and which, in turn, explain the consequent peer structure, the attitudes of teachers in schools with predominantly working-class students, and the objective outcomes regarding levels of additional education, and subsequent job distributions.[10]

(d) Mechanisms which give us an understanding of materials available to students in the construction of their beliefs, including mechanisms of identity formation which include, in turn, mechanisms of peer formation and mechanisms at work in households, especially, in this instance, how gender attitudes and attitudes of parents toward white-collar work produce belief.

Willis offers powerful hints about many of these in the course of his narrative, including the mechanisms of identity formation, but some are simply taken for granted, such as the generative mechanisms of capitalism and the mechanisms which explain the existence and conditions of working-class schools. Plainly, this is to be expected.

But it is easy to see also that the mechanism which is the focus of Willis's study can be applied widely, albeit with differences in the specifics. A similar mechanism is at work in several studies of drug use among ghetto

---

[9] See McAdam et al., 2001: 27, citing Gambetta, 1998. McAdam and Gambetta offer accounts of mechanisms which differ from mine.

[10] There is, of course, a host of good work on this even while there is a strong tendency to search for single causes or to suppose that quantitative methods can provide relative importance of "factors." For a recent excellent review, see Rothstein, 2004.

youth. Following earlier work by Terry Williams (1989), Phillipe Bourgois (1997), having immersed himself in an inner-city neighborhood, discerned a mechanism at work in which the parties were "frantically pursuing the American Dream." As in the Willis study, the local dynamic is structured by the dynamics of the international political economy, taken for granted by Bourgois. It provides the objective conditions which are the starting point for the development of the model. The critical point is to understand how inner-city youth understand the situation they find themselves in, and why they do as they do. This requires an ethnography from which we can construct the typical actors and their characteristic goals and capacities. Typically, "the underground economy and the culture of terror are seen as the most realistic routes to upward mobility" (1997: 70). But while the abstract model is not filled in in specific detail, and remains incomplete, it does give us considerable understanding. In particular, it does not "account for the explosive appeal of a drug like crack . . . This involves the conflation of ethnic discrimination with a rigidly segmented labor market, and all the hidden injuries to human dignity that this entails . . . It involves in other words, the experience of many forms of oppression at once, or what I call 'conjugated oppression'" (1997: 72). That is, in terms of the foregoing analysis, several mechanisms – including pharmacological – are at work.

A similar approach offers understanding of the often claimed link between drug abuse and violent crime. Extensive fieldwork by Goldstein, *et al.* (1997) led them to develop three different explanatory models. The psychopharmacological model is the most straightforward: it offers that drug use causes temperamental changes in individuals which lead to violence. The economic compulsion model offers that craving drugs, persons feel compelled to engage in economic crimes to finance their drug use. Here there is a clear goal by users along with a judgment on effective available means. The systemic model "suggests that violence stems from the exigencies of working or doing business in an illicit market – a context in which the monetary stakes can be enormous but where the economic actors have no recourse to the legal system to resolve disputes" (1997: 116). This model joins neatly with the Bourgois model. The authors then offer some statistical data to test the models. Examining a sample of 414 homicides, they show that only 7.5 percent were caused by the effects of drugs, 2 percent were motivated by economic gain and 39.1 percent were clearly the outcome of the systemic factors, violence between dealers or dealers and users. One might notice here that 47.5 percent of the sample (which reports only homicides) were not drug-related. There are, of course, also the mechanisms which produce and reproduce an ideology regarding drug use, an ideology which mystifies reality and which is promoted by perhaps even well-intentioned media.[11]

Promissory notes

Ogbu's now classic analysis of "caste minorities" (1978) offers another useful example which need not be developed here. On this model racism figures hugely. Of course, to speak of racism is to offer but a promissory note, to be filled in with an account of the social mechanisms which produce and reproduce racist outcomes. Promissory notes very often serve as quasi or suggestive explanations in the social sciences. Sometimes, the promissory note is left entirely empty and no mechanism is identified. The reader is left to imagine one. But as regards understanding the processes of nature, in social science, promissory notes have some explanatory value.

More confusing is their appearance in contexts where their explanatory value is inconsistent with the explicit explanatory effort of the writer. Thus, in his much discussed book, *Bowling Alone* (2000), Robert D. Putnam seeks to explain "the collapse and revival of American community," the subtitle of his book. He offers that in each of several domains, "we shall encounter currents and crosscurrents and eddies, but in each we shall also discover common, powerful tidal movements that have swept across American society in the twentieth century" (2000: 27). This is surely causal language and we might easily suppose that there is some pervasive mechanism at work here, e.g. commodification, globalization, urbanization. Presumably these explain Americans' "engagement in their life of their communities," a process that was reversed "a few decades ago – silently, without warning". Thus, one might argue that as large corporations and well-funded interest groups came to dominate civic life, individuals were simply not permitted access to participatory institutions. Indeed, an account of such mechanisms is not found anywhere in the book. Rather, for Putnam, social capital becomes a sort of intervening variable: when it is strong so too is community, and conversely. He offers a wealth of generalizations which test degrees of social capital. These, he notes, rest "on more than one body of evidence" (2000: 26). Chapter 3 then offers "a wide range of possible explanations" for changes in social capital – "from overwork to suburban sprawl, from the welfare state to the women's revolution, from the growth of mobility to the growth of divorce" (2000: 27). Again, one might say that these are promissory notes, yet to be filled in. But again, we are disappointed. For him these factors

---

[11] For some discussion of this, see Morgan and Zimmer, 1997 and Glassner, 2000.

represent correlations not mechanisms. And the assumption is that where
there is a strong correlation, we have an explanation; where it is weak, the
factor is not important in the explanation. He concludes: "some of these
factors turn out to have played no significant role at all in the erosion of
social capital, but we shall be able to identify three or four critical sources
of our problem" (2000: 27). For example, "pressures of time and money"
are not significant causes since his quantitative analysis shows that correlations of these variables are not significant. His "best guess" is that
"no more than 10 percent of the total decline is attributable to that set
of factors" (2000: 283). Rather, "generational change" is "the powerful
factor," "accounting for perhaps half of the overall decline" (2000: 283).
But the fact that generational change is correlated with measures of social
capital tells us nothing about causality. Thus, what are the changes in the
beliefs and conditions of persons of different generations, why did they
change, and how do these result in changes in "social capital"? No effort
is made in this direction.

The point here is not to raise questions about the generalizations or the
evidence cited for them, but rather to illustrate a critical point of difference in strategies of explanation. Generalizations, including significant
correlations, provide neither explanation nor understanding; they need
explaining. Oddly, there are places in the book where, in passing, Putnam
not only uses the idea of a social mechanism but, inconsistent with his
explicit methodology, he provides a sketch of one. Thus, he argues that
social capital may be better than medication in fighting illness and trau-
mas (2000: 289). He writes: "to clarify how these mechanisms operate
in practice, consider the following stylized example, which while technically fabricated, depicts reality for many parents. Bob and Rosemary
Smith, parents of six-year-old Jonathan live in an urban community . . . "
(2000: 289). He provides a sketch of their beliefs – for example, they
support public education and like the diversity of the public school –
and of the existing conditions, for example, the school is a shambles. He
then pursues the logic of the mechanism by which social capital is the
critical factor in whether they will succeed in founding a PTA, and how,
if they succeed, this will give new resources, and so forth.[12]

Sometimes the promissory note has more promise since some of the
mechanism is suggested. Examples are very easy to find, often in contexts which make reference to processes, or dynamics, or sometimes
to the logic of a process or system. Thus, writers speak of "urbanization," "centralization," "mobilization," "state building," "monopolistic

---

[12] For a series of essays which do make the effort to give us this understanding, see McLean
et al. (eds.), 2002.

competition," and so on. Typically, these will involve a complex of mechanisms. Thus in glossing an argument from Tocqueville, Boudon notes that "the macroscopic statement, 'centralization is a cause of agricultural development' appears as entirely acceptable, because it is supported by [an] individualist analysis" – a social mechanism. As he says, "though centralization is a complex process, it is identified with precise 'parameters' that affect the situation of decision making of the actors, here the landlords" (1998b: 823). Boudon may be generous in holding that the "parameters" are "precise," but perhaps they are as precise as they need to be.

Sometimes, promissory notes are offered as explanations with negligible effort to fill in the details, to identify the typical actors, their motives, their resources and their relations. Thus, Tilly (1992) offers that "the processes that accumulate and concentrate capital also produce cities." He writes:

> To the extent that the survival of households depends on the presence of capital through employment, investment, redistribution or other strong link, the distribution of population follows that of capital . . . Trade warehousing, banking, and production that depends closely on any of them all benefit from proximity to each other. Within limits set by the productivity of agriculture, that proximity promotes the formation of dense, differentiated populations having extensive outside connections – cities. (1992: 153)

The logic here is fairly straightforward. Persons need to be employed to maintain life. Businessmen seeking to minimize costs will seek environments that promote this. Persons seeking employment, accordingly, will gravitate toward those environments. Filling in even these rough pieces of the story was perhaps needless – depending upon our interests. It is important to emphasize this. Understanding and explanation are pragmatic notions so that what is demanded will be a function of what is needed and wanted. It may well often be the case that a promissory note will be sufficient.

Still, there are real dangers in failing to fill in the promissory notes, but especially, the danger of suggesting a spurious explanation. Thus, racism includes a variety of social mechanisms. The most straightforward mechanism is simply to show that those in a position to exclude have decided to exclude persons on the basis of race and that nothing prevents them from doing so. Likely involved in this mechanism is the belief on the part of the excluders that those to be excluded are inferior in this way or that. But evidence may show that the actors do not hold such beliefs and that no decision has been made to exclude. It would be easy to conclude, accordingly, that racism is not involved in the outcome. But there are more subtle forms of racism often lumped together under the heading of "institutional racism."

Unfortunately, "institutional racism" is a misleading term for the phenomenon since it suggests that the outcome can be understood by examining the social mechanisms at work in some institution, for example, a corporation or university. But this inappropriately restricts the problem. It is not hard to see that, as regards many outcomes, the problem regards the causal relations of several institutions. Perhaps a better term would be "systematic" or "historical racism." Thus, nobody needs to decide that a neighborhood school will be disproportionately African-American. The mechanisms here are interrelated but familiar enough: disproportionately poor African-Americans seek low-income housing which exists in neighborhoods which are already disproportionately low-income African-American. Of course, unexplained in this sketch is the fact that African-Americans are disproportionately poor. And again, explaining this will require some other interconnected mechanisms, including the Ogbu hypothesis, the work of Claude Steele and many others.

Thus, what Rosabeth Moss Kanter (1977) (following Wilbert Moore) calls "homosexual reproduction" is a mechanism relevant to explaining disproportionate numbers of white males in upper management positions. Assume first (and safely) that there is a mechanism which explains why managers earn more than janitors. (There are, it is important to notice, alternative mechanisms which can account for this. One, of course, is the familiar neo-classical model.) Then, in the corporate structures in which managers function, because of irresolvable uncertainties affecting their positions and roles, social similarity becomes important. Looking for the "right sort of person," a white, male, Ivy league-educated manager, for example, will prefer a white, male, Ivy leaguer to work for and with him. As Mills had earlier observed: "To be compatible with the top men is to act like them, to look like them, to think like them; to be of and for them" (1959: 141). This effort to minimize uncertainty by reproducing oneself in the workplace need not be self-conscious. The actors need not be self-conscious racists or sexists, even if behavior leads to racist and sexist outcomes.

Similarly, there are mechanisms which explain the higher incomes of college graduates in comparison to those lacking college education. (Again, there are the mechanisms detailed by neo-classical economics and there are competing accounts – to be considered in chapter 6.) For present purposes, we need only note the fact that persons with bachelor's degrees earn more, on average, than those who lack such degrees. Similarly, there are complicated mechanisms which explain who gets degrees, but we can assume that ability to perform on standardized tests is relevant to admission to institutions of higher education. Claude Steele (2004) has suggested a social / psychological mechanism (related to the array of self-confirming mechanisms) which helps to explain poor performance in standardized tests by African-Americans. Because of widely prevalent attitudes that they are cognitively inferior, these groups learn to lack self-confidence in their preparation and capacities and this causes them to perform poorly. Steele tested the mechanism through a series of experiments in which randomly selected African-American students from Stanford were told that the test measured personal attributes. They were reminded of their race by asking them to check this off on the questionnaire. Another group of black students, also randomly selected, were told that the test was simply psychological research and no mention was made of race. The first group did appreciably poorer than the second group. Other studies of women and Asians have confirmed Steele's theory of "stereotype vulnerability." The mechanism does not, however, explain why loss of confidence has the effects that it evidently has.

Mechanisms as providing the micro-foundations of the macro

Putting aside psycho-sociological mechanisms of the sort just noticed, it is important to notice that as analyzed here, social mechanisms do not divide into the macro and the micro. As analyzed here, they link the micro and the macro – or if you will, they provide the micro-foundations for the macro. Thus, aggregated capitalist unemployment is understood in terms of the decisions of agents in corporations, firms and labor markets. That is, on the present view, the macro / micro view is untenable and all mechanisms assume typical agents engaged interactively in producing outcomes. Social mechanisms can, however, be theorized as applying locally or globally and thus in terms of varying degrees of abstraction.

For example, the mechanisms of capitalism are highly global and thus highly abstract. Marx generated his model by abstraction from mid-nineteenth-century British capitalism, but he is clear in seeing that societies with different histories could be capitalist, or, following Adam Smith (and well before Wallerstein), one could also apply the model to a global capitalist system. In Marx's model, there are only two sets of actors, capitalists and wage workers, defined relationally. There are no families, no schools, no banks, no gender or racial differences; while everyone is a potential consumer, there is no one engaged in marketing or advertising; finally, government functions only to establish the legal and infrastructural conditions of a monetary economy. Flesh-and-blood agents are entirely absent, but certain beliefs and motivations, derived by abstraction, are attributed to them as typical actors. For example, wage workers, structurally compelled to sell their labor power, know that they will not eat unless they can secure employment. Capitalists know that in production, surplus is derived from value-adding labor power. But for Marx, neither group fully penetrates the conditions of capitalist reproduction, in particular that commodities are fetishized – that a relation between persons manifests itself as a relation between things. Marx offers also a sketch of theory of how this occurs. Although these mechanisms (and others built on them) apply in any capitalist society, there will be huge differences in actual capitalist societies, precisely because as actors are more concretely theorized, other mechanisms and other beliefs and motivations will be compounded in generating outcomes. This is tantamount to applying the model more locally, from, say, a region, to a nation, to a production facility in Dearborn, Michigan.

An excellent example is the work of Dipesh Chakrabarty (1989). Following Marx, for Chakrabarty, there is a capitalist social relation only if the labor power of workers is experienced as a commodity in Marx's carefully discriminated sense. This is not, to be sure, a subjective phenomenon. It is as objective and real as anything can be. Indeed, given the conditions outlined in Marx's model, it is quite inevitable. That is, the entire analysis of fetishism is meant to show how it is possible – and necessary – that workers actively and uncoercively reproduce a system in which they are exploited. The conditions for this are not merely juridical, the wage-form, but, as Chakrabarty says, laborers must *live* in accordance with norms defining "formal freedom," and "equality before the law," rights, as E. P. Thompson had argued, which were the rights of "a free-born Englishman" – "as Paine had left him or as the Methodists had moulded him" (Thompson, 1978: 221). It was thus that Marx believed that England, a society "where the notion of human equality has already acquired the fixity of popular prejudice," was the best place to decipher the logic of capitalism.

In Chakrabarty's analysis, the jute workers of Bengal were certainly wage laborers, but they were not proletariat in Marx's sense. If this is correct, the implications need to be pressed. Briefly, Marx builds assumptions regarding culture – the politics of "equal rights" – into his model in *Capital*. These assumptions simply do not obtain in India. Accordingly (and quite apart from the critical facts of colonialism), we can hardly expect that capitalism in India would take the same form as, presumably, it did when Marx was writing about England. Moreover, because of this cultural difference, it is not surprising that class consciousness did not emerge among Indian jute workers. More generally, while there is the high abstraction, capitalism, concretely, there are only capitalisms, differing as least as much as there are differences in historical experience.

Tilly's "Coercion, Capital and European States" (1992) provides another convenient example. Tilly's aim is to offer a way to understand state-building in Europe. He begins with a highly abstract theory which represents "the logics of Capital and Coercion." These are mechanisms which are meant to apply trans-historically. Thus, we can divide populations into those who have capital (understood by Tilly in non-Marxist terms) as "any tangible resources, and enforceable claims on such resources" (1992: 153),[13] and those lacking such. "Capitalists, then, are people who specialize in the accumulation, purchase and sale of capital." "They occupy the realm of exploitation" vis-à-vis those lacking such resources. Surpluses produced are captured by capitalists. Similarly, by virtue of their position in social relations, persons or groups can dominate others. Tilly makes no effort to spell this out in any further detail, but it is easy to see that as regards both mechanisms, some very elementary assumptions are being made: for example, that those lacking the means of life must produce for those who have the resources. Nor is Tilly interested in theorizing the wide variety of mechanisms which, in specific times and places, allow for the accumulation and capture of surplus. Feudal mechanisms in Western Europe were different from the mechanisms of capitalism (as Tilly would agree). His interest here is at a higher level of abstraction.

In the concrete world, the mechanisms work conjointly, but effectively using the tools of comparison. Tilly offers that one can theorize three processes which produce states: "a coercion-intensive process, a capital intensive process, and a capitalist coercion path." Thus, "in the coercion-intensive mode, rulers squeezed the means of war from their own populations and others they conquered, building massive structures of extraction in the process" (1992: 164). In their phases as tribute-taking empires, this path was taken by Brandenburg and Russia. "In the capital-intensive mode, rulers relied on compacts with capitalists . . . to rent or purchase military force, and thereby warred without building vast permanent state structures. Typically, city-states and urban federations took this path. Finally, rulers can do some of each, typically producing full-fledged national states earlier than the coercive-intensive and capital-intensive modes did" (1992: 164–165).

---

[13] Marx is definite in restricting capital to a social relation between owners of the means of production and wage workers who are compelled to sell their labor. To be sure, in all historical societies surpluses are captured by those who own or control the means of production. But how this is accomplished requires some specific, different mechanisms. A "general theory" of exploitation would not be very informative. See appendix C.

Another mechanism is introduced (without explicit notice): "Driven by pressures of international competition (especially by war and preparation for war), all three paths eventually converged on concentrations of capital and of coercion all out of proportion to those that prevailed in AD 990" (1992: 165).

The account is highly abstract but nevertheless illuminating, going well beyond the claim, for example, that the modern state is the product of war – or of capitalist development. But as Tilly recognizes, if this provides abstract understanding of state-building, the devil is in the details. In his appeal to Lorenzo, Machiavelli saw that his city-state could not stand up to the aggrandizing motives of the new "empires," but we need Italian and English history to see why England achieved fully-fledged nation-state status by the seventeenth century and Florence did not. We need more than mechanisms here, a problem to be considered in chapter 5.

Work by Stinchcombe (1998) provides another useful illustration both of the idea that a fundamental mechanism may be employed in different institutional contexts, and of the putative macro–micro gap. He theorizes a mechanism titled "monopolistic competition" which by virtue of strong analogy, explains "the continuity of status of corporations in markets, or universities in prestige system, [and] of world power systems" (1998: 207). The basic mechanism needs to be stated at a relatively high level of abstraction to cover these divergent contexts, and Stinchcombe does not make much effort to articulate in detail the model in terms of the specific types of actors and the structures they are working with. Thus, he argues that "in fields of markets, prestige systems, and world systems, some organizations perform better than others, and they always do this not by becoming rentiers choosing their investments. Instead, they organize networks of collective action, create networks of suppliers, build or buy capital resources, and give people incentives to do all these successful performances" (1998: 270). While it is sometimes convenient to speak of organizations as agents, it is clear that it is the top management of these organizations who, by virtue of prevailing conditions suggestively sketched, are enabled and motivated to "appropriate the benefits of their competence as long as the opportunity continues to pay off, or if competitors develop competitive competences so that monopoly is no longer defensible" (1998: 271). Stinchcombe's account, of course, is more illuminating than the bare bones summarized here, but when all is said and done, a good deal more might be said about the mechanisms he has identified.

By contrast, the mechanisms analyzed in Goffman's *Asylums* (1961) apply pointedly only to "total institutions." Goffman's model is not made explicit, but it is far richer than Marx's model exactly because it is quite concrete. We can identify the key elements. Goffman identifies two entirely antagonistic types of actors standing in a well-defined social relation: the managers and the managed (professionals versus clients, staff versus inmates). By virtue of their place in these social relations, there are resources available which enable the construction of their identities and their social relations, including having appropriate credentials and dress, along with a number of specific capacities characteristic of the institution. Abstractly, the managed must be constructed as something less than a full person, while the manager is constructed as competent to "treat" the managed. Thus, "social distance is typically great and often formally pre-scribed" (Goffman, 1961: 7). Each of the two parties has goals (which "provide a key to meaning") and each has a system of beliefs (for the managers, an interpretative scheme which includes a theory of human nature). For each group, there are structured capacities for achieving their goals. Typically, the managed undergo mortification, the construction of a different self; role dispossession (1961: 14–15); "personal defacement" (1961: 20–21); "contaminative exposure" (1961: 23); and a diminishing of the capacity of the managed to control action. A mechanism employed in the stripping of power is "looping," where a disruptive response from an agent becomes the target of the next attack (1961: 35–36). But as with Willis, the managed also have resources. Resistance by them takes on a number of forms, including contesting the meaning of rules, "frater-nization," and "playing it cool" (1961: 61–65). Institutional ceremonies, including, for example, a newsletter produced by inmates, an annual party and an open house, are regular events in the life of the institution. These are intended to produce a joint commitment to the official goals, even if everyone "on the inside" knows better.

Goffman very convincingly shows how the beliefs of actors, true and false, promote behaviors which have as their outcome the reproduction of an institution in which there is a manifest disjunction between the official goals of the institution and the actual outcomes, and how, as in the Willis account, actors unintentionally act in self-defeating ways that sustain the conditions of their own oppression.

Goffman's model is of a total institution, but it offers insights into "near total institutions," for example, a boarding school, and even to institu-tions not nearly as "total," for example, a factory or university. Extended in this way, of course, the model needs to be amended to address the differences in the real concrete between these sorts of institutions. Bosses and classroom teachers do not stand in the same relation to the man-aged as staff to inmates. But there will be social mechanisms at work in these places that can be identified and that gives us an understanding of outcomes.

Worth mention here are the family of mechanisms generally termed "self-fulfilling prophecies" or as Schelling (1998) suggests, "self-realizing expectations." As he says, a coffee shortage, an insolvent bank, and going early to get a seat, would seem to be explained by the same mechanism. The critical step is the fact that acting on the pertinent expectation is sufficient to produce the outcome: if people expect a coffee shortage, many will engage in hoarding, and there will indeed be a coffee shortage. Similarly, if people believe that a bank is insolvent, they will withdraw their savings, ultimately rendering the bank insolvent.

Generalization, abduction and assessing theories of social mechanisms

It was noted that generalizations do not explain, that they need explaining. It is easy enough to see also that generalizations[14] will be the point of departure for a theory of a mechanism. That is, where there is some pattern or regularity, there are but two possibilities: either the regularity is the product of some mechanism or combination of mechanisms at work, or it is not. So compare, "A relatively small proportion of children from poor neighborhoods in the UK continue into higher education," and "For the past three months, as the prices of real estate in Honolulu went up, so too did movie attendance." Both propositions might be true, but there is little reason to believe that there is a mechanism at work which could explain the latter. The correlation is wholly accidental, perhaps a statistical anomaly. Where the regularity seems not to be accidental, Lawson (1997) suggests the idea of a "demi-regularity," or "demi-reg" for short. He defines it as "a partial event regularity which *prima facie* indicates the occasional, but less than universal actualization of a mechanism or tendency, over a definite region of time-space" (1997: 204). "Demi-regs" *prima facie* suggest a mechanism exactly in the sense that based on what we know, the connection is not likely to be accidental. Of special interest, then, are what he calls "contrastive demi-regs." He gives a number of examples, some commonsensical, some not so obvious: "Women look after children more than men do." "Average unemployment rates in the western industrial societies are higher in the 1990s than the 1960s," "In the 1990s UK firms are externalizing or 'putting out' more parts of the production process than twenty years ago," "Government persons tell more lies in war-time." As Weber rightly noted, there are countless numbers of these functioning both in ordinary life and in more sophisticated

---

[14] Generalizations here include both universal and statistical assertions, "All Fs are Gs," "Most Fs are Gs" are patterns and regularities which can always be expressed in these forms.

science. We can offer a number of important observations regarding such generalizations.

First, theory construction does not begin from nothing. Not only is it problem-driven, but the theorist has a stock of knowledge which will be the materials of the effort. Struck then by what is an interesting (and well-established) "demi-reg," inquiry into the possible mechanism or mechanisms begins.

Second, the demi-regs may well be the product of descriptive work, either quantitative or qualitative. Stephen Kemp and John Holmwood (2003) have argued that identifying unknown patterns is a particularly important task of statistical techniques. Thus, drawing on work by Stewart and his colleagues (Stewart *et al.*, 1980) they ask whether there is a mechanism to explain the unclear relationship between class background and type of school with the number of years a student pursued education. Kemp and Holmwood argue that regression techniques were effectively employed to show that the strongest pattern regarded class and high-status schools, a pattern not discernible without the use of these methods. But, of course, on the present view, the inquiry could not stop here. It is unfortunate that so much solid descriptive work is so often mistakenly taken to be explanatory when it is not (see appendix A). Given the identified pattern, the problem now becomes what explains it. Indeed, some aspects of the pertinent mechanism would seem to be involved in some of our previous examples. The interested reader might well test her theoretical ingenuity.

Third, contrastive demi-regs force inquiry into looking for differences which point to the probable causally relevant features. "[We] notice the effects of sets of structures through detecting relatively systematic differences in the outcomes of *prima facie* comparable types of activities (or perhaps similar outcomes of *prima facie* different activities in different space-time locations, or differences in types of position-related activities on comparable space-time locations, and so forth" (Kemp and Holmwood, 2003: 208–209). So, as is obvious enough, differences in domestic responsibilities between men and women suggest powerfully that we need to understand the mechanism which explains the existing division of labor. There are, no doubt, mechanisms of gender discrimination at work, but as with racism, these need to be spelled out and confirmed. Similarly, increased unemployment rates suggest differences in productivity or rates of profit which in turn suggest changes in mechanisms explaining productivity or the rate of profit.

The idea of contrastive demi-regs is at the bottom of considerations regarding comparison, long recognized to be a tool of macro- and historical sociology. That is, where outcomes are different, we seek differences in the causes. Comparative inquiry provides opportunities to identify the pertinent mechanisms at work in one case but not the other, or to identify pertinent differences in a similar mechanism which explains the differences in outcome (see chapter 5 and appendix C).

Finally, as in natural science, the mode of inquiry here is neither deduction nor induction, but what C. S. Peirce called "abduction." Given a demi-reg, can we identify the causal mechanism which explains it? And if there are several plausible mechanisms, can we arrive at some valid, if still fallible, conclusion? A host of difficulties attend this, including, as already noted, the fact that experiment is generally not possible in the social sciences.[15] The absence of the possibility of controlled experiment is an important difference between the natural and social sciences, but it need not lead to the conclusion that a human science is quite impossible (Collier, 1994).

Two lines of argument may be noted. First, there is the sort of evidence produced by Goldstein, *et al.* (above) to test their three different explanatory models. This is more or less direct. Second, among competing explanatory mechanisms, there are different consequences and these are testable. Hernes offers a wonderful example: the effort to explain why, as reported by Norwegian media, women are stung by wasps more often than men. It shows clearly how, on realist grounds, a theory of generative social mechanisms might be tested.

[15] So-called "natural experiments" are not experiments in any useful sense. But there are what are sometimes termed "quasi-experiments." An excellent example is the longitudinal study, "Lifetime Effects: The High/Scope Perry Preschool Study Through Age 40." As summarized by David L. Kirp, "From a group of 123 South Side neighborhood children, 58 were randomly assigned to the Perry program, while the rest, identical in virtually all respects, didn't attend preschool. Most children attended Perry for two years, three hours a day, five days a week. The curriculum emphasized problem-solving rather than unstructured play or 'repeat after me' drills. The children were viewed as active learners, not sponges; a major part of their daily routine involved planning, carrying out and reviewing what they were learning. Teachers were well trained and decently paid, and there was a teacher for every five youngsters. They made weekly home visits to parents, helping them teach their own children." "Random assignment is the research gold standard because the 'treatment' – in this case, preschool – best explains any subsequent differences between the two groups." Data was collected every year from age 3 through 11, then at ages 14, 15, 19, 27 and 40. The results are quite remarkable in terms of every relevant outcome: literacy, completion of high school, crime, and marriage and divorce rates. Indeed, at age 40, "nearly twice as many have earned college degrees (one has a Ph.D.). More of them have jobs: 76 per cent versus 62 per cent. They are more likely to own their home, own a car and have a savings account. They are less likely to have been on welfare. They earn considerably more – $20,800 versus $15,300." See David Kirp, "Life Way After Head Start," *New York Times Magazine*, November 21, 2004. But, of course, we remain unclear as to what in the experience of these students explains these differences in outcomes. It will certainly be a complicated story.

He offers four possible explanations:

(1) *The Rambo theory*: "Women are a more *tender* species than men . . . For a real man it would be disgracefully effeminate to call a doctor for a dinky distress" (Hernes, 1998: 76). The mechanism has it that men fail to report bites.

(2) *The outdoors theory*: "Women spend more *time* in the open air than men, walking their babies and playing with their children." This mechanism involves gender differences in roles.

(3) *The hysteria theory*: Women panic when they see a wasp, agitating them to sting. Men do not panic. The mechanism here makes women the cause of increased biting.

(4) *The scent theory*: Women use fragrances which "beguile wasps, but which then sting because they become aroused and then aggrieved when they discover that the bouquet stems not from flowers and react to frustration by aggression" (1998: 77). Critical to this mechanism are assumptions about wasp behavior.

Each of these *could* explain the outcome. But which, if any, is true? Hernes points to standard methodology: take the Rambo theory. *If* women are more tender, *then* they should be less tolerant of pain. Does any research support this? For each of these theories, we can test the truth of assumptions with evidence and argument. Very often this requires drawing out the implications of the assumptions, and accordingly, it requires a strenuous effort to see exactly what those assumptions are. Unfortunately, not only will this not be easy, but it is easy to fail to notice that assumptions which may be critical are being made.

Lawson (1997) also provides a wonderful example. He cites Leamer's account (1983) of the predicament of the applied econometrician:

The applied econometrician is like a farmer who notices that the yield is somewhat higher under the trees where birds roost, and he uses this for evidence that bird droppings increase the yield. However, when he presents his findings . . . another farmer . . . objects that he used the same data but came up with the conclusion that moderate amounts of shade increase the yields . . . A bright chap . . . then observes that these two hypotheses are indistinguishable, given the available data. (1997: 214)

Lawson answers:

The obvious response of course, albeit one that econometricians occupied with fitting a line to *given* sets of data rarely contemplate, is to add to the 'available data.' Specifically, the aim must be to draw consequences for, and seek out observations on, actual phenomena which allow the causal factor responsible to be identified. If, for example, bird droppings are a relevant causal factor then we could expect higher yields wherever birds roost. Perhaps there is a telegraph wire that crosses the field which is heavily populated with roosting birds, but which provides only negligible shade . . . Perhaps too there is a plot of land somewhere close to the farm house which is shaded by a protruding roof, but which birds avoid because of a patrolling cat . . . The fact that it is not possible to state categorically at this abstract level the precise conditions under which substantive theories can be selected amongst, i.e., without knowing the contents of the theories themselves or the nature or context of the conditions upon which they bear, is an unfortunate fact of all science. (1997: 214)

Lawson's more general conclusion deserves quoting(1997: 214): "Science is a messy business. It requires an abundance of ingenuity, as well as patience, along with skills that may need to be developed on the job."[16]

One final point needs to be considered here. It is the question of the role, limits and / or advantages of *verstehen* in the construction and evaluation of social mechanisms. In a well-known passage, Weber asserted that in the human sciences, "we can accomplish something which is never attainable in the natural sciences, namely the subjective understanding of the component individuals" (1968: 15). In one sense, this merely points to a huge difference in the nature of theorized mechanisms in the natural and human sciences. Since persons are the critical causes of what happens in society, a social mechanism must appeal to their beliefs and motivations. But is this an advantage?

Some writers, perhaps including Weber, have thought so. There is no argument, perhaps, that it is an advantage when it comes to building a model of a mechanism. As Bhaskar notes,

How, then, given the mishmash nature of social reality, is theory-construction accomplished in social science? Fortunately, most of the phenomena with which the social scientist has to deal will already be identified, thanks to the *concept-dependent* nature of social activities, under certain descriptions. (Bhaskar, 1979: 63)

Thus, we know what it is to cash a check and to need a job. As already suggested, theory construction must, inevitably, draw on common stocks of knowledge. As Schütz (1970) rightly noted, the explanation must be comprehensible to the lay person.

One might also argue that considerations of plausibility enter into our assessment of hypothesized social mechanisms. An account may be plausible in the sense that it confirms widely available beliefs and understandings (prejudices?). Clearly there is a manifest danger here. Fifty thousand Frenchmen can be wrong. On the other hand, in order to understand one another, we must have some understanding of the motivations and goals of others even if we can be mistaken on any given instance. Still, if the

---

[16] See also Sayer, 1992: chapter 7.

account is plausible and can be sustained evidentially, we may legitimately have some confidence in it.

But there remains the problem that actors can be mistaken about the social world which their activities sustain. Does not this suggest a disadvantage for theory construction in the human sciences? This objection would seem to rest on a misunderstanding of how the mechanism explains. There are two problems to be solved. There is the problem of understanding the beliefs of members. This obviously requires evidence. But there is also the problem of explaining the beliefs and actions of members, of discovering the existing conditions and consequences of action – which may or may not be known or acknowledged. This, too, requires evidence. It may be that the members do grasp reasonably well the social world that their action sustains. As in the work of Willis and Goffman, to take two outstanding examples, the mechanism may be able to show that the outcome would not be what it is unless the actors had false or partial beliefs about the conditions and consequences of their actions. That is, in these cases, explaining the outcome requires seeing that the actors failed to have an adequate grasp of the social world that is the ongoing product of their actions.

I have so far argued that in both the physical and the social sciences understanding requires identification of the generative mechanisms of outcomes. In chapter 3, it was argued that it was implausible to believe that we could improve on our ordinary capacities to understand the actions of concrete persons. Without social science, we can have an entirely adequate understanding of why your boss expects punctuality, of why your spouse wants to visit family at Christmas. In this chapter, it was argued that theory abstracts from the concrete reality of the actors and situations to get at the logic of a social process, for example, to achieve an understanding of an increased divorce or crime rate. But more needs to be said about how social mechanisms function in explanatory contexts. This takes us back to considering the goals of social science and forces us to address the question of the relation of history to social science. The question of "historical sociology" has been the battleground for this debate. The next chapter takes this debate, historically and currently, as its point of departure.

5 Social science and history

Introduction

One could argue that the classical sociologists, Montesquieu, Comte, de Tocqueville, Marx, Weber, even Durkheim, were historical sociologists. All of them worked with historical materials and all shared in the idea that this was essential to what they were doing. They did their work before sociology emerged in the twentieth century as a distinct discipline. Even though Marx disapproved of much work which had been done by people who identified themselves as historians, he believed, indeed, that history was *the* human science.[1] Similarly, Weber seems to have believed that sociology was, as he put it, a *propaedeutic* for historical work. That is, sociology could provide the tools and concepts for good historical inquiry, but was not itself an independent body of knowledge.[2]

Beginning in the so-called *Methodenstreit* (battle of methods) toward the end of the nineteenth century, the literature has tended to employ a distinction formulated by Windelband in 1894 between two kinds of inquiry: "nomothetic" versus "idiographic." It is generally held that the natural sciences are nomothetic – they are engaged in the search of laws, while the human sciences, including history, are idiographic – their object of concern is the concrete particular in its uniqueness. But there is considerable disagreement as to whether the grounds for this difference are methodological, epistemological or ontological. In what is perhaps its most recurring form, two kinds of explanation are at issue: on the nomothetic view, explanation is in the form of the covering law model. It is just this that is rejected by defenders of the idiographic view. For them, the

---

[1] In the *German Ideology*, Marx and Engels write: "We know only one science; the science of history." Quoted in Simon, 1994: 107.

[2] On Weber, there is a vast literature, of course. For some critical and historical background, see Manicas, 1987: 127–140, and more recently, Fritz Ringer, 1997. Also see notes 7 and 9 below. My effort pursues themes set out by Weber.

Durkheim had a different take. For him, "history can only be a science on condition that it raises itself above the particular; but then it ceases to be itself, and becomes a branch of sociology. It merges [as Comte would have said] with dynamic sociology" (1972: 78).

human sciences, including history, require a distinct form of explanation in which the goal is to grasp the meaning of human action. For the nomothetic sciences, general theory is essential, and induction and deduction are the primary tools; for the idiographic sciences, the structure of explanation, as in history, is narrative and there is no role for theory in the sense assumed in the natural sciences.

Except for some very important exceptions, historical sociology was very nearly extinguished by the middle of the twentieth century. Although the story would be complicated, this was largely a consequence of disciplinary specialization coupled with the vigorous effort on the part of modern sociologists to model their work on lessons presumably learned from natural science. From this perspective, since it did not seek "general explanatory variables," history was not nomothetic, hence not a science. Sociologists, accordingly, could leave narrative to historians and get on with their own important efforts at discovering "general explanatory variables."[3]

Such a view was, at best, a distortion of genuine science – a distortion which, fortunately, the classic writers did not need to confront. The writers who continued to practice historical sociology were not in the mainstream of academic sociology, even when their work was recognized as significant. One thinks here of some of the work of writers with variant understandings of the work of Weber, for example, Benjamin Nelson, Reinhard Bendix, C. Wright Mills and Barrington Moore. One thinks also here of some Marxists who were historians, including Christopher Hill, Eric Hobsbawm and M. I. Finley, and of historians influenced by Marxism, for example, Marc Bloch, and of a few others even harder to classify, such as Norbert Elias and Karl Polanyi.

Since the 1970s, however, sociologists have again begun "to reach for history." As Tilly writes:

Historical analyses of industrialization, of rebellion, of family structure began to appear in the journals that sociologists read. Departments of sociology began hiring specialists in something called "historical and comparative analysis."

---

[3] It is also important to examine the role of Talcott Parsons in the current (mis)understandings of Weber. See Grathoff (ed.), 1978; Wagner 1983; and Camic 1987. In his 1979 *New York Times* sympathetic reflection on the legacy of Parsons, Daniel Bell noted that charges against Parsons's style of sociology rested on a misunderstanding of the difference between history and sociology. Following a version of Durkheim, but certainly not Weber, Bell asserted, "there is no science of the particular; it is necessary to generalize. In the sciences the aim is to establish the invariant features of phenomena." Parsons repeatedly warned his readers that he was not dealing with concrete phenomena but with "'analytical abstractions,' a set of logical categories into which all social actions would fit." Parsons's "integration" of Weber, accordingly, vitiated the core of Weber's views on social science (see below).

Sociological authors began to write as if *when* something happened seriously affected *how* it happened. Some few sociologists actually began to learn the basic historical skills: archival exploration, textual analysis, and the like. History began to matter. (Tilly, 1982: 38)

One suspects that this rediscovery of history was due, in part at least, to the onslaught against the conventional wisdom in the philosophy of science, to the eclipse – at least officially – of the dominating work of Talcott Parsons and of structural functionalism, and perhaps also, as Tilly suggests, to the new skepticism regarding progressivist theories of modernization and development.[4]

The recent past

Books about historical sociology by Stinchcombe (1978), Tilly (1982, 1984), Abrams (1983), Smith (1991) and Skocpol (1984, 1994), not to mention a host of important books in historical sociology by both younger writers and well-established authors, demonstrate a continuing vitality and, I hasten to add, a continuing disagreement over strategies for joining history and sociology. There was even a "counter-revolution" against the very idea of joining the two. Goldthorpe (1991) strenuously defended the covering law model and insisted on a sharp division between history and sociology. Most recently, we have two important collections of essays: one, edited by McDonald (1996), *The Historic Turn in the Human Sciences*, has a broad scope; another, edited by Mahoney and Rueschemeyer (2003), *Comparative Historical Analysis in the Social Sciences*, focuses on comparative methods. There is also a new and useful handbook on historical sociology (Delanty *et al.*, 2003). This volume covers most of the ground and concludes that "historical sociology is deeply divided between explanatory 'sociological' approaches and more empirical and interpretative 'historical' approaches." Finally, there is lively debate in both *The American Journal of Sociology* (1998) and in a recent book (Gould, 2004) between Margaret Somers and advocates of rational choice theory regarding the role, if any, of "general theory" in historical sociology. (See appendix C, below.)

---

[4] Craig Calhoun (1996) provides a useful sociology of historical sociology. Important here is his observation that the work of the 1970s and 1980s made the effort to legitimize historical sociology by arguing that it could be as rigorous as other forms of sociology. Presumably "other forms of sociology" more nearly approximated the methods assumed to be true of natural science. Theda Skocpol's effort to employ Mill's methods is a good example. See appendix B for critical discussion. For additional reflections on the sociology of historical sociology, see Skocpol, 1994 and Delanty *et al.*, 2003.

Symptomatic of confusion over the relevant issues, writers disagree even on their understanding of what some of the better-known studies were doing. At one extreme we find Stinchcombe arguing that "the difference between Trotsky's Marxism, Smelser's functionalism, and de Tocqueville's conservative despair makes hardly any difference to any important question of sociological theory" (1978: 2). Thus, "when they do a good job of historical interpretation, Marx and Weber and Parsons and Trotsky and Smelser all operate in the same way." This is surely puzzling: perhaps they rarely "do a good job" or what counts as "the same way" is very fuzzy – despite Stinchcombe's interesting readings of the authors he discusses.

Although entirely different in aim and approach, Dennis Smith's *The Rise of Historical Sociology* (1991), which gives an account of eighteen noteworthy writers, puts him, ultimately, near to Stinchcombe as regards differences between historical sociologists. He gives even-handed descriptions of each of his eighteen selected writers, usually in pairs, usually arranged by topics: for example, under "old empires, new nations," he discusses Eisenstadt and Lipset, and under "two critical rationalists," we find Barrington Moore and E. P. Thompson. In his last chapter he identifies four relevant issues: "whether historical sociologists have operated as 'outsiders', or as members of the relevant 'establishment'; the way they handle problems of involvement and detachment; third, their orientations toward theory, empirical generalization and primary exploration of historical data; and fourth, the strategies of explanation they adopt." Important as these notions are, they seem to be almost afterthoughts: they do not drive the accounts of the writers he discusses. More importantly, perhaps, he is very uncritical of notions of theory and explanation. And on all four of the issues, he finds no clear lines at all, offering instead four "strategies of explanation": competitive selection, system contradictions, infrastructural capacities and dominant routes of social change.

However, these are not best construed as "strategies of explanation," but as theoretical orientations, predicated very much on very different notions of the nature of history and of society. In any case, he finds some combination of these in all the writers he has discussed. Presumably Smelzer's work exemplifies the dominant route strategy – a stage theory – but in a less pure form, it is also found in Runciman, Wallerstein, Lenski, Moore and Anderson. With Moore and Anderson, however, it is complemented with evolutionist assumptions, and, in the case of Moore (Anderson is not mentioned), "great attention to the infrastructural capacities of dominant and subordinate classes within agrarian polities." He thus meets Mann, who, as it turns out, shares with Lenski "a location between infrastructural capacities and dominant routes." One could go on. The upshot is the feeling that historical sociologists are quite messy beasts and that as far as method or strategy is concerned, an eclectic anarchy is to be recommended. On the other hand, one wonders whether the problem resides more in the way that the material is being conceptualized by these commentators. It may be that, as with much talk about science, the problem stems from an inapt theorizing of the actual practices.

Modes of comparison: individualizing, universalizing and variation finding

A similar generosity is found in Tilly's suggestive, but ultimately unhelpful, classification. Tilly identified four approaches to historical sociology. For him the key difference is the mode of comparison: individualizing, universalizing, variation finding, and encompassing comparisons. Thus,

> a purely individualizing comparison treats each case as unique, taking up one instance at a time, and minimizing its common properties with other instances. A pure universalizing comparison, on the other hand, identifies common properties among all instances of a phenomenon . . . [Variation finding] is supposed to establish a principle of variation in the character or intensity of a phenomenon by examining systemic differences among instances. (Tilly, 1984: 81–82)[5]

While Tilly's account of comparison is provocative, it suffers, as he seems to acknowledge, in part, because writers are anything but clear or consistent as to whether they are individualizing, universalizing or variation finding. Indeed, he undermines his own classification by remarking:

> If we needed a pedigree for individualizing comparison, its use by Max Weber would suffice. When Weber started elaborating his great taxonomies, he bowed toward generalization. When he spoke of rationalization and charisma, he gestured toward universalizing comparison. But his wide comparisons of religious systems served mainly to specify the uniqueness of the achieving, accumulating, rationalizing bureaucratic West. To a large degree, Max Weber used comparison for the purpose of individualizing. (1984: 88)

Weber is a critical figure in the literature of historical sociology and his work has been put to a number of uses. In what follows, we will argue that his work remains fundamental for any plausible version of a historical sociology. However, "individualizing" cannot serve as a way to distinguish these often inconsistent efforts. When Reinhard Bendix and Perry Anderson are both identified as individualizers we may suspect that we

---

[5] "Encompassing" is sufficiently unlike "comparison" to omit it from discussion here. Tilly defines it as follows: "[Encompassing] places different instances at various locations within the same system, on the way to explaining their characteristics as a function of their varying relationships within the system as whole" (1984: 83).

have missed what is essential in comparing their work. Moreover, as later chapters in Tilly's very useful book show, no writer fails to do some individualizing, some universalizing and some variation-finding. As is plain enough from Tilly's own formulation of these strategies, one is tempted to say that Weber could not help both individualizing and generalizing since individualizing presupposes generalizing. Thus, we need to see what counts as a bureaucracy – a step in generalizing – and then to see how the bureaucracies of China differed from bureaucracies in modern capitalist societies – an individualizing step.

Much confusion, unfortunately, attends the idea of generalization. In the first place, it is quite indispensable. Whenever we use an abstract noun, we are committed to a generalization, however vague, however open textured or ideal-typical. Thus, when we identify an institution as a bureaucracy, we assume that there are some properties connoted by the term which enables us to call institutions of China and institutions in modern capitalist states bureaucracies. On the other hand, it is true, but trivially so, that every concrete particular is unique, so the real question is whether the individualizing is non-trivial – essential to our interest in understanding the particular concrete under study. Thus, what features of pertinence distinguish bureaucracies in capitalist societies from those of China? Similarly, variation finding requires both individualizing and generalizing, finding differences along a continuum.

There are several real questions here. One, clearly seen by Tilly, is the question of whether our interest is in what is distinctive or in what is common. Weber insisted that physical theories, for example, the physics of masses, apply to all masses at any time and place, and such highly abstract knowledge is interesting to us. When it comes to the human sciences, it is the concrete in all its individuality which interests us. Thus, he wrote famously: "the type of social science in which we are interested is an *empirical science* of concrete reality (*Wirklichkeitswissenschaft*). Our aim is the understanding of the characteristic uniqueness of the reality in which we move" (1949: 72). For him, even if social science were to model itself as an abstract science, like physics, and offer general theories and propositions true of all human groupings, such knowledge would be neither useful nor interesting.

This turns out to be no small matter, especially as regards comparison. On this view, comparisons are not employed primarily to find generalizations – what is true, for example, of all bureaucracies – but rather to sharpen one's understanding, for example, of "the uniqueness of the achieving, accumulating, rationalizing bureaucratic West." More importantly, on Weber's view of the matter, the goal is not to settle for the generalization, for example, that in pre-revolutionary France and pre-revolutionary China, "peasants were the critical class component," but to see as precisely as one can, the differences in peasant relations in these two cases. Finally, while there can be little doubt that at some level of abstraction, there will be resemblances both in the types and in the sequences characteristic of, say, commercialization or state-building, differences in outcomes can be explained only by identifying different causes in these similar sequences.[6] The comparative method becomes, on this view, both a method of discovery and a way to test hypotheses about causes. I will return to this below.

Second, and as important, there is the question of what one does with generalizations. Tilly's classification suffers mainly from the fact that it gives us no help in seeing what comparison is doing for us. In particular, is it the main goal of a historical sociology to seek generalizations (and law-like statements) in order to explain by covering laws? Presumably, it is just this that distinguishes sociology as a science and separates it from history – the familiar "nomothetic / idiographic" divide.[7]

It is important to see here that Weber (1975) revised the prevailing nomothetic / idiographic bifurcation and insisted that "the logical peculiarity of 'historical' knowledge in contrast to 'natural-scientific' knowledge . . . has nothing at all to do with the distinction between the 'psychical' and the 'physical,' the 'personality' and 'action,' on the one hand, and the dead 'natural object' and the 'mechanical processes of nature,' on the other (1975: 184–185). The key difference is in the goals of two kinds of science: the nomological or abstract sciences employ laws which are unconditionally and universally valid. The sciences of concrete reality aim at knowledge of the particular. "Because of the logical impossibility of an exhaustive reproduction of even a limited aspect of reality . . . this must mean the following: knowledge of those aspects of reality which we regard as *essential* because of their individual *peculiarities* (Weber, 1975: 57). In turn, we can then identify what in the infinitely complex causal history of the concrete explains it (see below).

---

[6] In *The Protestant Ethic*, Weber notes that he "treated one side of the causal chain," while in his more extensive studies of religion, in order to "find points of comparison with the Occidental development," he aimed at finding causal relationships "to economic life and social stratification." "For only in this way is it possible to attempt a causal evaluation of those elements of economic ethics of the Western religions which differentiate them from others, with a hope of attaining even at tolerable degree of approximation" (1958: 27). Too often Weber is read as giving a "culturalist" (and monocausal) explanation in response to "socio-economic" (and also monocausal) Marxist accounts.

[7] Charles Ragin and David Zaret (1983) have argued for a version of Weber which focuses on the particular features of concrete cases and rejects as impertinent a Durkheimian search for general explanatory variables.

There are, as already noted, at least two other functions of general-ization. First, it is presupposed in individualizing: we identify critical differences in a set of outcomes or sequences which at some level of abstraction resemble one another. For example, we see that in Case 1, unlike Case 2, the peasants had property rights and that this made a difference in the outcomes, exactly because different choices were pos-sible. Second, hypotheses generated by comparative study will serve as promissory notes calling for explanation. Thus, comparative study may yield the generalization: "In a highly bureaucratic absolutist state, the landed nobility has little political power." Such generalizations, if true, may provide some explanation, depending on the question of interest. But, in turn, they demand explanation: what are the mechanisms that explain the generalization? The analogy to the natural sciences is exact: molecular theory begins with unexplained generalizations, most of which are common to ordinary experience. Sugar dissolves in water; iron rusts. Molecular theory tells us why. In the writings of historians and historical sociologists, one encounters a host of generalizations, many indeed which come directly from ordinary experience, for example, "It is not easy to challenge a bureaucracy," or "Bureaucracies are not easy to control." If true, there will be reasons for this and these will be given in terms of causal mechanisms which regard the capacities, beliefs and behavior of bureaucrats.

Tilly offers that the relative value of the strategies he identifies "depends upon the intellectual task at hand." This is certainly the case as to whether the particular problem calls for individualizing, generalizing or variation finding. But he also sees that the value of strategies "depends on the nature of the social world and the limits to our knowledge of that world" (Tilly, 1984: 145). Indeed, one of most powerful parts of his book is his epistemologically and ontologically sensitive analysis of the "pernicious postulates," for example, that "a single recurrent social process governs all social change" (1984: 33), or that "abstractly specified processes such as differentiation or concentration, mark out the limits for intelligible analysis" (1984: 50). As he would probably agree, if we want to iden-tify strategies for inquiry, it is desirable to provide a classification which takes for its criterion of demarcation a feature which cuts deeply into methodological, epistemological and ontological issues. While there are some serious problems with it, Theda Skocpol's (1984) classification of approaches in terms of explanation strategies is exactly what is called for. A review of this will also allow us to see more clearly how the argument of the present volume relates to existing literature on the question of history and sociology.

A taxonomy of explanation types

Skocpol offers a trichotomy of strategies that might be termed "function-alist universalist," "analytical historical" and "interpretative historical." Skocpol is also unwilling to risk dogmatism and finds that writers very often mix strategies – assuming, presumably, that no problems of coher-ence arise?

The basic orientation of the first subtype, "functionalist universalist," is expressed well by S. M. Lipset:

From an ideal-typical point of view, the task of the sociologist is to formulate general hypotheses, hopefully set within a larger theoretical framework, and to test them. His interest in the way in which a nation such as the United States formulated a national identity is to specify propositions about the general process involved in the creation of national identities in new nations. Similarly, his concern with changes in the pattern of American religious participation is to formulate and test hypotheses about the function of religion for other institutions and for the social system as a whole . . . These are clearly not problems of the historian. History must be concerned with the analysis of the particular set of events or processes. Where the sociologist looks for concepts which subsume a variety of particular descriptive categories, the historian must remain close to the actual happenings. (quoted in Tilly, 1982: 5)

The basic idea is clear. The task of the (historical) sociologist is to use theory to generate some general hypotheses which, if true, would explain the particular event under examination. For the functionalist, the theory will be a version of structural functionalism.[8]

In Lipset's example, we have hypotheses about "the general process" of nation-building. We might argue that a key modernizing process is differ-entiation, including the increasing division of labor in society, increased institutional separation and thus accentuated individualism. For example: "Whenever a society undergoes modernization, there is an increasing divi-sion of labor in society." Coupled with other hypotheses, for example, "When religious institutions are weakened, there is a loss of normative control," we are led to the conclusion that an essential requirement for the continuing stability of the social system is the development of organs of "authoritative interpretation and enforcement" – a legitimated legal system and the coercive forces of the police. With this theory, then, one goes into history and examines nation-building in a variety of contexts.

Skocpol provides some powerful criticism of functionalist universal-ism. First, "the model itself has to be taken as given prior to its historical

---

[8] Rational choice theory is another candidate for such a general theory. See below appendix C.

application" (Skocpol, 1984: 365). It is important to stress what this must assume. It assumes that there are universal principles of social reproduction and social change, even if the particular forms they take are historically variable. If, however, as Mills (1959) long ago insisted, we do not know of any such universal principles, that these vary with the social structure we are examining, then this criticism is fatal. Second, how can we be sure that different investigators would concretize such abstract concepts as "differentiation" or "mass organization" in the same way? Here the problem is the wobbly character of critical general terms. Perhaps indeed, in order to save functionalist assumptions about change, almost anything can be made to count. Finally, and following on this, perhaps historical facts are omitted or distorted to fit the preconceived theory.[9]

For the functional universalist, histories are case studies meant to elaborate and demonstrate the validity of universally valid theoretical ideas. Case studies allow the theorist to move from the abstract to the concrete. By contrast, the analytic sociologist "aspires to generate new explanatory generalizations through comparative historical analysis," or alternatively, to "discover causal regularities that account for specifically defined historical processes or outcomes, and explore *alternative* hypotheses to achieve that end" (Skocpol, 1984: 362). For example, while Skocpol hopes to induce a general theory of modern revolution from studies of cases, Lipset hopes to test his general theory against cases. They thus differ fundamentally in the use to be made of history.

For Skocpol, analytic historical sociologists "acknowledge the desirability of generalizable explanatory principles" (1984: 375), but they stand between those who seek "a single overarching model" and those who restrict themselves to "the meaningful exploration of the complex particularities of each singular time and place" (1984: 374).[10] This is certainly plausible. But like the functionalist universalist, Skocpol is committed to the covering law model of explanation.[11] We have argued that

[9] This line of criticism applies also to a good deal of what goes under the name of Marxism. There are other problems of functionalist theory (Marxist and non-Marxist), some familiar since at least Nagel, 1961 and Hempel, 1965 scrutinized reigning Parsonian theory. For criticism of functionalism in sociology, see Anthony Giddens, 1979, 1981. Functionalist theory still commands attention. See Alexander, 1998; Münch 1987; and Luhmann 1997.

[10] Moore, 1966 and Anderson, 1974 take this route, but do not assume the covering law model. Paige (1999) asserts that Skocpol, contrary to her claims to the contrary, is committed to the search for "universal causal laws" (1999: 791). But it is her commitment to the covering law model which misleads Paige. See below.

[11] For her, "the distinctive causes of the social-revolutionary situations in France, 1789, Russia, 1917, China, 1911" (Skocpol, 1984: 154) reduce to two: if a state organization susceptible to administrative and military collapse is subjected to intensified pressures from developed countries abroad *and* there is widespread peasant revolt facilitated by

this mode of explanation cannot be sustained in any science and will not repeat those arguments here. In any case, as a number of critics have shown (Burawoy, 1989; Sewell, 1996), Skocpol's use of Mill's methods does not allow her to produce the necessary explanatory generalizations – "the sufficient distinctive causes" – of the French, Russian and Chinese revolutions.[12]

Interpretative historical sociologists (on Skocpol's taxonomy) eschew causal explanation and seek what is called "a meaningful interpretation." This leads such writers to pay especial attention to ideas, and to the intentions of actors. Since causal explanation is rejected, description and explanation, which take the form of narrative, tend to collapse. Interpretative historical sociologists are skeptical of the sort of theory employed by both generalists and analytic historical sociologists, but many find useful Weber's conception of the ideal-type. In their comparative work, interpretative historical sociologists are interested in individuating and in establishing significant differences between what is compared. As Reinhard Bendix says:

> By means of comparative analysis I want to preserve a sense of historical particularity, as far as I can, while still comparing different countries. Rather than aim at broader generalizations and lose that sense, I ask the same or at least similar questions of divergent materials and so leave room for divergent answers. I want to make more transparent the divergence among structures of authority and among the ways in which societies have responded to the challenges implicit in the civilization accomplishments of other countries.[13]

We can illustrate this briefly with reference to his impressive *Kings or People* (1978). Like Barrington Moore (below), Bendix is interested in modernization, but the difference in orientation is clear from the very first pages:

> It is easiest to define modernization as a breakdown of the ideal-typical traditional order: Authority loses its sanctity, monarchy declines, hierarchical social order is disrupted. Secular authority, rule in the name of the people, and an equalitarian ethos are typical attributes of modern society. (Bendix, 1978: 10)

"The traditional order" is ideal-typically defined in the sense that the several features singled out are true more or less of pre-modern society,

---

agrarian sociopolitical structures, then there will be a social revolution. In 1789, France was subjected to such pressures and had an agrarian social political structure. Hence there was a social revolution in France (1984: 154). Similarly, we can substitute Russia and China in the second premise and "explain" their revolutions.

[12] See appendix B for detailed analysis of this.

[13] Quoted by Theda Skocpol (1984: 370), from Reinhard Bendix, "The Mandate to Rule: An Introduction," *Social Forces* 55 (1976): 247.

some may be present, some, sometimes absent. Ideal-types do not pretend to be strict definitions. Indeed, while they are not fictions, nothing really corresponds to them. Following Weber, they represent "some valid point of view" that is culturally significant for us. In Bendix's study, considerable emphasis is put on Christianity, Hinduism and Confucianism. This is a version of Weber, but without Weber's fundamental concerns with causality. Moreover, as Tilly remarks, "ordinary people disappear from Bendix's history, except as a breeding ground for new elites and as a field in which those new elites sow their implicitly revolutionary ideas." Indeed, "the pivotal events are not alterations in the structure of production or of power [as in Moore], but changes in prevailing ideas, beliefs, and justifications" (Tilly, 1984: 93). And these remain unexplained.

Critical problems can be anticipated with each of these strategies. There is good reason to reject the idea of a general theory that can be applied to historical instances,[14] but there is also good reason to be clear about one's meta-theory – one's epistemological and ontological assumptions about inquiry in the human sciences. Thus, are there historical laws? What explanatory role do individuals, Napoleon or George W. Bush, play in the effort at explanation? Is culture an explanatory variable or does it require explanation? Finally, there is good reason to insist, as Weber had long ago argued, that attention to the particular and to identifying meaning are, in the human sciences, an essential part of the causal problem. But then we must be clear about our sense of causality.

It is possible to articulate a conception of a historical sociology which responds to these questions, meets these desiderata, draws on the work of Weber – and is both coherent and plausible. Indeed, it turns out that this is an answer to the more general problem of explaining concrete social events or episodes. If it is a critical task of a social science to provide explanations of events, then a good deal of sociology is historical, in the sense that sequence is critical.[15] We can suggest along the way that what we take to be successes in the efforts of historical sociologists are successes mainly because their work manifests, albeit unclearly and perhaps even incoherently, the conception to be defended here. It must also be emphasized that the issue is not that one cannot find valuable insights in many of the major efforts in historical sociology. It is rather that these are often accidents in the sense that they were not only not promoted by the

---

[14] See appendix C for further discussion of this.

[15] Of course, all sociology is historical in the sense that social forms are historical products. But in addition to explaining events, there is also a sociological interest in understanding in the sense of chapter 1. That is, as understanding in the physical sciences comes with a theory of generative mechanisms, a theory of social mechanisms gives us understanding, for example, of why working-class kids get working-class jobs, of capitalism or state-building. This does not require history in the sense of historical sequence. See below.

explicit strategy of the author, but would in fact not have been there at all had the author been clear about his or her commitments.[16]

A realist historical sociology

The conception to be defended here begins with two fundamental observations. First, we assume a realist conception of causality: causes are productive powers that bring about outcomes. Second, the primary[17] causal agents in history are persons. We need to consider the important role of social structures – as the ongoing product of activity – but we cannot say that social structures are causal. As virtually existing, they do not determine action, even though, to be sure, they both constrain and enable action. In every instance, persons must operate with "materials at hand", "rules and resources" in Giddens's formulation. What powers and capacities they have will be very much a function of the resources available to them in acting. As Marx rightly insisted, we make history – though not with materials of our choosing. But as C. Wright Mills (1956) observed (probably with the Marx text in mind), "the fact is that although we are all of us within history, we do not all possess equal powers to make history." For example, the decision of the US president to invade Iraq was a decision of monumental importance exactly because it changed the world in ways that would be quite impossible for most ordinary people. He could make war, but wars begun cannot be undone. Options are foreclosed and new choices are demanded.[18] Nevertheless, this decision was enabled by the actions of many persons who acted in terms of social mechanisms they did not create.

There will then be an analogy in historical explanation to explaining an event in the natural sciences. Consider the simplest case: we want to explain the fact that this morning in Sam's kitchen, a spoonful of salt dissolved in a pot of water. We can appeal to the generalization, "salt is water-soluble," and to the fact that somebody put the salt into the pot. Both implicate causes: the promissory note of a mechanism and the

[16] Several writers have argued that Skocpol's most influential *States and Social Revolutions* (1979) is an excellent example of an incoherently wrought success. Put briefly, she allows us to believe that her use of Mill's methods generated explanatory generalizations. In fact, her explanations involved examining causes, understood in realist terms. In addition to what follows, see appendix B for further discussion.

[17] Again, natural events and processes very often play critical causal roles in history. Donald McNeil Jr. recently asked, pertinently, "What follows in the wake of a tsunami? The death of a nation? Secessionist warfare or, conversely, the unexpected drift of warring parties toward a peace table? A surge in Islamic fundamentalism?" (*New York Times*, January 2, 2005)?

[18] There is, obviously, a parallel to biography. Some decisions are of major personal importance: they alter "the path we are on," foreclosing some options and opening others.

effect of human action. Consider an analogous case in social science: why didn't Jones get the job for which she seemed to be eminently qualified? We notice that Jones is a female and that Sam is a sexist. We have an explanation since "sexist" is functioning as promissory note.

Neither case is remarkable. Such problems as explaining the collapse of the Twin Towers or the outcome of the American presidential election in 2000 are more interesting. But the basic task remains the same. One must identify and trace the ensemble of causes, both singular causal statements regarding the eventful acts of key agents, for example, the nineteen terrorists who commandeered the aircraft, and foreign policy decisions of key actors in the US government. The narrative will include an account of both past and currently existing social mechanisms, for example, processes which generate enemies of the USA, including the mechanism which produces terrorists,[19] CIA intelligence practices and processes of foreign policy decision-making in the USA. None of this will be easy and much of it will be contestable. (Explaining the collapse of the Twin Towers would require also identifying of the causal role of the pertinent *physical* mechanisms, for example, the incapacity of the structure to resist the heat generated by explosions of jet fuel.) Taken together these produced the outcome.

Time will be critical, since the sequencing of causes is essential. In the case of the election, this nexus of causes will involve the acts of key agents whose decisions and actions had identifiable causal consequences, mostly unintended, for example, the actions of the opposing candidates and their advisors, the acts of Katherine Harris and the Supreme Court.[20] But it

---

[19] To engage a "war on terror" it is essential, of course, that the mechanism which produces terrorists be understood. Without attempting to even sketch this mechanism, one may reasonably suppose that invading Iraq would not only not address this problem, but might, indeed, exacerbate it. Compare here the too often failure to consider the mechanisms which produce criminals, or the failure to notice that the mechanisms which produce youthful drug dealers are not the same as the mechanisms which produce white-collar criminals.

[20] Struggling with many of the same problems of this chapter, Marshall Sahlins (2004) offers a distinction between two types of "structural agency," "systemic agency" and "conjunctural agency". By virtue of institutional position, the acts of a systemic agent, such as Napoleon, "are fateful whatever strategic decision he took" (2004: 158). Bobby Thompson (whose home run in the bottom of the ninth inning won the 1951 World Series of baseball) or Katherine Harris (whose decision as Florida Secretary of State, powerfully influenced the presidential victory of George W. Bush) are "conjunctural agents." Thompson and Harris were "circumstantially selected for [their] historic roles by the relationships of a particular historical circumstance" (2004: 157). There may be some utility to such distinctions as they are employed in the narrative, but as Sahlins acknowledges, explaining outcomes requires seeing that the acts of both depend upon capacities made available by their "positions" and that in both cases, their actions are essential to explaining the outcome. Of course, as Sahlins notes, had either done differently, their names would have dropped out of history and this is not true of Napoleon.

will also involve the acts of theorized typical persons: rural whites in Middle America; media people; politicians; publicists and pundits; ministers; gay and anti-gay activists; union members; and campaign financers; all of whose beliefs, motives and situations explain their decisions. But the social scientific task does not end there: we also need an explanation of why typical actors have the beliefs they do. Getting a handle on this will not be easy and, as above, the account may well be contested. On the other hand, why should we suppose that the causal story will be uncomplicated? One needs to be reminded of the limits of meteorology and indeed, more generally of physics – the abstract science *par excellence*.

The basic outline of this view of inquiry is already present in the work of Max Weber.[21] Guenther Roth ably summarizes:

Both sociology and historiography proceed from causality inherent in human action. When Weber defined sociology as "a science concerning itself with the interpretative understanding of social action and thereby with the causal explanation of its course and consequences," he meant to affirm that in history only men act, not social organisms or reified collectivities.[22] The construction of socioeconomic models, such as patrimonialism or rule by notables, is possible because, in principle, we can understand the intentions of men and causally explain the course and consequences of their actions. (Roth and Schlucter, 1979: 205)[23]

---

[21] There are some important differences between Weber and contemporary "realisms," but the critical point here is that he was anti-positivist both in rejecting the Humean analysis of causality for an account in which causes produce effects, and in rejecting the idea that social science pursues laws which presumably explain the real concrete. See, among many texts, "Objectivity" in *Social Science and Social Policy* (1949). For example, "Where the individuality of a phenomenon is concerned, the question of causality is not a question of *laws* but of concrete causal *relationships*; it is not a question of subsumption of the event under some general rubric as a representative case but of its imputation as a consequences of constellation" (Weber, 1949: 78f.). "The conclusion which follows . . . is that an 'objective' analysis of cultural events, which proceeds according to the theses that ideal of science is the reduction of empirical reality of 'laws' is meaningless" (1949: 80). More generally Weber rejected the Laplacean metaphysics wherein (following Dilthey's critique) the "ideal goal" was "a sort of 'astronomical knowledge'" (1949: 73).

While this cannot be argued here, despite positivist readings of Marx (via Engels), Marx would agree to this. See Sayer, 1979, 1987. Similarly, while Weber would agree that persons can (and often do) act on beliefs which are false or distorted, this is not given the attention that Marx gives it.

[22] Compare Marx: "History does nothing, it possesses no immense wealth, it wages no battles. It is man, real living man, that does all that, that possesses and fights; history is not a person apart, using man as a means for its own particular aims; history is nothing but the activity of man pursuing his aims" (Marx, 1956: 125).

[23] See also Fritz Ringer, 1997, 2002. Ringer offers a most useful account of Weber on causal analysis. He focuses on Weber's notions of "interpretation" and "adequate causation," for Weber, the effort to identify the change in the existing state of affairs which produced an outcome. *Verstehen* is critical since persons are causal agents who act for reasons which we need to identify: "historical agents envisage the results that they hope to achieve, along with the means to achieve them, and that is what moves them to act. The specific characteristic of 'this kind of cause'. . . is that we can 'understand' it" (Ringer, 2002:

Roth distinguishes socio-economic models from what he terms "secular theories." On the present view, both are easily construed as social mechanisms. There is little to dispute as regards the main line of argument:

The socio-economic models as well as the secular theories are not intended to explain what is happening in a given situation. One model alone cannot adequately describe a given case: a battery of models or hyphenated types, such as a patrimonial bureaucracy, can provide a better approximation. Their utility lies in serving as base lines for identifying the distinctiveness of the case. While secular theories attempt to trace a long line of causation, they too have limited usefulness as regards a given situation. Theories such as those of democratization and industrialization diminish in explanatory value when we look at the relatively short span of a few years or even two or three decades, because they are concerned with long-range structural change. (Roth and Schlucter, 1979: 198)

The real concrete, whether it be a specific exchange between two parties or a civilizational whole, like Modern Western Capitalism, is complex and the product of complex causes, some of very long historical genesis. Our models are always abstract, even though, importantly, they will be of varying degrees of abstraction. The causal account of nineteenth-century democratization might well begin with the Greek *polis*, even if understanding nineteenth-century democracy will require a causally linked series of configurations, each getting us closer to the real concrete which needs to be explained.[24] As Weber insisted:

Every individual constellation which it "explains" or predicts is causally explicable only as the consequences of another equally individual constellation which has

169). Moreover, "as both Simmel and Weber showed, a singular relationship does not and cannot be specified as a set of connections among the elementary constituents of two successive total states . . . The logic of causal analysis does not change with the generality of the historical developments and outcomes that are to be explained" (2002: 175). That is, the same logic applies whether the explanandum is Modern Western Capitalism or "the defenestration of Prague."

Two problems with Ringer's account may be noted. First, Ringer offers that Weber employed counterfactual reasoning *and* comparative analysis, especially after 1909 in developing causal arguments. No doubt counterfactual reasoning is useful in seeking to identify causes, and is especially useful in getting an understanding of real possibilities available at some time and place. Too often, actual choices and their outcomes are made to seem inevitable. But there is no way to test a counterfactual in history, so that Ringer's analysis (graphically represented in diagrams) cannot be sustained. That is, one cannot compare the actual course of events with an *imagined* difference. For example, while it is clear that the rejection of the Confederation was critical as regards nation-building in the USA, that the choices by the SPD in Germany were fundamental as regards ensuing German history, and that Hitler's decision to invade Russia was important as regards the course of World War Two, we can only speculate on what might have occurred had the US Constitution failed to be ratified by the States, had the SPD not compromised in 1918, and had Hitler not invaded Russia. See Manicas, 1989.

[24] In his *General Economic History* (2003), of course, this is precisely what Weber sets out to do. See Collins, 1980.

preceded it. As far back as we may go into the grey mist of the far-off past, the reality . . . always remains equally individual, equally *undeducible* from laws. (1949: 73)

Weber is no methodological individualist. Indeed, if anything, his substantive investigations (in contrast to his methodological arguments) are very "macro-oriented" involving social mechanisms of "typical actors" working with materials at hand. Moreover, he appeals infrequently to the causal consequences of actions of key actors.[25]

Moore's now classic account in *Social Origins of Dictatorship and Democracy* (1966) is a fine illustration. Moore writes:

To sum up as concisely as possible, we seek to understand the role of the landed upper classes and the peasants in the bourgeois revolutions leading capitalist democracy, the abortive bourgeois revolutions leading to fascism, and the peasant revolutions leading to communism. The ways in which the landed upper classes and the peasants reacted to the challenge of commercial agriculture were decisive factors in determining the political outcome. (1966: xvii)

This is a highly abstract summary of what was theorized to be the key mechanism – the role and relations of lords and peasants. The analysis, then, would aim at understanding precisely what these concretely were and what were their outcomes. The analysis is in terms of typical actors at particular times and places. Typical differences in their relations and conditions give us an understanding of the problems that were set, the beliefs which defined their choices and the consequences of their actions, intended and mostly unintended.

Moore's work is fundamentally individualizing: as he moved closer to the concrete, comparison led to his seeing differences in the relations of lord and peasant in each of his cases.[26] This involved bringing in details and sometimes also seeing connections of causally related mechanisms, for example, "market forms" versus "labor-repressive forms." Thus, was

[25] Roth suggests usefully that this is the third level of analysis, what he terms "situational analysis," typically in his important political writings. See especially Weber (1968), "Parliament and Government in Reconstructed Germany."

[26] In certainly one of the very best reviews of Moore's book, Skocpol (1994) notes: "Moore (rather unsystematically) elaborates and interrelates *three key variables* in order to explain (a) differences among the sequences characteristic of the major Routes, and (b) differences among the 'Bourgeois Revolution' cases. His overall 'explanation sketch' seems so unsystematic not only because he fails to define variables and spell out their roles in explaining sequences of structures and events, but also because so much of *Social Origins* is taken up with case accounts for individual countries. This fact has even led one reviewer to assert that Moore's method is 'idiographic'!" (1994: 28). This is correct *and* unobjectionable. The use of the term "variables" by Skocpol, so characteristic of hard science orientations, may be excused here, except that one suspects that it was the attractiveness of these methods which led Skocpol astray in her important *States and Social Revolutions*. See appendix B, for extended discussion.

surplus that accrued to the landed classes, derived from rents or from the sale of produce? Moore concludes: "In comparison with their counterpart in England during the eighteenth century, the French nobility lived very largely from dues collected in kind or in cash from their peasants" (1966: 41). The pertinent mechanism here involved differences in the extent of commercialization, itself a promissory note and consequence explained by differences in England's early advantages in international political economy. Similarly, what were the prevailing social relations, the attitudes of typical actors, peasants and aristocrats?

Moore is self-conscious regarding the idea that explanation requires identifying the actual motives and beliefs of actors. He writes: "We cannot do without some conception of how people perceive the world and what they do or want to do about what they see" (1966: 487).[27] Thus, in order to explain the reproduction and transformation of lord / peasant relations in France (especially in section 5 of chapter II), Moore identifies the perceptions of peasants, the poorest and the less poor, as best as his documents will allow, and offers an account of why they held the beliefs they did. For example, "by 1789 the large majority of rural proprietors did not have enough land to live on and had to work for others or find some auxiliary trade" (1966: 71). That they expressed concern in securing more land is easily explained. By contrast, the situation of the richer peasants led them to acknowledge "the social position and special privileges of the nobility," a "fact which suggests that they could not understand any general connection between the privileges of the nobility and their own problems" (1966: 73). Similarly, despite opinions to the contrary, Moore offers that the data do not support the view that the French ruling classes had beliefs which led them to forgo commerce. But the mechanism which gave the nobility rental income had consequences, including tenancy: "The best solution, at least for many, appears to have been to throw the burden of cultivation as much as possible on those tenants who would manage large units or, more directly on the

---

[27] But he sees a large problem with making "ideas" causes. He continues: "To detach [the conception of the] how people perceive the world from the way that people reach it, or to take it out of its historical context and raise it to the status of an independent causal factor in his own right, means that the supposedly impartial investigator succumbs to the justifications that ruling groups generally offer for their most brutal conduct" (Moore, 1966: 487). This is, of course, Marx speaking to Hegel in the famous texts of the *German Ideology*. Indeed, as Moore insists, "to maintain and transmit a value system, human beings are punched, bullied, sent to jail, thrown into concentration camps, cajoled, bribed, made into heroes, encouraged to read newspapers, stood up against the wall and shot, and sometimes even taught sociology" (Moore, 1966: 486). Compare Bendix, above. More generally, understanding both the reproduction *and* transformation of structure requires specifying a social mechanism. This will include, probably, not only the uses of violence, but if participants have false beliefs about their condition, why they have these beliefs. One may wonder about the pedagogic role of too much social science?

peasant" (1966: 73). He offers that this compares neatly to the English case.

Tenancy, too, had consequences: "By the time of the Revolution, peasants possessed close to *de facto* property rights" (1966: 42). While the revolution "began with an offensive by the nobility" – a fact also in need of explanation – "the three great popular upheavals" were provoked by the *sans-culottes* of Paris, and "succeeded as long as it could draw on active support from the countryside" (1966: 77). Here we need to understand the situation and expectations of peasants in the countryside such that they gave (or did not give) active support to the *sans-culottes*. Throughout his book, Moore develops arguments about mechanisms, none as complete as it might be, but mostly more than promissory notes. On the other hand, as noted earlier, whether an explanation is satisfactory depends on the question asked and the interests of those offered the explanation.

Moore's explanation of the three different routes – only hinted at here – is a narrative (actually, each chapter offers one), but it is important to emphasize what is intended by the use of the term "narrative." If one defines "narrative" as "an account of some process or development as a story, in which a series of events are depicted chronologically,"[28] there is a temptation to ignore causality or, more usually, to restrict causes to singular causes, the specific acts of specifiable individuals. Such narratives, accordingly, ignore causal mechanisms, the "materials" of action. This is the typical historian's approach. But as argued here, we need both causal mechanisms and singular causes woven together chronologically in a story. Narrative in this sense is no mere chronicle, nor can it ignore the context – the ongoing causal mechanisms – which enables and constrains the decisions and actions of agents. Moore's account gives an understanding of three paths to three culturally significant outcomes and, as in Weber, he makes the effort to do this in terms of "*the causes of their being historically so and not otherwise.*"

History and sociology

The foregoing suggests that there are a number of tasks for sociology that do not require history and there is at least one important task that does.

First, a great deal of very good and important sociological work is descriptive: either qualitative or quantitative.[29] A good ethnography or a

---

[28] I follow Andrew Sayer, 1992: appendix.

[29] On description, see Sayer, 1992: appendix. As he notes, "thick description need not be seen as antithetical to theory, or synonymous with narrative. It could be the product of a concrete research which combines and works up the insights of a range of theories dealing with particular aspects of the object" (1992: 262). See also appendix A of the present volume.

good statistical study is an important achievement. *But they do not offer explanations of concrete events or episodes, nor do they give us an understanding of the processes at work in society.* One might say that a good ethnography gives us an understanding of the system of belief and practices of a group, but if it stops there, it does not give us an understanding of why these particular beliefs and practices are what they are. To do this one requires causal analysis – an account of the mechanisms at work; and it requires history – an account of the genesis of those mechanisms.

This suggests another sort of inquiry – one which can ignore history. We may have a pattern which requires explanation, as illustrated in chapter 4 with examples from a variety of writers. Understanding, as in the physical sciences, aims at identifying the mechanism which explains a generalization, for example, a discovered correlation between drug use and homicide, or between schooling and employment. Or we might be seeking to understand a process or set of processes, such as economic development, state-building or gentrification. These parallel processes in the natural sciences like oxidation or growth, except that, to be sure, we cannot assume that social processes will everywhere be the same. Or we might look at abstract mechanisms which make intelligible a relatively bounded system, including the reproduction of social institutions, for example, capitalism, a health care delivery system or the international system.

Perhaps paradoxically, having identified the pertinent social mechanism, one can achieve understanding without history and without appeal to concrete agents.[30] The typical actors of the mechanisms suffice. While what is to be understood is located in time and space, the passage of real time is not relevant here. Thus, Tilly's account of the pertinent mechanisms gives us some understanding of modern state-building; but it does not explain the genesis of the modern state in England or anywhere else. That is not the goal of the inquiry. The concern is to identify the relevant key mechanisms and not the particular trajectory of state-building as it concretely occurred in a particular place. Similarly, Marx's *Capital* is a work of theory, aiming at identifying the mechanisms of capitalism and capitalist reproduction. If we accept this account, it gives us understanding, just as molecular chemistry enables our understanding of a host of chemical outcomes. Just as molecular theory cannot of itself explain any particular outcome, for example, a fire in a hotel in Las Vegas, Marx's *Capital* cannot of itself explain the success of Japanese capitalism in the 1980s – or its more recent stagnation. In the present formulation, these are (loosely) episodes – the proper task of a historical sociology.

---

[30] An early version of this argument can be found in Manicas, 1981, a review essay of Skocpol's *States and Social Revolutions*.

Again, we are close to Weber's view of the matter as summarized by Roth. He finds in Weber three levels of historical analysis: sociological, historical and situational, this last not of immediate concern here. Roth writes:

The three levels are all historical in a general sense, but in Weber's terminology the first is that of sociology – of type or model construction and of rules of experience – whereas the second level, the causal explanation of past events, is labeled by him "historical" in quotation marks, or sometimes "developmental" (*entwicklungsgeschichtlich*). (Roth and Schlucter, 1979:197)

To sum up: In Weber's practiced methodology "sociology" is the generalized aspect of the study of history and contrasts with the causal analysis of individual phenomena – the task of "history." Both sociology and historiography proceed from the causality inherent in social action. (Roth and Schlucter, 1979: 205)[31]

The generalized aspect which defines the goals of sociology often takes the form of generalizations: "When religious institutions are weakened, there is a loss of normative control," or "In a highly bureaucratic absolutist state, the landed nobility has little political power." Understanding comes with the unpacking of these: the development of a model which explains the generalization.[32]

As noted in chapter 1, the terms "understanding" and "explanation" are often interchangeable, depending on the context. Allowing for considerable arbitrariness, we can say that explanations in historical sociology are paradigmatically of episodes (or events located in time and space)[33]: The Bolshevik Revolution; World War Two; the Great Depression; the Civil Rights movement; a change in female participation in the labor force; a rising crime rate; an immigrant pattern; the victory of the Christian Democrats in the German elections of 2004. Explaining an episode requires an understanding of the pertinent mechanisms, but since

---

[31] In *Economy and Society*, Weber writes: "We have taken it for granted that sociology seeks to formulate type concepts and generalized uniformities of empirical process. This distinguishes it from history, which is oriented to the causal analysis and explanation of individual actions, structures, and personalities possessing cultural significance" (1968: vol. 1, 19).

[32] This would include what Sayer calls "analysis." "By analysis I mean the explanation of concrete cases by the direct application of abstractions or theoretical models of what are believed to be widely replicated structures and mechanisms. As such it tends to abstract from particular historical sequences" (1992: 259).

[33] "Event" suggests a sharply limited time-frame: the attack on the Twin Towers. An episode is a relatively extended piece of history. Weber was quite right to see that the characterization of what is to be explained, whether it was a sharply limited "event" or a relatively amorphous civilizational construct, was determined pragmatically, had political meaning, and that a causal explanation was then called for. McAdam *et al.* (2001) would seem here to follow Weber in holding, rightly, that the naming and labeling of an episode is an interpretative, theoretical *and* political act.

sequences in real time are here critical, it will also require history. Explaining an episode calls for a narrative – a history – in which one needs to show what actions, events and mechanisms combined sequentially to produce the outcome. Explaining episodes, like explaining the collapse of a bridge, requires a narrative which identifies the causes open-systemically at work in the world, where perhaps none is either a necessary or sufficient condition. Very much work in the social sciences is historical in this sense.

It would be churlish to suppose that inquirers in the social sciences do not also move sometimes somewhat uneasily between these two paradigms. Just as much quite good social science offers us quite incomplete suggestions of mechanisms at work, much quite good social science offers but sketches of causal histories. More generally, quite good social science is dealing with problems which, as Weber insisted, were both concrete and terribly complex. Unlike the "pure" theorists of the physical sciences who can deal with high abstractions, who can deal with causality in a highly stratified way, and who can subject their theories to rigorous experimental test, this is not possible in the human sciences.[34]

Indeed, in the social sciences as in the natural sciences, we can very often come to a quite satisfactory understanding of some process or system. In none of the sciences (*pace* the D-N "ideal") can we hope to find a complete explanation of an episode since there will always be bits and pieces in its unique causal history yet to be identified. Indeed, there is a sense in which providing causal explanations in the human sciences is both easier and harder. It is easier in that human action is absolutely critical to what happens in history. But it is more difficult in that there are immense (theoretical) difficulties in identifying the social mechanisms which, taken together, enabled and constrained actors, a consequence of the absence of the capacity to construct system closure: to experiment.

Similarly, the range of complexity will be a direct function of the question asked. Thus, one can get an understanding of capitalism from Marx's *Capital*, but understanding American capitalism requires not only an understanding of the mechanisms which define capitalism, but of a complicated nest of other mechanisms true of contemporary American society. One can understand capitalism without considering gender discrimination or racism, but since these mechanisms function in capitalist

[34] Lawson (1997) distinguishes "pure," or "abstract" or "theoretical" explanation, from "applied," or "concrete" or "practical" explanation. The former task regards "the identification of underlying structures, powers, mechanisms and their tendencies" (1997: 220), while the latter task "entails *drawing upon antecedently established knowledge* of relatively enduring structures and mechanisms (rather than revealing them), and investigating the manner of their joint articulation in the production of the novel event in question" (1997: 220). There is certainly no objection to his alternative formulation.

markets, they will of necessity be part of the account of American capitalism. Finally, explaining the global posture of American capitalism in the past decade requires not only a grasp of the relevant mechanisms, but a narrative of how contingent events, and the actions of key agents, working with materials at hand, combined to produce that outcome.

In the next chapter, we turn to an examination of a family of social mechanisms familiar to social science since at least Adam Smith. It is the family of social mechanisms we call "markets."

6 Markets as social mechanisms

Introduction

There is a long history of theorizing markets as social mechanisms in exactly the sense of the previous chapter. This began at least with Adam Smith's account in *The Wealth of Nations* (1776). As Smith saw, market outcomes could be explained as the joint product of the actions of persons interacting in society. It is easy enough to see that Smith constructed his mechanism by making assumptions about persons, their beliefs, aims and interests, about what they know, and what they can do. The outcome of their activity was, for example, a market price. The idea was beautifully developed in neo-classical micro-economic theory. This maintained the fundamental assumptions of the "classical" theory, but was able to develop the analysis by generalizing the idea of the "marginal" to cover both production and consumption. All of this could then be articulated in terms of continuous variable mathematical models specifying the relationships between what are considered the key variables. Following the assumptions of the deductivist (D-N) account of theory, the consequences of the assumptions laid down by the theory would then be rigorously deduced.[1]

But there is a paradox here of some importance. On the one hand, by virtue of the sophistication of the models produced by economists, it is

---

[1] Very briefly, the pertinent history is this: neo-classical theory is distinguished from classical theory by virtue of the introduction of marginality which enabled theory to overcome the puzzlement generated by the distinction between exchange value and use value. W. S. Jevons, Carl Menger and Leon Walras each quite independently arrived at the main ideas which became widely accepted with Alfred Marshall's *Principles of Economics* (1890). It is the heart of what today is called "micro-economics." Walras, along with Pareto and then Pigou, is generally credited with introducing into this body of theory the idea of general equilibrium. See Schumpeter, 1954: 892–944, chapter 7. The ability to formalize these models with mathematics was a decisive additional step, generally attributed to Samuelson (1947), Kenneth Arrow, Gerald DeBreu and Frank Hahn. It fit beautifully into the dominating empiricist notion of theory as a deductive system in which outcomes are "explained" as entailments from the premises. For a valuable account of the contingent facts leading to the use of mathematics in economic analysis, see Mirowski, 1991. For an excellent account of developments from Hayek on, see Boettke, 1997.

very often said that economics is the most advanced or scientific of all the social sciences. Most recently, a number of political scientists and some sociologists have adopted the generalized version of this sort of model-building under the heading of "rational choice theory" (RCT).[2] But the problem is not that markets are not social mechanisms which, if properly modeled, could give us an understanding of outcomes by appeal to the actions of persons – the bogeyman of methodological individualism – but that the mathematical model-building of mainstream theory, encouraged by a false idea of science, has lost nearly all touch with reality. This line of criticism is not new. For example, in 1982, Nobel prize winner Wassily Leontief had this to say:

Page after page of professional economic journals are filled with mathematical formulas leading the reader from sets of more or less plausible but entirely arbitrary assumptions to precisely stated but irrelevant theoretical conclusions . . . Year after year economic theorists continue to produce scores of mathematical models and to explore in great detail their formal properties; and the econometricians fit algebraic functions of all possible shapes to essentially the same sets of data without being able to advance, in any perceptible way, a systematic understanding of the structures and the operations of a real economic system.[3]

These mathematical models are perfect examples of deductivist theory construction. But if this idea of science is misconceived then these models are, on their face, a poor choice for thinking that economics is an advanced social science. Since a good deal of the foregoing has been a criticism of this positivist or neo-positivist conception of science, we need not repeat the arguments here. In what follows we concentrate on the assumptions of the models themselves.

The account of social science (developed in chapters 3, 4 and 5), can be brought to bear directly on the criticism that neo-classical model-building has enormously oversimplified its analysis of markets. This problem was identified by the earliest critics of the neo-classical model.[4] They saw it as failing to acknowledge that economic actors are social beings who

---

[2] See appendix C. For extensive criticism of its use in political science, see Green and Shapiro (eds.), 1996.

[3] Leontief, 1982: 104, quoted by Lawson, 1977: 4.

[4] The long history of criticism of the neo-classical model begins with Durkheim (see Lukes, 1972), and in Germany with the *Methodenstreit*, conveniently dated from the 1893 publication of Carl Menger's *Untersuchungen über die Method de Sozialwissenschaften und der de Politischen Ökonomie insbesondere*. Weber, of course, played a key role, too often misunderstood. One then needs to include Thorstein Veblen and a long line of "institutionalists," from John R. Commons to John Kenneth Galbraith to many contemporary "economic sociologists." Useful anthologies of essays by representative writers include: Etzioni and Lawrence, 1991; Granoveter and Swedburg, 1992; Swedburg, 1993; Smelzer and Swedburg, 1994; Biggart, 2002; Dobbin, 2004. See also Dugger, 1992. We exclude here any discussion of Marxist criticisms.

are socially situated, that economic institutions, as all else in society, are historical and social constructions, profoundly related to a host of other institutions and that, unlike the example of celestial mechanics, processes in time are critical. Thus, on the mainstream view, persons are conceived as atomized individuals and as socialized exclusively as historically indifferent "rational beings" who make choices in an unchanging environment. Not only do they have approximately similar motivations, but they have more or less equal powers and capacities and they have broad scale knowledge of the market conditions in which they act. Clearly there are a number of problems here: CEOs of corporations, Mom and Pop Chinese restaurateurs, heart surgeons, immigrant farm workers – legal and illegal – non-unionized plumbers and unionized auto workers, part-time female salesclerks, NBA superstars, public school teachers and drug dealers (one could go on), simply do not have the same beliefs or capacities – either as "producers" or as "consumers." Nor, as importantly, are they atomized (although one could argue that capitalism is doing the best it can to make them so), nor do they have the knowledge and information required of them by the theory.

In what follows, we draw on some of the now familiar criticisms of the model. These are all well known, but in part, at least, because the model has the authority of mainstream empiricist philosophy of science, the economics profession has largely been content to reproduce their practices and ignore these critiques.[5] In this chapter, having restored persons as historically situated beings, it is also argued that there are different

For some exceptional doubt offered by the discipline's most leading lights, see the AEA Presidential Addresses of Leontief, 1971, Tobin, 1972 and Solow, 1980. Similar themes have been expressed by other notable insiders, for example, Thurow, 1983, Balough, 1982, Hirshman, 1985 and Sen, 1977. For a variety of critical analyses, see also the Progressive Economics Forum (www.web.ca/~pef).

Business school professionals are also critical as regards the usefulness of microeconomic models for business decision-making. See Oxenfield (ed.), 1963. For example, "market models admit time considerations only in a limited and contrived manner . . . But investment represents the concern of major executives, rather than clerks, for the very reason that markets are dynamic and are buffeted by many forces that vary over time . . . In other words, executives who are estimating the pattern of revenues and costs over the life of an investment – and the length of its life – get relatively little help from market models of price theory" (Oxenfeld (ed.), 1963: 63). See also Lazonick, 1991 and Hayek's critique, below.

[5] For most economists, the model is justified in terms of its putative predictive value or as a "useful" approximation of concrete reality. See below. There is no argument as to the usefulness of these models for ideological purposes. See Stiglitz, 2002, and for different sort of "usefulness," see Davis 2004. Davis writes that "a majority of AEA members" who responded to a survey he conducted, admitted, "at least privately, that academic research mainly benefits academic researchers who use it to advance their own careers and that journal articles have little impact on our understanding of the real world and the practice of public policy" (2004: 359).

kinds of markets which differ in fundamental ways, and that once the
effort is made to construct models which are closer to reality, it becomes
clear that, while these models must sacrifice the elegance of mathematical
models, they can aid in understanding market processes. But explaining
most outcomes, for example, current unemployment, requires engaging
history – just as with the explanation of a terrorist attack or a war.

The problem, it must be emphasized, is not that abstraction, simpli-
fying assumptions and model-building are inappropriate for a human
science (Boettke, 1997: 13). As argued in chapter 1, to understand the
concrete one must offer abstractions from it: we understand why iron
rusts because abstraction has yielded a representation of the causal powers of the theoretical (but real) entity, Fe. Similarly, as regards the social
mechanisms which give us an understanding of our social world – including, then, the focus of this chapter: the mechanism of markets.

The neo-classical model of the market

The basic ontology of neo-classical theory postulates rational individuals engaged in interaction, either as consumers or producers (firms) (see
appendix D). Their attributes and situations are formally defined in terms
of a familiar set of postulates. For example, if an agent prefers x to y and
y to z, then she prefers x to z: revealed preferences are transitive. The
general equilibrium model adds a number of further assumptions: that
there is perfect information available to all parties, that there are many
buyers and sellers in every market, that each may enter and leave easily,
that everyone has the relevant information, that there is an interdepen-
dence among the many markets, that commodities (including labor) are
infinitely divisible, etc.

The majority of economists would seem to agree that most of these
assumptions, at least without severe qualifications, are false.[6] People are
not rational in the relevant sense, decisions about preferences are not
made pairwise, commodities are not indifferently substitutable in all situations,[7] firms do not always maximize profits, transaction costs are totally

---

[6] There are important writers who take the very heroic stand of insisting that the model
sufficiently well approximates reality to be a valid description of it. These include the
so-called Chicago School economists, Milton Friedman, George Stigler, Gary Becker
and Robert Lucas. See Boettke, 1997.

[7] That is, it is not true (as asserted by, for example, Debreu, 1984) that "commodity space
has the structure of a real vector space"– a critical assumption for formalization. Mirowski
(1991) relates the story of the shepherd who agreed to accept two sticks of tobacco for one
sheep but became confused when given four sticks for a second sheep. For the economist,
this shows that the shepherd does not understand arithmetic. But indeed, it shows that
the economist does not know sheep!

ignored,[8] information is never anywhere near perfect, etc. Moreover, the formalized theory leaves no room for the effects of the passage of time and the fact that, in the real world, the economic situation is continually changing because of decisions made by ordinary people, corporate heads, managers and government officials – from heads of state to the secretary of the treasury.

Starting from scratch

One could argue that even if the assumptions of the mechanism are not true, then as Weber suggested, the model can nonetheless provide a useful heuristic. *But if the goal is to understand or explain outcomes, then it is hard to see how the model can do this.* Understanding, like explaining outcomes, requires that the assumptions of the mechanism be more or less true. Thus, for example, the equilibrium price of a commodity is that price exactly because in the theorized causal mechanism, individuals are making decisions in accordance with the assumptions of the model. If, indeed, this is not true, then even if the model does has predictive capacities, the outcomes are not explained.[9] We must then ask, can we build better models, even if, perhaps inevitably, they will lack the rigor provided by formalization?

We should, at the outset, acknowledge that the neo-classical theory may illuminate outcomes in some markets. We spoke earlier of Chinese restaurateurs. In most cities in the USA, they are small firms in a genuinely competitive environment. Operators know what their costs and their sales are and must make decisions which seek to produce profits. While it is contestable that they think in terms of opportunity costs and have the concept of marginal productivity, it is not implausible to hold that these theoretical ideas help us to understand their actual behavior and thus, assuming that their customers are seeking quality at the best price, the actual prices in Honolulu of items on the menus of Chinese restaurants.[10] But even if this is true, this environment is not typical.

---

[8] R. H. Coase (1995) has famously argued that the existence of transaction costs "implies that methods of coordination alternative to the market, which are themselves costly and in various ways imperfect, may nonetheless be preferable to relying on the pricing mechanism, the only method of co-ordination normally analysed by economists" (1995: 8). This was Coase's 1991 Nobel Laureate Address. Transaction costs, for example, contracts to be drawn up, inspections to be made, arrangements to settle disputes, processing costs, are the least of it. See below.

[9] It is highly contestable whether neo-classical theory survives the test of "good predictions." Fundamentally at issue is the quality of the "empirical" tests. See appendix A.

[10] We say "may illuminate" outcomes since we need to say here that if operators do not think in terms of opportunity costs as defined by the theory, they are thinking something quite similar. As Schütz insisted, to explain action one must identify actual beliefs and motivations, not ones imposed on actors by social scientists.

Put aside for the moment the very different conditions and behavior of CEOs of large corporations,[11] and consider here Charles Smith's important work on auctions (1989). Auctions are an important kind of market, not least because they appear to illustrate the general equilibrium model.

Smith offers a rough classification of kinds of markets. Auctions must be distinguished from "fixed-price" exchanges in which buyers confront prices which have been established and are "fixed" in the sense that they are stable over substantial periods of time. This is certainly the most typical sort of market. Finally, there are "private treaty" forms of market exchange in which buyer and seller "actively negotiate the price between them" (Smith, 1989: 15). Generalized in terms of supply and demand curves (appendix D), the private treaty form is the conceptual ideal for neo-classical theory. Where buyers and sellers "actively negotiate the price between them," informational problems may be solved, and if a deal can be made, since the actors are rational, no one gets cheated. We consider below "fixed-price" markets and argue that there are several ways that the prices confronting buyers are fixed.

Not only are fixed-price markets, private treaty exchanges and auctions very different kinds of markets, but there are also several kinds of auctions. Critically, there are important differences in the social mechanisms of these variant forms – differences which need to be established empirically. Smith groups auctions into three subtypes: "commodity/exchange," "collectable/dealer," and "art/one-of-a-kind." Among the features which make for differences between these and other kinds of markets are the importance in determining price of a wide variety of factors; the importance of historically stable practices and changes in these; the "rules" which are constitutive of the process; collective consensus regarding value or the absence of such consensus; uncertainties regarding costs; differences in individual taste and judgement; and even "the will to possess."

Consider, for example, two instances of bizarre price fluctuations. In 1985, the all-time record for a thoroughbred yearling was set at $13,100,000 for one horse while in the next two years the highest price paid was $3,600,000 and $3,700,000, respectively. In the recent past, the Dow Jones average went from 800 to 2,700 in about five years, only to drop 1,000 points within a week. In neither case had these changes much to do with changes in variables analyzed by the neo-classical model. The first is explained in terms of "the will to possess," and the head-to-head competition between a handful of buyers, the sheikhs from Dubai and Robert Sangster (Smith, 1989: 192). By 1986, they were no longer in competition.

---

[11] The literature is large. But see, for example, Chandler, 1962; Berle and Means, 1968; Galbraith, 1968; Barnet and Müller, 1974; Lazonik, 1991; Dugger, 1992; Geneen, 1984; Bakan, 2004. See also the discussion of "imperfect competition," below.

The stock market fluctuations had no such competition, and more importantly, not much to do with changes in the shape of the economy or the "real" value of stocks. Rather, the introduction of new computer-based trading programs that made use of financial futures and option contracts enormously complicated trading practices and opportunities such that key "decisions" were made, in fact, by computers programmed to respond to specific indicators, such as capital flows. None of this would have been possible, even given the technology, if the rules governing the stock market did not establish the rights required for trading financial futures, option contracts and "derivatives." We will return to this extremely important point.[12]

The point to be emphasized here, however, is that in each of these variant forms of markets, there are specific social relations, rules and practices, mostly unarticulated, which constitute and legitimate the conditions of the exchange, and which, accordingly, enable and constrain the participants and, as such, the results. While, as noted, the conditions set out by neo-classical theory are sometimes sufficiently close to concrete reality to be illuminating, this is not the case in general.

Defining a market

It is profoundly paradoxical that while it is the central concept of modern economics, the concept of a market is either taken for granted, unanalyzed, or more likely, defined, tautologically, in terms of the theory such that, if the conditions set out by theory are not satisfied, then there is no market! As Dyke noted, if, for example, "the market must fulfill the condition of the independence of irrelevant alternatives, then a market hardly ever exists" (1981: 116) (see appendix D). But plainly, explaining markets requires that our theory confront *actual* markets. Although the concept of a market is a high abstraction, we need a workable definition.

There is a widely available intuitive sense of a market: a place where there are many sellers of various goods, either of one sort or of many different sorts, and there are many shoppers. One thinks of Covent Garden in London, the Mercado Centrales in Managua, even the Swap Meet in Aiea, O'ahu. Markets of this sort have existed for a very long time, and almost everywhere. Sadly, this image is anything but helpful when one talks about industrial markets, labor markets, the stock exchange, or even Keeneland Thoroughbred horse auctions.

A standard sense (to be rejected here) defines markets as:

---

[12] For detailed description of the social process which produced equity option markets and sponsored word / phrase Internet search engine markets, see Smith (forthcoming).

A social institution in which people freely exchange commodities (goods, resources, services) generally through the medium of money.[13]

The definition trades on the intuitive image, but there are two problems. One regards the role of money, the other the idea that "people freely exchange commodities." What can "free" mean here?

"Free exchange"

The weakest (and most widely held sense) would seem to be that there is no coercion in the sense of legitimate or illegitimate threats of force. Giving up one's wallet to a gunman is not a market exchange. But what of state-enforced requirements on a minimum wage, an eight-hour day or regulatory agencies and anti-trust laws? These are surely legally enforceable constraints on exchange. The ideological point is clear enough: The myth would have it that there is a clear separation of state and economy. Markets are presumed to be autonomous institutions, ideally unconstrained by state action. But this idea leads to total conceptual confusion since in all modern societies, the state is essential to the very constitution of markets.

To take one obvious but much overlooked example, property rights are surely critical as regards exchange. Indeed, thoroughly undermining the image of a market with which we began, Coase (1995) argues that rights to perform certain actions are what is traded. It is hard to overstate the importance of this in a world where actions by economic actors can have monumental consequences as regards health and safety and the environment, and where financial markets have taken on extraordinary forms. He concludes: "As a result, the legal system will have a profound effect on the working of the economic system and may in certain respects be said to control it" (1995: 11).

The question, then, is not whether the state must act in constituting markets; the question rather is, what is the character and what are the consequences of widely varying forms of that constitution, of who benefits and who (and what) does not? For many people today a "free market" is a market constituted so that entrepreneurial actors are not hindered by laws or regulations aimed to protect employees, consumers, the environment, or public goods not provided by the market. One might argue that such a market is desirable, perhaps because it is efficient. But indeed, even if this were true – and it is not difficult to show that the idea is fatally flawed (appendix D) – there are a host of hard-won legal constraints, for example

---

[13] Outhwaite and Bottomore, 1992: 359. The text is paraphrased from the authoritative and useful *Blackwell Dictionary of Twentieth-Century Social Thought*.

on child labor and the length of the working day, which no reasonable person would want to see repealed.

A stronger (and more plausible) sense of "free" would require that no coercion of any sort was involved in generating the exchange. But if so, markets exist only when the parties are in a condition such that they need not exchange. Autarchy would be the ideal. But obviously whenever there is division of labor, people are not autarchic; and if one accepts the idea (shared by Weber and Marx) that wage labor is defined by the fact that as Weber put it, workers are *compelled* to sell their labor power to some employer or another, then obviously coercion is a systematic aspect of labor markets.[14] The ideology is also clear here: neo-classical theory would have us believe that we are all buyers ("consumers") and sellers ("firms") who are free to reject any and all exchanges. This idea, of course, is fully reinforced by the intuitive sense with which we began.

Voluntary exchange

We had better abandon any notion that markets require free exchanges. All sorts of constraints and differential resources – and thus inequalities of power and freedom – are perfectly consistent with markets. But there is an important point perhaps confusedly seen by those who argue for "free" exchange and build economic models based on that assumption. Markets do require that exchanges be *voluntary* in the standard sense that the exchanges are not legally compelled. The extraction of surplus from feudal peasants is not a market exchange. Nor, plainly, is slavery.

It may be, indeed, that the idea of free wage labor contributes substantially to the confusion being addressed here. It might be held, for example, that although workers sell their labor power, this is not voluntary if the only choice is to starve. He or she is thus in this sense compelled.

It is critical that we do not think of choices as involuntary simply because all the choices are undesirable. This would drain the notion of voluntariness of any usefulness. We need here a conception of freedom

[14] This is almost never noticed; sometimes, when it is, as by Charles E. Lindbloom (1977), the point is obscured. He sees that "freedom depends upon the character of the alternatives" and thus, "the generalization . . . is that exchange best supports freedom when every party can choose among offers that do not greatly differ in value from each other or from no exchange at all" (1977: 49). He then suggests that this condition is met in either of two circumstances: exchange is limited to small values or "no single act of exchange is greatly more advantageous to either party than other available exchange opportunities. In neither circumstance can anyone be coerced, since he can, without great loss to himself, easily refuse any offer" (1977: 49). This is a manifest *non sequitur* since persons with only their labor power to sell can refuse any particular offer, but must accept *some* offer. They *voluntarily* accept the best offer because they are not *free* to reject all offers. See below.

which precludes this collapse. Roughly, one is free insofar as one can do (be or have) what one wants to do (be or have). So construed, freedom is very unequally distributed in society, even though everybody has some freedoms and nobody is absolutely free. Thus, for example, if Sally lacks the money to buy a ticket to Maui, she cannot go. Harry has the money but he cannot go because his boss will not give him the time off. Louis is free to go to Maui because nothing prevents him from going.[15] In this context, one acts voluntarily in taking a terrible job, but if one could do as one pleased, one would not take the job even if it were the best of the awful alternatives. It is easy to see also how confounding "free" with "voluntary" contributes to the ideological association of markets and "individual freedom."[16]

To see how voluntariness figures in defining a market, a comparison with practices in the former Soviet Union, where there was no labor market, is useful here. Every Soviet citizen had to work; one could be deported to Siberia or receive other punishments if one chose not to. Workers were confined to localities by the internal passport system and controlled through the use of labor books and personal files that could be used punitively. Labor was, in this sense both unfree *and* involuntary. As

---

[15] In a liberal society, people may have equal rights, but be unequally free. Following Gerald Feinberg (1973), we should think of freedom as a triadic relationship:

A (some agent) is free from *C* to be able to do (or be, have, not do, etc.) *F* where *A* is the name of some person or group, *C* is a specification of constraints, obstacles, lacks and *F* is an action, e.g., going to New York for a holiday, a state of being, e.g., being a lawyer, or a possession, e.g., a house on Maui, a Mercedes, etc.

Constraints can be classified roughly as follows:

(1) Internal positive constraints such as compulsive desires and neuroses. Thus *A* can't quit smoking. Each time *A* lights up, it is correct to say that *A* acted voluntarily. But if *A* simply can't quit, there is something about *A*'s mental state which keeps *A* from quitting. From the point of view of social theory, these are least interesting sorts of constraints.

(2) Internal negative constraints, such as ignorance or deficiency of skill. For example, *A* can't read. Some of these, of course, are socially remedial.

(3) External positive constraints. Like those in (2) these depend upon humanly constructed social arrangements. They include physical coercion and the threat of physical coercion, constraints always noticed by liberal social theory. These constraints make acts both unfree *and* involuntary, a fact which helps promote the collapse of the two ideas. But often overlooked are constraints which are rooted in social relations, e.g., class, racism and sexism. One can say, accordingly, that the propertyless worker is not free not to work, that glass ceilings restrict opportunities (and thus choices) for females and African-Americans who would otherwise have such choices.

(4) External negative constraints, such as lack of money, tools, friends, etc.

Some of these, of course, are causally related: if you are born into a poor family, likely you will live in a poor neighborhood, go to poor schools and thus lack knowledge and skills which would otherwise be available. Thus, finally, you will lack the money, social ties, etc., which would give you greater freedom. Again, if liberal society assures equal rights, it surely does not assure equal freedom.

[16] See also Dyck, 1981: chapter 7, who offers a range of conceptions of freedom.

Ticktin (1992: 84) argues, we lack a useful way to talk about many of the relations in the "actually existing socialisms." Following Oleg Bogomolov, Ticktin writes that labor in the USSR was "semiforced." That is, workers did not sell their labor power even if it was alienated in a particular (and historically novel) form. Less obvious, but as critical, wages were not really wages since, as Ticktin writes, "money is not money in the USSR." Though we need to develop what this means, here we can say that wages were nearly meaningless, replaced by party and bureaucratic relations, the networks which really mattered in getting housing, automobiles and opportunities to travel and to participate in amenities of life.

But command economies also restrict voluntary exchanges in other important ways. Still involuntary are exchanges made between producers under instruction from a central planning authority. Again, failure to follow the plan brought sanctions. Thus, for example, planners decide for manufacturers what component parts, electric power, etc. they will get and whom they get them from. As Nove (1989: 242) writes: "Managers are tied to *one* supplier, cannot exercise choice, and cannot go elsewhere." Moreover, since there is no stock market, there is no opportunity for individuals or groups to exchange shares in the material resources of production, which, for some at least, is the key issue regarding markets. Of course, command economies do not altogether eliminate voluntary exchanges. They are minimized in areas of the economy where both individual consumers and suppliers are excluded. Of course, as consumers, people engage in voluntary exchanges at food markets, shops and so on, even if, given contingent circumstances of development, the imperatives of production for war, the low priority given to consumption, the failures of the planning system, etc., choices among consumables are severely restricted.

More generally, then, it is a key feature of market economies that exchanges be voluntary. But all choices, including decisions to exchange, are enabled and constrained by existing social relations and the positions of individuals in them. Even where most exchanges are voluntary, as in all capitalist political economies, people engage in voluntary exchanges under very different circumstances. As argued in chapter 4, to build a model we need to know who are the actors, what they want, what they know and what they can do. What they can do includes identifying alternatives, constraints and options as these are structured by class, race and so on. That is, variation in social structure, political and legal systems and relations, all thoroughly suffused with culture, make for huge differences in the conditions of voluntary exchange. It is a critical part of the empirical problem of understanding markets to be clear on just what these conditions are. It should go without saying, here, that the implications for ideological critique and for normative social theory are huge.

Capitalism and market economies

The foregoing definition of a market as a social institution in which people "freely" exchange commodities continues with this sentence:

The market presupposes a social division of labor and (at least) de facto private ownership of the means of production.

If we accept this definition, "market socialism" would be a contradiction in terms. If we mean by socialism some form of community ownership of the means of production, we must, accordingly, reject the view that markets require private ownership of the means of production. It may be that the so-called market socialisms cannot solve the problems of market capitalisms or perhaps, depending on the nature of the market, they can. In any case, the foregoing definition confuses market economies with capitalism because it fails to recognize that capitalist property rights are not the only sorts of rights available which will enable exchange. And as already noted, market economies can take on many forms; the differences may make all the difference. Compare the USA, Germany, Italy, Japan, Indonesia and Brazil. At some level of abstraction these are all market economies (as well as capitalist), but one needs to explain why, for example, US school teachers with fifteen years' experience earn an average of $36,219 compared to Switzerland's $62,052 and among OECD countries (thirty nations including most of Europe, North America, Japan, South Korea, Australia and New Zealand) only the Czech Republic, Hungary, Iceland and Norway pay teachers less relative to national income (*New York Times*, June 13, 2001). The point is precisely that these outcomes can be explained only if we acknowledge that the prevailing market mechanisms in these economies are very different.

Prices and money

What, then of the second objection to the original definition, the idea that generally, money is the medium of exchange. Here again, there is a subtle but important point that is probably being obscured. Money is surely a medium of exchange, but the critical idea as regards most forms of markets is this: *the price system is the mechanism for coordination.* Roughly, everything has a price and buyers and sellers make choices among priced items.

Following Karl Polanyi (1992), we can identify three main forms of coordination / integration in the exchange of goods and services: (1) reciprocity, (2) redistribution and (3) a price system. Each of these presupposes different sorts of mechanisms of coordination and control. For example, where reciprocity prevails, there are (if Polanyi is correct), symmetrical groupings, for example, a kinship system as a fundamental ordering principle. Similarly, redistributive forms require allocative centers of authority – from the systems of ancient Egypt to contemporary command economies. Price systems differ from these in that everything has an exchange value and prices provide information regarding allocative and distributive decisions. Concrete societies may involve some mixing of these three (ideal-typical) forms of coordination / integration, although as above, generally, one will tend to dominate.

The definition with which we began misses the main point. It is not the use of money as such which characterizes markets. As Polanyi argues, money has three critical uses: as payment, as standard, and as measure of exchange. Money can function as payment and standard where the market is not the main or essential mode of coordination / integration. Thus, "bride price" or fines are payments in money. The "standard" or accounting use of money is essential (Polanyi argues) for redistributive systems of organization. Here a "price" is fixed, usually once and for all, for specific purposes, including, for example, managing the staples of the community. Equivalences are established, but they do not function as in exchange systems and are not, strictly, exchange values. Thus, "they designate the quantitative relationship between goods of different kinds that are acceptable in payment of taxes, rents, dues, fines, or that denote qualifications for a civic status dependent on a property census" (Polanyi, 1992: 49). Also, the equivalency can set the ratio at which wages or ratios in kind can be claimed, at the beneficiary's choosing. Similarly, "under reciprocative forms of integration . . . equivalences determine the amount that is 'adequate' in relation to the symmetrically placed party" (1992: 49). As Polanyi emphasizes, "clearly the behavioral context is different from either exchange or redistribution" (1992: 49).

The capacity of money to represent relative values is, of course, essential to markets, for it allows for extended *indirect* exchanging. Money must come to represent a value which allows for commensuration of very different sorts of objects of exchange – including concrete labor.[17] This is "commodification." In capitalism, we have the universalization of the

---

[17] Because money makes possible generalized exchange, for Marx, it is a precondition for alienation. Briefly, from the point of view of the producers, "the relations connecting the labor of one individual with that of the rest appear [i.e. manifest themselves], not as direct social relations between individuals at work, but as what they really are, material

commodity form. With extended exchange, then, prices are critical in determining what choices will be made by capitalists and by workers as job-seekers and consumers, and hence, in determining the overall shape and direction of the economy. But to anticipate: it is critical to see here that we need a mechanism if we are to understand how prices get fixed and that neo-classical theory is not the only possibility.

Reference again to the former USSR is useful here. When Ticktin (1992) writes that "money is not money in the USSR," the force of this is precisely that rubles make little difference. First, it is not a store of value or representation of exchange value. In addition to what we have already said regarding real distributive processes in the (former) USSR, workers in the same sector tend to have similar real incomes, irrespective of task, skills or attitudes toward work. Planners do not think of prices as opportunity costs or signals of relative scarcities and, as a result, production targets were based on physical indicators. Whatever real money there is in the system is, of course, foreign currency precisely because it does represent exchange value. To summarize: command economies, in contrast to market economies, restrict voluntary exchanges in many ways; labor is "semi-forced" and planners determine authoritatively a host of economic decisions. But in neither are choices generally "free." Similarly, in command economies, in contrast to market economies, prices are not used for coordination since in these economies, there is no "real" money.

Markets provide a coordinating mechanism for economic activity. That is, in any market system, price will be a dominant consideration for most participants. It is hardly an earthshaking observation that a potential consumer will not buy if he deems that the price is too high, or that a potential investor will not borrow if the interest rate is too high.[18] Changes in relative prices also provide information. If the price goes up, participants

---

relations between persons and social relations between things" (Marx, 1970: vol. I, part I, Section 4). It is interesting to note also that in chapter 5 of his *Two Treatises*, Locke argues that "consent" to the use of money (prior to the contract which constitutes civil society) overcame God's limits on appropriation from nature, and had, as its unintended consequence, class inequality in exactly Marx's sense.

[18] Of course, there are buyers for whom "money is no object": "If you have to ask the price, you cannot afford it." And, worse, there are needs so great that any price will be paid, for example, medication or life-saving surgery. Since (for most people at least) price is an obstacle to consumption, it represents an "opportunity" cost: the higher the price the greater its opportunity cost in terms of other goods that cannot be purchased. Thus, also, a price reduction will ordinarily spur sales. But as with many other ideas in the neo-classical toolbox, this was well known before Adam Smith (Oxenfeld, 1963: 72). See the discussion of elasticity, appendix D.

More generally, we need to be on guard in believing that some theory is true because it catches a small piece of what was available quite independently of the theory.

may consider economizing. Ex post, prices reveal the profitability or unprofitability of economic decisions. Good judgements are rewarded and poor judgements punished (Boettke, 1997: 26).

Neo-classical price theory

So far, so good. Any market model will acknowledge the foregoing. But this says nothing about how prices are determined. It is just here where the troubles begin. On the neo-classical model, demand and supply for the market can be represented by curves which relate price to quantity. On the demand side, the higher the price, the less that is demanded; on the supply side, the higher the price the greater the amount of the good to be supplied. The curves are merely (sic) the aggregation of the curves which represent the preferences of the individual consumers or suppliers. There is nothing empirical about this, although econometric statistical study does seek to elucidate them. Rather, the curves get constructed from the premises of the theory, for example, that persons have known preferences, are rational maximizers, etc. The intersection of the curves, the equilibrium price, is, *ceteris paribus*, the market price and, as such, the social optimum (see appendix D). This is, of course, the utopia of "free market" fundamentalists – utopia because not only does it not exist, but because it almost certainly could not exist.

Indeed, the falsity of the premises does not stand in the way of an even greater benefit to the capitalist market as comprehended by neo-classical theory. On the theory, market coordination results in efficiency: "A distribution of goods or a scheme of production is inefficient when there are ways of doing still better for some individuals without doing any worse for others" (Rawls, 1971: 67). That is, not only is there coordination of all the many actions of the parties, but the coordination allocates and distributes so that given the resources, there is no better way to use them. For example, at equilibrium, workers are getting paid just what they "deserve" and employers are efficiently satisfying the wants of consumers.

It is easy to see the attractiveness of this theory of markets. Unfortunately, it is easy to show (appendix D) that even if the conditions set out by the model could be satisfied, a market result need not be efficient even in the restricted terms of the theory. Markets are important coordinating mechanisms, and indeed, as Hayek has insisted, real markets do better in rational allocation than planned economies *not* because prices do what neo-classical theory says they do, namely, guarantee "efficiency," but because by means of decentralization only a fraction of information about production possibilities and demand needs to be processed at any one time, in any one place (Hayek, 1978; Elson, 1988; Stiglitz, 2002).

Whatever stability and efficiency there is in capitalism depends critically on at least this much information being available.

This leaves us with this definition:

A market is a social institution in which people voluntarily exchange commodities (goods, resources, services) and coordination of those exchanges is accomplished via a system of prices.

This definition is admittedly abstract, but that is not a disadvantage since we must allow for different kinds of markets. All markets require prices and thus money, and that exchanges be voluntary, but, as noted, *we are not here committed to any particular theory about how prices get formed*, to the assumption, for example, that prices are equal to the marginal costs of production, nor are we committed to any particular assumptions about the participants in the market. There are many ways in which prices get established. Determining how in any concrete historical market they do so is a critical empirical problem since, indeed, it is precisely these conditions which enable and constrain voluntary decisions on the part of actors.

One or two general considerations may here be noticed. First, we need to recognize that in all market societies, the legacy of past practices, including non-market practices, will have direct effects on exchange values. History is here critical. This is emphasized by Polanyi (1992: 50) who notes that price systems

may contain layers of equivalences that historically originated under different forms of integration . . . Max Weber remarked that for lack of a costing basis Western capitalism would not have been possible but for the medieval network of statuated and regulated prices, customary rents, etc., a legacy of gild and manor. Thus price systems may have an institutional history of their own in terms of the types of equivalencies that entered into their making.

Indeed, one need not go back to the Middle Ages to see the vital importance of historical and non-economic factors in the pricing process. This is confirmed by Hicks (1989) who writes, "economic forces do affect wages, but only when they are strong enough to overcome . . . *social* forces." They are highly influenced by "custom . . . or by any other principle which affects the parties to the wage-bargain think to be *just* and *right*."[19]

Second, we can follow neo-classical theory and distinguish perfect competition from imperfect competition. This includes monopoly, the

---

[19] The text is quoted from Hamouda (1993: 119). Sir John R. Hicks, the first Briton to receive a Nobel Prize (1972), moved dramatically from the contributions which won him the prize. He offered that his famous *Value and Capital* (1939) "was the work of a 'neo-classical' economist now deceased."

limiting case of imperfect competition, and oligopoly, where several large firms dominate the market, there are barriers to entry and the suppliers produce relatively similar products. *In imperfect competition, prices are fixed independently by suppliers: suppliers are price-makers, not price takers* (appendix D). Nor, contrary to the assumptions of mainstream theory, in the real world, is this the "special case" (Galbraith, 1968; Baran and Sweezy, 1968).

Conditions of imperfect competition are still conditions of competition, but as mainstream theory acknowledges, price makers recognize that price competition would likely lead to a mutually destructive price war (Baran and Sweezy, 1968: 58). Many solutions are available to prevent this, from outright collusion, sometimes ignored and sometimes legitimated, to what is called "price leadership," where a dominating firm sets the price and the rest follow. Since price competition is seen to be destructive, it gives way to other forms of competition: variation of the products' appearance and packaging, planned obsolescence, continuous model changes, brand names, technological innovations and credit schemes. Indeed, "in an economic system in which competition is fierce and relentless and in which the fewness of the rivals rules out price cutting, advertising becomes to an ever increasing extent the principal weapon of the competitive struggle" (Baran and Sweezy, 1968: 115–116). It has long been recognized that advertising is not merely "informational" but is essential to the market process (Chamberlin, 1962). Indeed, if market capitalism is to be reproduced, new needs must constantly be created (Baran and Sweezy, 1968; Galbraith, 1968). As Schor put the matter, "consumerism is not an ahistorical trait of human nature, but a specific product of capitalism" (Schor, 1992: 117).

The labor market: an example

The labor market offers an excellent example of a market where (1) there are "crowds" of people seeking employment and there are employers (though not perhaps "crowds") who are seeking workers. There is, accordingly, competition, and supply and demand are critical to determining wages, and (2), as above, wages and salaries are real money: they are the primary means allowing for voluntary choices by employers as regards what wages attach to what jobs and what jobs potential employees will accept. That is, everything, including labor power, is a commodity – and thus has exchange value. But if supply and demand are pertinent to determining wages, the mechanism (or mechanisms) runs well beyond the one offered by neo-classical theory.

We can distinguish *ranking*, how jobs, and wages and salaries are created, transformed and destroyed, and *sorting*, the process whereby individuals get matched to jobs. As Granovetter and Tilly (1988), who I follow here, insist, ranking and sorting go on simultaneously and we must resist the temptation to reify skills, jobs and occupations as some abstract market process.[20]

For neo-classical theory, sorting is based on competition for available positions by workers who have different skills and competences. As the mythology goes, a worker's competences determine the job that he will get based on his marginal productivity to the firm. Presumably, employees have information on *all* jobs available, employers know exactly what they expect of potential employees and are able to assess the competences of the pool of potential employees. As rational, they hire the best person for the job. Ranking depends upon the imperative of profit maximizing with firms paying wages equivalent to their marginal products.[21] Wages and salaries are unequal because what people earn is commensurate with what they contribute.

Unfortunately, employees are often ignorant of job possibilities and, even if known, they are often out of reach; employers may have only vague ideas of what skills are actually needed; and they are very often unable to assess the competences of potential employees. Employers are also often "irrational" regarding whom they hire – allowing their prejudices, or commitments to friends, etc. to get in the way, but perhaps most importantly, the idea of a concrete marginal product on which wages are based is a mathematical fiction. Where the "product" is a cooperative product, as is the case in almost all real-world production, it is difficult, if not impossible, to assess the relative contributions of the cooperators. Indeed, this simple (and marvelously fair and efficient!) mechanism barely speaks to reality.

The reality of labor markets is extremely complicated and concretely specific. As Granovetter and Tilly show, talk of "markets" collapses a very

---

[20] As they emphasize, "skill" compounds personal capacities and substitutability: the ease and expense of replacing the worker. Skill, like productivity, is very difficult to measure, despite mythology to the contrary. Skill involves tacit knowledge and is not well defined (contrary to human capital theory). Athletes are the exception, not the rule. Similarly, jobs (and occupations) are continually being socially constructed (and reconstructed). As Granovetter and Tilly summarized matters: "What determines outcomes . . . are such matters as the resources, bargaining power, socialization, cultural and social structural patterns of negotiating groups, and the state of labor and product markets" (1998: 209).

[21] Marginal decision-making considers whether the benefits of "an extra amount" of something is worth the extra cost. Thus, the marginal product of labor is the extra output of an additional "unit" of labor. See appendix D.

complicated struggle by a host of parties – capitalists, workers, house-holds, states and organizations, for example, the American Medical Association, trade and labor unions – into a misleading abstraction. These actors have very different capacities, a function of their structural positions and relations in society. To take some obvious examples, the stunning differences in the range of income inequality in the USA and Japan, including inequalities in executive compensation, the critical importance of racism and sexism in the sorting processes, the flexibility in defining and redefining occupations, and thus requirements and wages, need to be explained in terms of the ways that parties have employed resources which are the product of historically developed structures and relations. All this is perhaps familiar enough. (Yet, if so, one may be rightly pressed to explain the grip of neo-classical assumptions on our thinking about markets.)

The labor market *is* indeed a market; prices provide information on choices, but neither jobs (nor wages) are "a function of" markets as these have been comprehended by neo-classical theory. If one wants to explain outcomes in labor markets, one needs to construct a model in which the beliefs, knowledge, motivations and capacities of typical people looking for jobs and of typical people hiring workers are identified. One needs also to identify the constraints imposed by history, gender and race relations, credentialing bodies, unions, etc. More generally, the outcomes in labor markets are the product of a number of interconnected social mechanisms, including pertinently, the political system and how it functions, the mechanisms which explain racism and sexism, and the mechanisms which give credentialing bodies and unions capacities to influence outcomes.[22]

But there is a further point to be emphasized. The neo-classical model is timeless, but in real markets, time is a critical factor.

Market as process

The importance of time in market processes was recognized by Hayek, von Mises, Lachman and others. In its most interesting (and radical) form it rejects the idea that there is or could be general equilibrium. As Lachman (1984: 304) writes:

The notion of equilibrium which makes very good sense when confined to individual agents, like a household or firm, is less easily applied to the description of human interaction. It still has uses when applied to a very simple type of market, such as Marshall's corn market. But "equilibrium of the industry" is a

---

[22] See also, for example, Tilly and Tilly, 1997.

difficult concept to handle. Equilibrium of the "economic system" is a notion remote from reality, though Walras and Pareto show its logical consistency. Equilibrium of an economic system in motion, "equilibrium growth" borders on absurdity.

The market is not (as per general equilibrium theory) an "end-state" tending, *ceteris paribus*, toward equilibrium, nor is it a closed system, analyzable ahistorically. The main point is that events occur in real time and what precedes alters conditions in ways which have unpredictable consequences on what follows. General equilibrium theory has time as a "variable" in very nearly the same sense that time is a variable in celestial mechanics.[23] Nor is it an "open system on which external change impinges in the form of 'random shocks' each of which the system, possibly with variable time lags, contrives to 'absorb'." As Lachman writes: "The existence of human action consciously designed to produce certain effects, prompted by expectations which may, and often do, fail, makes it impossible to look at the market process in this way" (1984: 305).

The point is that market outcomes are the unintended product of the conscious action of different actors each acting with very different materials at hand to bring about their economic goals. This is, of course, another way of stating what we said about labor markets. For Lachman, what propels the market as a continuous process is that there is a gap between actions based on plans embodying a mental picture of the future and the future itself. If the plans of all the interacting individuals were consistent (along with some other very strong assumptions, about, for example, conditions of competition), then a general equilibrium is logically possible; but because individuals have different mental pictures, there is continuous unpredictable change and hence no "equilibrium" in any useful sense. But there are patterns and this implies that there are social mechanisms that can be identified.[24]

---

[23] In response to this, so-called "complexity theory" has now been applied, if modestly, to economic model-building. See Anderson *et al.*, 1988, especially the essay by John Holland, "The Global Economy as an Adaptive Process." Insofar as he (still) finds valuable "equilibrium dynamics under uncertainty," Arrow represents the critical, but still unreformed leading edge of the mainstream.

For neo-classical theory each agent makes a judgement about future prices by means of a probability distribution. As Littlefield (1986: 28) summarizes this: " 'Tomorrow' can be characterized as a vector of random variables, where the range the values can take is known today, and more important, so is the set of variables itself." Sadly, this is so far-fetched as to not deserve comment.

[24] Lewis and Runde (forthcoming) have opened an interesting line of inquiry in their examination of the work of Lachman. As they see matters, Lachman addressed "the challenge inherent in attempting to advance a strong and consistent subjectivist view of human agency without at the same time undermining the possibility of providing a

Existing market-as-process theories define competition in the same way that it is defined in neo-classical theory as a condition of many buyers and sellers, each interested in realizing interests. But the function of competition is differently understood. For neo-classical theory, a condition is (fully) competitive only if at equilibrium, price equals marginal cost and markets clear. Competition serves, on this view, to make it impossible for producers or consumers to set prices. Imperfect competition gives the corporation discretion within a price / quantity range. Oligopolistic firms may be seen as cost economizers (including for Williamson and others, transaction cost economizers).

On the process conception, it is still assumed that competition makes it impossible for producers to set prices, but it is held also that competition is "a method of discovery." As Hayek (1978: 236) put it: "We have come to understand that the market and the price mechanism [as staticly analyzed by neo-classical theory] provides . . . a sort of discovery procedure which makes the utilization of more facts possible than any other known system, and which provides the incentives for constant discovery of new facts which improve adaptation to the ever changing circumstances of the world in which we live."

Three points bear emphasis. First, the Hayekian view remains in the thrall to the competitive model, certainly the marginal case. But this view does open up some alternative ways to think about markets. That is, not only does it reject the static equilibrium model, but it shows how price systems – even in conditions of imperfect competition – actually do function in coordinating economic action. It puts knowledge, more precisely the highly distributed forms of knowledge, at the center of coordination problems. As Hayek (1978: 182) writes:

Utilization of knowledge widely dispersed in society with extensive division of labor cannot rest on individuals knowing all the particular uses to which well-known things in their individual environment might be put. Prices direct attention to what is worth finding about market offers for various things.

Or as Boettke (1997: 30), following Kirzner (1985), summarizes matters:

The essence of the coordinating property of the price system lies not in its ability to convey perfectly correct information about resource scarcity and technological possibilities, but in "its ability to communicate information concerning its own faulty information-communication properties". . . Disequilibrium relative prices,

coherent account of social institutions and socio-economic order." They argue that while there are difficulties in Lachman's account, these could be remedied with a version of Bhaskar-inspired critical realism. If so, the result would be very close to what is being argued here.

imperfect as they are, nevertheless provide some guidance in detection and correction absent from formal models of economic "information" premised on static equilibrium.[25]

Third, and a presupposition of the argument for competition as discovery, is the fact that in market economies, the economic situation is ever-changing and unpredictable. "Competition is valuable *only* because, and in so far as, its results are unpredictable and on the whole different from those which anyone has, or could have, deliberately aimed at" (Hayek, 1978: 180).[26]

The process view of markets has much to recommend it even if Hayek's particular understanding is flawed (Lawson, 1997). Process theories are correct in seeing that there is a historical dynamic to market arrangements in which what has happened continually alters the conditions for future decision-making. And even in markets where competition is imperfect, the price system provides guidance in finding and correcting information essential to making economic decisions. Perhaps the most obvious objection to Hayek-inspired theories is the failure to notice (or at least to see through) the fact that decisions are structured and that, accordingly, individuals have widely different (and unequal) resources in making their choices, a failure carried over from neo-classical theory. These structures are also a legacy of past activities, currently being reproduced and transformed. Ignoring this, of course, both ignores the powerful ordering capacities of institutions (Lewis and Runde, forthcoming) and allows for the widely shared myth of competition.

---

[25] There is a historical connection here between Hayek's views and many of the ideas of Alfred Schütz. Of some importance, Schütz was a member of the Mises' Privat-Seminar in Vienna in the 1930s. See Augier, 1999.

   Boettke points out that new information economics, for example, the work of Stiglitz (1994) and Grossman (1989) remains committed to rational-expectations equilibrium analysis, concentrating on "market failure" – the failure of markets to achieve efficiency as defined by the model. Yet, Boettke notes also "their research on the informational role of prices has led to a fundamental recasting of many basic questions in orthodox economic theory" (1997: 29).

[26] Hayek notes that "the necessary consequences of the reason why we use competition is that, in those cases in which it is interesting, *the validity of the theory can never be tested empirically* . . . If we do not know the facts we hope to discover by means of competition, we can never ascertain how effective it has been in discovering those facts that might be discovered" (1978: 180). The defense of competitive markets is thus global and historical: "All we can hope to find out is that, on the whole, societies which rely for this purpose on competition have achieved their aims more successfully than others" (1978: 180). This is surely contestable, depending hugely, of course, on being clear about the "aims" of societies. But the point is probably moot since, in a world that has giant corporations, it may be quite impossible to secure and maintain competitive markets.

Better markets?

A number of important conclusions are suggested by the foregoing account. First, actually existing markets (and market economies) and *differences* in these – differences sometimes of considerable importance – are the historical products of agents working with materials at hand – and their present constitution can be explained (chapter 5).[27] It follows also that there is nothing "natural" about markets which, as human products, can be changed. As Dugger (1992: 237) writes:

According to market mythology, our fate is due to natural law – supply and demand in the market – and cannot be changed. In this way, the market myth weakens the credibility of those who would reform the market, dashes the hopes of those dispossessed by the market, and hides those who benefit from the particular way the market has been instituted.

Granting the constraints imposed by history and nature on the various market economies of the world, the role of government is here critical. While this is not the place for extended discussion, it is easy enough to see that there are a host of policy choices that have dramatic effects on the constitution of real-world markets. As argued, there is no way for government *not* to intervene so as to affect outcomes. In baseball, the height of the mound has consequences for pitchers *and* hitters. There is no way to be "neutral." So as regards markets, the "rules" inescapably benefit some at the expense of others. The only questions, then, are what are the goals, and are the means effective? Determining the goals, of course, is inescapably political. Given that there is no escaping *some* policy choice, and thus *some* concrete institutionalization of the market, we can only here list the most obvious policy areas and hint at their relevance:

> Monetary and fiscal policy. What should be the goals of macro-economic policy and how should they be carried out?
>
> Industrial policy. Should there be incentives for some industries, e.g., aircraft. How does the budget for defense shape critical markets?
>
> Labor policy, including the length of the working day, a minimum wage, the organization and capacities of unions, anti-discrimination policy, and laws regarding occupational health and safety.

---

[27] The task was begun by Marx and Weber, of course. There are a host of other examples representing differing theories but consistent with the analysis of chapter 5. These include Tawney, 1998; Polanyi, 1971, 2001; Shonfield, 1965; Brenner, 1977; North, 1981, 1990; Pomeranz, 2000; Davis, 2001; Harvey, 1987.

Environmental policy. Will the "costs" of destroying the natural environment be taken as "externalities" from private production, or will they be part of the cost analysis of the polluters?

Energy policy. Should some sources be given incentives or constraints? What is the most effective means to secure the least expensive, cleanest energy sources, to minimize waste of energy?

Farm policy. As with energy policy, how should these markets be structured? Can one justify subsidies to "agri-businesses"? To tobacco?

Financial market policies. Are current Securities and Exchange Commission rules encouraging investment or promoting waste and corruption?

Family policy. What are the rights of working women, including maternity leave policy, facilities for child-care, and safeguards against discriminatory practices?

Health policy. How should these markets be structured? Is a system of third-party payment justified?

Educational policy. What is the commitment of the government to creating workers with the necessary skills and how should this be done? Is privatization of mass education, through, for example, vouchers, feasible or desirable?

Transportation policy. Commerce depends on transportational infra-structure. Are there ways to utilize properly structured markets to achieve what is necessary and desirable? Should these be public monopolies?

Immigration policy. What are the consequences of alternative policies on labor markets?

To be sure, none of these problem areas has lacked serious inquiry – despite the obstacles of disciplinary fragmentation.[28] But the neo-classical model of economic behavior and markets has badly misdirected much intellectual effort in this regard. It is hoped that the foregoing chapters provide a useful way to conceptualize inquiry in the social sciences and to avoid some of the more obvious pitfalls. As regards the argument of the present chapter, it is irresponsible for social scientists to ignore the fact that markets are differently constituted and that the ideal described

---

[28] The problems, of course, are severely compounded by what is termed "globalization." There are also global markets and these, too, are historical products. Again, the topic is huge, but see, for example, Barnet and Müller, 1974; Robertson, 1992; Barnet and Cavanaugh, 1994; Appadurai, 1996; Bauman, 1998; Sassen, 1999; Mittleman, 2000; Ritzer, 2004; Steger, 2005. For an account of the American role in recent globalization, see Gowan, 1999; Stiglitz, 2002; Brenner, 2003.

by neo-classical general equilibrium theory fails to gives us an adequate understanding of capitalist markets. Indeed, general equilibrium theory is the myth that "weakens the credibility of those who would reform the market, dashes the hopes of those dispossessed by the market, and hides those who benefit from the particular way the market has been instituted."

One final point: the foregoing insisted that the neo-classical theory of markets was fatally flawed, but it also noted that conceiving of markets as social mechanisms had distinct benefits if properly understood. We might note here that the criticism of general equilibrium theory leads also to a critique of centralized planning. The extent to which ideas of centralized planning depend upon general equilibrium theory is remarkable. As Diane Elson (1988) argued in her critique of Mandel (1986, 1988), in attempting to achieve an *ex ante* equilibrium, the planners play the role of a Walrasian auctioneer. But not only must the planner know more than he could, but things change through time, so theoretically speaking, the auctioneer could never close shop; he never fixes a price – a point made by the Austrian critics of general equilibrium theory. Historical experience suggests that centralized planning cannot be made to work – although obviously, our historical experience is limited to undemocratic regimes. But one must confront the argument that it is theoretically impossible for a centralized planner to have all the pertinent information.[29] On the other hand, various forms of market socialism remain, at least, consistent with these arguments.

More generally, the argument of this volume should encourage us to believe that if social science is sometimes part of the problem, it is, of necessity, essential to the solution.

---

[29] The formal theoretical similarity of planned and market economies was first noticed by Barone (1908) and Pareto (1909). For an account of the misunderstandings of their work by Samuelson and the formalists, see Boettke, 1997. Boettke notes also that most current forms of market socialism suffer from sharing assumptions of general equilibrium theory, but it remains contestable, versus Hayek, whether there are some genuine real-world alternatives to private property and idealized competitive markets. For a defense of a distinct and historically novel form of market socialism, see Elson's remarkable – and ignored – essay (1998).

Appendix A The limits of multiple regression

It is too often thought that multiple regression overcomes the problem of isolating causes and allows us to weigh their importance to outcomes. Even careful writers often confuse the following ideas:

1. A (some "variable," e.g., IQ) correlates with B (some other variable, e.g., income)
2. A "predicts" B
3. A "explains the variance" in B
4. A "explains" B
5. A "causes" B

We can handle 4 and 5 together. We can say 4, "A explains B" only if we can say "A causes B." But, first, correlations do not establish causes. Causes are "mechanisms" which produce outcomes. We can have a correlation where there is no conceivable mechanism, e.g., the price of eggs in a Beijing market and the price of Microsoft on the New York Stock Exchange. Second, there are always many causes of any outcome. In order to make a fire, we need, in addition to some combustible material, a source of heat and oxygen. Absent any of these, no fire. So which is more important? We get a fire only if the *right combination* is present. (It takes a good deal more heat to ignite a vinyl fabric than it does to ignite cotton.) If we pick out a source of heat as "the cause," that is because we assume the presence of oxygen and the combustible material. We forget about the oxygen and say, the spark "caused" the fire. (Weber called this "adequate causation," the difference in the existing state which brought about the effect.) This is both convenient and unsurprising. But the fact remains: *all* the factors are important: you will not get a fire if *any* are absent. Consider then Sarah's ability to score big on the SAT. What is "the cause"? Which of the "factors" (causes) will be more important? Sarah may be "bright," but she also was well-motivated, got some terrific education – and she felt good on the day of the test.

1 and 2 also can be treated together. A correlation between A and B can be between 0.0 and 1.0. 0.0 is no correlation; 1.0 is a perfect correlation:

for every change in A there is a commensurate change in B. Perfect correlations are rare indeed. This raises the question: when is a correlation (or in multiple regression, a "coefficient of correlation") "significant." But we need here to distinguish "policy" or "scientific significance" from "statistical significance" – roughly, measures designed by statisticians to ensure "a good fit."[1] A statistically significant finding may or may not have some policy or scientific significance. This generally will be a judgement about causality.

Where we have a statistically significant correlation, we can predict. If there is, for example, a positive correlation of 0.7 between the winner of the Super Bowl and the political party which won the presidential election, then we can predict the winner once we know the winner of the Super Bowl. There is no suggestion that there is a causal connection here. The correlation is a statistical fluke. But for purposes of prediction, the relation is all that I need. Nor because there is no causal mechanism involved here, can I *explain* the presidential victory by pointing to the team which won the Super Bowl.

Smoking and cancer is a good example. There is *some* causal mechanism at work in cancer production, likely several, and smoking is related to this in ways that we do not yet understand. Some people do smoke all their lives and never get cancer. And some people who never smoke do. But we know that the probability of getting cancer significantly increases if you smoke: A "predicts" B.

Sophisticated scientists are very often careless when they speak about 3, "explaining the variance." What they intend by this can be briefly summarized. Assume that there are a number of "factors" which taken together presumably "determine" some outcome. The idea then is to find out how significant each factor is in "producing" this outcome. The language of "producing an outcome" or "determining an outcome" is causal language. But indeed, such language is entirely inappropriate. We need to go a little deeper to see what is at issue here.

Assume first a standard regression equation, a set of dependable, meaningful independent variables $(a, b \ldots)$ with a linear relation to the dependent variable (Y).

$$Y = a + b_1 + b_2 + b_1 b_2 + e \text{ (Equation 1)}$$

---

[1] On "good fit," see below. Ziliak and McCloskey (2004: 333) showed that "of 137 relevant papers [in the *American Economic Review*] in the 1990s, 82 percent mistook statistically significant coefficients for economically significant coefficients." Indeed, things were getting worse. In their earlier study (1996), 70 percent of papers published in this distinguished journal did not distinguish the two, "and fully 96 percent misused a statistical test in some (shall we say) significant way or another" (2004: 332). Such is the power of positivist theory of science.

"Y," the "dependent variable," presumably is "determined" by the independent variables, "$a + b_1 \ldots$" The problem is then one of variable selection. The goal of the analysis is a "good fit." If we do our work well, what we end up with is "a useful statistical description defensible against plausible alternative interpretations" (Achen 1982: 13). It is critical to emphasize that *the very best result is a statistical description*, a point nearly always missed. At best, the result is a highly simplified picture, a statistical snapshot, of a fantastically complicated concrete social situation. For example, as an abstract ratio, the crime rate represents a picture of crime in the real world. It leaves much out – obviously. On the other hand, as Achen remarks: "A picture of a friend is useless if it covers a football field and exhibits every pore. What one looks for instead is an interpretable amount of information, with the detailed workings omitted" (Achen, 1982: 13). As regards the crime rate, the "detailed workings" include, of course, the specific structured actions of *everyone* in society: both criminals and non-criminals. While it would be agreed that a crime rate is such a snapshot taken from a very long distance, the same is true of all other statistical results, including the results of regressions.

A useful description – a good fit – is not so easy to come by. One test of this is the "coefficient of correlation," R^2. It is usually said that R^2 gives "the percentage of variance explained" in the dependent variable by the regression. But as Achen comments: this is an expression that, "for most social scientists, is of doubtful meaning but great rhetorical value" (1982: 58f.). The rhetorical value lies in the supposition that, first, a large R^2 guarantees "good fit" and, second, in the more radical confusion, that the number represents the causal importance of the factor in the regression.

Neither supposition can be sustained. As Achen says, R^2 "is best regarded as characterizing the geometric shape of the regression points and nothing more" (1982: 59). It is easy to see why it is nothing more than this. Achen says: "The central difficulty with the R^2 for social scientists is that the independent variables are not subject to experimental manipulation"(1982: 59). In the natural sciences, one tests theories about causality with an experiment. The experiment seeks to "control" the conditions to see if the hypothesized cause actually produces the outcome which the theory predicted. This is not possible in the social sciences. "Regression," which presumes to "control" variables, *mathematically*, is often thought to be an adequate substitute for experiment.

There are several lines of argument that it is not. One regards the problem that "variances are a function of the *sample*, not the underlying relationship" (Achen, 1982: 59). That is, the linear model (Equation 1) is a *local analysis* whose result depends upon the actual distributions of the variables in the population sampled. Thus, "in some samples, they vary widely, producing large variance; in other cases, the observations are more tightly grouped and there is little dispersion" (Achen, 1982: 59). (One needs some further understanding of statistical analysis to fully grasp this criticism.) For this reason, then, "they cannot have any real connection to the 'strength' of the relationship as social scientists ordinarily use the term, i.e., as a measure of how much effect a given change in the independent variable has on the dependent variable" (Achen, 1982: 59).

Second, there is the problem of assuming that the measured variables "add up" to 1.0, the problem of "additivity" and independence. Achen offers an example:

If the regression describes, say, domestic violence in countries as a function of violence in prior years plus economic conditions, can one say which variable is more important in causing violence? For most purposes the answer is no. The units of one variable are violence per amount of prior violence; the units of the other are violence per amount of economic dislocation. One can say only that apples differ from oranges. *As theoretical forces abstracted from any historical circumstances, they have no common measure.* (1982: 70)

Equation 1 makes us believe that the variables are both additive and independent (with b_1 b_2 taking into account the interaction effects of the variables).[2] But this is never the case. The best sort of example to illustrate the general principle is to see the confusion in the mostly meaningless discussions of the relative effects of heredity and the environment. Consider a parallel (idealized) biological study, a study that requires a controlled experiment.

Take a genotype replicated by inbreeding or cloning. This minimizes genotypic individuality. Place them in various carefully controlled environments. It is then possible to establish rough tables of correspondence between phenotype on the one hand and genotype-environment combinations on the other. The results, called the "norm of reaction," are *never* predictable in advance.[3] They are not predictable since genetic and environmental factors are not additive (and hence cannot be represented by linear equations). They are causes in transaction in exactly the sense that

[2] See also "path analysis," an extension of regression which makes the same assumptions as does regression, but where "a regression is done for each variable in the model as dependent on others which the model indicates are causes, direct and indirect." "Path coefficients," then, are "used to assess the relative importance of various direct and indirect causal paths to the dependent variable."

[3] This follows Lewontin, 1974. See also Lewontin, 1982 for a fuller account of the importance of "norms of reaction" and their absence in human quantitative studies: "Except for such traits as the presence or absence of blood-group antigens . . . we do not have a norm of reaction for any human trait" (1982: 22).

genes cause different phenotypical outcomes in different transactional environments.

If such norms could be experimentally established for persons in their development, then across the range of controlled environments and (cloned?) genotypes, one could relate the variances in outcomes with the changes in the independent variables. This would still not provide the *proportion* of causation since causation does not suddenly become additive. But one could talk sensibly about their relative "importance." One could "explain the variance" sensibly. More dramatically, as Achen says, we might conduct an experiment in which we put some children in middle-class homes and the others in closets. There surely will be differences in cognitive ability, personality, etc. Almost certainly, most of the differences in these realized capacities will be "explained" by environment. Conversely, put them all (*per impossible*) in the *same* environment, most of the variation surely will be "explained" by heredity. The foregoing explains, of course, the importance of (identical) twin studies – and their limitations.

It is obvious that except for identical twins, not only are no two genotypes the same, but that in the concrete real world, there is not any way *in principle* to specify all the relevant environmental "variables," exactly because *these are not independent.* The social world is real enough, but the mere fact that *necessarily* it is mediated by the consciousness of agents makes it impossible to say how a condition will be experienced and understood by the agent, and thus what effect it will have on him and his behavior. Accordingly, not only will multiple regression not give the proportion of causality involved in some outcome, but in general, it will not even allow us "to explain the variance." Indeed, there are differences between individuals which are rooted in our genes, but if, for example, we want to explain inequalities in the real world, we had best find some other way.[4]

But all this is not to say that quantitative methods have a minor place, or more outrageously, that they have no place in social science. First, they are enormously useful in providing descriptions of facets of the society. Second, we need to have numbers of all sorts of things, demographic, economic, political and sociological: the number of Americans or Hawaiians,

[4] Whitfield and McClearn recognize that "the causal nexus for any particular phenotype may be viewed as a complex network with inputs from multiple genetic loci and from multiple environmental factors" (2005: 106). But they nevertheless put confidence in the idea that "increasingly sophisticated statistical designs of structural equation models in quantitative genetics can be enormously amplified by incorporating measurements of theoretically relevant environmental variables, specific genetic loci, and physiological mediators of the causal nexus" (2005: 112).

the income distribution, the number of voters, by income, by ethnicity, etc., crime rates, etc. Of course, there are considerable methodological and indeed epistemological issues here, best handled by sophisticated methodologists. We need only repeat that there is considerable danger in confusing causal explanation with description. Description is an essential first step and lacking an adequate picture of social reality, explanation is pointless even where it is not dangerous.

Second, these methods give us capacities to generalize, including generalizations discoverable *only* through the use of regression and similar methods. As Kemp and Holmwood (2003: 12) argue, "quantitative and statistical techniques may be used to reveal patterns . . . that are obscured by the range of influence operating on them . . . Likewise, statistical techniques can sometimes be used to extract revealing patterns in data even when the precise parameters of the various influences are not known prior to analysis."[5] As argued, generalizations are materials for explanatory inquiry: for example, how do we explain differences in variance regarding ethnicity or income in voting behavior, etc. As above, identifying such patterns does not give us causality, but as Kemp and Holmwood write, "'the existence of such a pattern suggests that there may be structural influence at work, a claim that can be investigated further to examine its plausibility" (2003: 12).

[5] See also Olsen and Morgan (forthcoming).

Appendix B   Comparison, Mill's methods and narrative

Historical sociology typically employs comparison as a research strategy. In what follows we concentrate on the idea of comparison and try to get clear on its use – and misuse. Inspired by Theda Skocpol's influential *States and Social Revolutions* (1979), recent sophisticated discussions argue that the methods codified by John Stuart Mill are appropriate techniques toward advancing a more "scientific" approach to comparative analysis. Finally, as part of this, we look at the idea of "narrative" as a mode of explanatory sociology. The issues are at the heart of a lively recent debate between Skocpol and William Sewell.[1] While the two writers seem often to be talking past one another, once the key assumptions and confusions are clarified, a resolution is readily available.

We can develop these issues by considering the ideas put forward by James Mahoney (1999) regarding "Nominal, Ordinal, and Narrative Appraisal in Macrocausal Analysis," the title of his important essay.[2] Mahoney is interested in identifying explanatory generalizations and offers that the three strategies identified in the title of his essay can be, and are, employed jointly by researchers, despite the view often taken that the work uses only one strategy. On his view, "each of these three different strategies represents a *different* technique that can be used for assessing the same causal relationship." Thus *States and Social Revolutions* is wrongly taken to employ one basic strategy, "nominal appraisal." Mahoney argues that, indeed, Skocpol employs successfully all three. Mahoney provides by far the most sophisticated attempt to sustain this view. We conclude by arguing that his effort fails, and that, indeed, while Skocpol did use these three different "strategies," this introduced incoherence into her

---

[1] See Sewell, 1996. The essay won a prize in 1991 and, still unpublished, was vigorously attacked by Skocpol in the concluding essay of her *Social Revolutions in the Modern World* (1994).

[2] See also his "Strategies of Causal Assessment in Comparative Historical Analysis," in Mahoney and Rueschaemeyer (eds.), 2003. Portions of this essay in this volume were adapted from an earlier essay, "Strategies of Causal Inference in Small-N Analysis," *Sociological Methods and Research*, 28 (May 2000).

account, and remarkably, gave her book a persuasive power which was quite alien to some critical specific claims regarding the use to which she put nominal and ordinal methods.[3]

Nominal comparison

Mahoney writes: "Nominal (or categorical) comparison entails the use of categories that are mutually exclusive cases . . . and collectively exhaustive" (1999: 339). Thus Skocpol's concern is revolution versus non-revolution. Following John Stuart Mill, she hopes to establish "valid causal associations." To do this, one can seek to establish what several cases have in common with the phenomenon to be explained – Mill's Method of Agreement. Or one can contrast cases in which the phenomenon to be explained and the hypothesized causes are present to cases where both the hypothesized cause and the effect are absent, but which are otherwise similar. This is Mill's Method of Difference. As regards macro-historical phenomena, Skocpol notes that "in practice . . . it is often possible, and certainly desirable, to combine these two comparative logics" (1979: 37).

She has three positive cases to be explained, the social revolutions in France in 1789, Russia in 1917 and China in 1911. In very interesting chapters she undertakes a comparative-historical analysis in which she considers these, and though briefly, three "negative" cases, or situations where there was no social revolution. While her emphasis is on the positive cases, strictly, she employs Mill's joint method.[4] She concludes that the three positive cases have in common "(1) state organizations susceptible to administrative and military collapse when subjected to intensified pressures from more developed countries abroad and (2) agrarian sociopolitical structures that facilitated widespread peasant revolts against landlords" (1979: 154). Taken together, she concludes that these are "the sufficient distinctive causes" of these revolutions.

---

[3] To anticipate, in an early essay review of her book, I argued that her "narrative" made her argument convincing, but that it was, indeed, incoherently joined to what Mahoney calls "nominal appraisal." See Manicas, 1981. This is substantially the criticism that has been reasserted by Sewell, 1996. I consider this below.

[4] Schematically,

$$\text{ABC } (x_1, x_2 \ldots) \quad \rightarrow \quad \text{E } (y_1, y_2 \ldots)$$
$$\text{ADF } (x_1, x_2 \ldots) \quad \rightarrow \quad \text{E } (y_1, y_2 \ldots)$$
$$\text{GH } (x_1, x_2 \ldots) \quad \rightarrow \quad \text{not-E } (y_1, y_2 \ldots)$$
$$\text{MN } (x_1, x_2 \ldots) \quad \rightarrow \quad \text{not-E } (y_1, y_2 \ldots)$$

Probably A is cause (or "determining condition") of E

Indeed, this better fits Skocpol's use of Mill's methods.

The logic is clear enough. One hypothesizes various potential "causes," then eliminates some as neither necessary nor sufficient. Mahoney argues that nominal methods provide "a sound logical basis for eliminating potential necessary and sufficient causes" (1999: 241f.). Unfortunately, this is an unduly optimistic conclusion, for many reasons.

We can begin with the Method of Agreement. In Mill's own words:

If two or more instances of a phenomenon have one circumstance in common, the circumstance in which alone all the instances agree is the cause (or effect) of the given phenomenon.

Schematically,

$$\text{ABC}\,(x_1,\ x_2\dots) \rightarrow \qquad \text{E}\,(y_1,\ y_2\dots)$$
$$\text{ADF}\,(x_1,\ x_2\dots) \rightarrow \qquad \text{E}\,(y_1,\ y_2\dots)$$

Probably A is cause ("or determining condition") of E

Capital letters ABC etc. are hypothetically identified possible "causes" of E. The small letters in parenthesis represent unknowns present in the situation but not part of the analysis. The inference to A as the probable cause depends on the assumption that B, C, D and F are not *necessary conditions* (since E occurs when they are absent) and that E is *not* the product of the joint operation of ABC, BC, DF and ADF. These have not been eliminated as *sufficient conditions for E*.

Mill's method of difference aims at eliminating conditions as not sufficient. In his words:

If an instance in which the phenomenon under investigation occurs and an instance in which it does not occur have circumstance in common save one, that one occurring in the former, the circumstance in which alone the two instances differ is the effect, or the cause, or an indispensable part of the cause, of the phenomenon.

Schematically,

$$\text{ABC}\,(x_1,\ x_2\dots) \rightarrow \qquad \text{E}\,(y_1,\ y_2\dots)$$
$$\text{BC}\,(x_1,\ x_2\dots) \rightarrow \qquad non\text{-E}\,(y_1,\ y_2\dots)$$

Probably A is cause ("or determining condition") of E

In the real world, it is next to impossible to find cases satisfying this method. Indeed, Sewell (1996) is quite correct to insist that Skocpol assumes what he calls "experimental temporality," and that, "in order for Skocpol's revolutions to be subjected to her comparative method, they must be conceptualized as analogous to separate 'trials' of an experiment. This means that the trials must be both equivalent and independent" (1996:

258). But it is quite impossible to satisfy these conditions. It was just this problem which led Mill to offer his Joint Method, a method which is *not* a combination of the methods of agreement and of difference. Mill's point precisely was that it was the fallback method when one did not have conditions of closure optimally demanded for the method of agreement and all but required for the method of difference. The point is that since most outcomes are not the product of a single non-trivial sufficient condition, the methods can offer little help with trying to sort this out. On the other hand, while they can offer some confidence in eliminating factors as not necessary, *if there are alternative paths to outcomes*, this will not be of much help either. This is the point about equivalence. Consider, for example, alternative paths to modernization (Moore, 1966). That is, at some point in time, given existing conditions, some condition may be "necessary" for some outcome. But it may not be necessary at some other time and place given *other* existing conditions. For example, at some time and place, breaking the capacity of a landed nobility to resist private property may be necessary for there to be commercial development, but at some other time and place, given (say) abundant merchant capital in cities, this is not necessary.

But there is a far more serious problem. Mill intended his methods to be used to establish causes in Hume's understanding of causality: *a* is the cause of *b* means that there is law-like, but contingent, association ("constant conjunction," "invariant relation") between *a* and *b*. The realist conception developed in chapter 2 has it that *a* causes *b* means that *a produces* or brings about *b*, and the relation is not contingent. On the Humean reading, causality can be analyzed in terms of necessary and sufficient conditions; on the realist reading, it cannot. Mahoney is not insensitive to the problem which this objection presents, even if he fails to see that it is fatal.

As he says, "even if logical methods exist for identifying necessary and sufficient causation, some analysts contend that it is still not a productive way to think about causation" (1999: 348). Why not? To say that C is a sufficient for E is to say: "If C, then E" with the "if . . . then" analyzed as a material conditional: the conditional is false only when C is true and E false. C is a necessary condition for E means, "If not-C, then not-A." (It follows, logically, that if C is a sufficient condition for E, then E is a necessary condition for C – they are contrapositives.) Thus, paying your parking tickets is a necessary condition for graduation; graduating is a sufficient condition for having paid your parking tickets.

The analysis of causality in terms of necessary and sufficient conditions suffers from being both too wide and too narrow. It is too wide since it includes cases where there is no suggestion of causality. One doesn't graduate *because* one pays one's parking tickets and graduating did not *cause* the paying of the parking ticket. On the other hand, and more seriously, genuine causes may be neither necessary nor sufficient conditions.[5] Consider an example where causation (and explanation) is at issue.

Suppose that you are Louis Pasteur interested in determining the cause of fermentation. You select a variety of fermented liquids, including beer, wine, vinegar and cider. Microscopic examination shows that each has a characteristic micro-organism (which, as it turned out, was *Mycoderma aceti*, a kind of yeast). You conclude that this micro-organism is the cause of the fermentation. Compare, then, Skocpol's use of Mill's methods.

First, in both examples, it is clear that considerable theory is involved since theory is essential if we are to have an idea of what to look for, the character of the likely causes and how they are to be identified. Pasteur looked for micro-organisms; Skocpol looked for "structural conditions" with particular reference to the political economy, the institutions of the state and the international political and economic environment. She could have surely looked elsewhere. She might, for example, have not looked at "structural conditions" or merely put them in the background. She might, instead, have looked at the psychology of actors. Or she might have theorized "structures" differently, and instead of focusing on political economy, she might have considered long-term cultural facts, e.g., the role of the Catholic Church, the Reformation, etc.[6]

Second, *Mycoderma aceti* is the cause of fermentation in a very ordinary sense. It is an identifiable "thing" which, in appropriate circumstances, *produces* fermentation. It is the difference in the prevailing state of affairs which *brings about* change in the wine. Is there an analogy in Skocpol's account? Skocpol recognizes, of course, that her "sufficient distinctive causes" are not at all like Pasteur's *Mycoderma*. Indeed, if anything compares to the *Mycoderma*, it might be King Louis XVI! She herself writes: "as everyone knows, the summoning of the Estates-General [by the king]

[5] More generally, causality does not submit to an extensional analysis. Thus, on the extensional analysis, inconsistent counterfactuals are both true: "Had Hitler not invaded Russia, he would have won the war" and "Had Hitler not invaded Russia, he would have lost the war" are both true, since the antecedents of both are false.
[6] Her structuralism, of course, was specifically in response to what she termed "*aggregate psychological* theories" (1979: 9). But as I argue subsequently, she could not escape assumptions about motivations. Similarly, like many who advocate structuralist (and causal) accounts, her anti-interpretativist bias leads her to dismiss "culture" as a critical part of the account. See McDonald, 1996. But as argued in chapter 3, despite the bias shared by Parsonians and structuralist Marxists, "culture" can hardly be separated from "structure" properly understood.

served not to solve the royal financial crisis but to launch the Revolution" (1979: 65). "Launch" is causal. Could not one say, as many historians would, that this was a cause of the Revolution (Hexter, 1971)? Of course, he did not *intend* "to launch a Revolution" and we can only guess at how things would have developed had the king chosen to do otherwise (as he surely could have). On the other hand, there is something right about Skocpol's interest in structural conditions, even if, in no stretch of the imagination can we think of them as causes in Hume's sense, and even if they *are*, for her, causes in the realist sense. That is, the king's decision to summon the Estates-General had the consequences it did *because* of the existing "structural conditions." Compare a fire: the "structural conditions" are the presence of combustible materials and plenty of oxygen. To have a fire, then, one needs only a lit match. In both cases, there were pertinent causes at work, both events and causal mechanisms, and once we see how they came together, we can explain the outcome.

Third, in the *Mycoderma* example, the analysis of causes in terms of necessary and sufficient conditions utterly breaks down. We noted earlier that the method of agreement eliminated conditions as not necessary. In this case, can we say that the *Mycoderma aceti* is a necessary condition for fermentation? In fact, we cannot. That is, there is a whole set of organisms which, in the right environments, produce fermentation. "Fermentation" is an abstract term and we need to be aware that there are also very different kinds of fermentation. We see, accordingly, the pertinence of the unknowns in our schema, $y_1, y_2 \ldots$

Nor (even assuming we now employ the method of difference) can we say that *Mycoderma aceti* is a sufficient condition for fermentation for in addition to a fermenting agent, fermentation requires the presence (or non-occurrence) of many other conditions as well. Some of these may be too obvious to make a fuss over, e.g., the presence of a fermentable liquid; others may be less obvious, e.g., a temperature range which will permit the process to begin and proceed, or a host of non-events, e.g., the absence of an accident in the laboratory which would affect the outcome.

Mahoney acknowledges this problem by introducing Lieberson's example of the drunk driver. He writes: "These methods correctly show that drunk driving by itself is neither a necessary nor a sufficient condition for an automobile accident" (1999: 349). But indeed, in some particular case, drunkenness was the *cause* of the accident, and one surely does explain it by noting that the driver was drunk.

This also suggests severe limits on providing true and non-trivial causal generalizations. Thus it is false that "Whenever a driver is drunk, he has an accident," "People with cancer are all smokers," "If you put salt in water, it dissolves." Consider, then, the structure of Skocpol's covering law "explanation" of the three social revolutions:

If a state organization susceptible to administrative and military collapse is subjected to intensified pressures from developed countries abroad *and* there is widespread peasant revolt facilitated by agrarian sociopolitical structures, then there will be a social revolution.

In 1789, France was subjected to such pressures and had an agrarian social structure which facilitated widespread peasant revolt.

Hence, France in 1789 had a social revolution.

The first premise is the "explanatory generalization." We can replace China or Russia for France in the second premise and thus also "explain" their social revolutions.

The argument is a perfectly valid deduction and hence if the premises were true, then assuming the covering law model, Skocpol would have achieved her hoped for "valid, complete explanation of revolution." But if the conditions are not sufficient, the first premise is false. Thus a collapse of the state coupled with widespread peasant revolts, along with inevitable other conditions, *could* lead to a restoration of the old order and not "the emergence of new sociopolitical arrangements." Consider, for example, Iran in 1953 where Mohammed Mossadegh's revolutionary attempt was thwarted with assistance from the CIA. On the other hand, one could have a social revolution even where the state has not "collapsed," for example, the Cuban or Sandinista revolution which succeeded because armed insurgents were able to defeat the forces of the existing state.[7] On the other hand, one could "save" the explanation by providing pertinent *ceteris paribus* clauses, for example: "If a state organization susceptible to administrative and military collapse is subjected to intensified pressures from developed countries abroad, then *unless it receives support from other international actors . . .*" But there is now the real danger of trivializing the account.

Which is not to say that we can never offer true non-trivial generalizations expressing necessary and/or sufficient conditions: "Whenever there is combustion, oxygen is present"; "When a bullet passes through the brain, the person dies." The presence of oxygen is a non-trivial "factor" in combustion; bullets through the brain are sufficient "causes" of death. In both cases, it is worth emphasizing, we do not need inductive arguments to have confidence in these generalizations exactly because we have an excellent understanding of the pertinent causal mechanisms.

---

[7] For critical discussion along these lines, see Burawoy, 1989 and Sewell, 1996, drawing on Burawoy (1989). Skocpol (1994) takes issue with these criticisms, but she seems unwilling to acknowledge that, given her explicitly stated goals, they are entirely fair.

Ordinal comparison

Mahoney could reply that the foregoing argument shows only what he
acknowledges, that nominal methods are not sufficient. On his view, these
need to be supplemented with ordinal comparison.

> Ordinal analysis involves rank ordering cases using variables with three or more
> values based on the degree to which the phenomenon is present. This kind of
> analysis facilitates the use of J. S. Mill's method of concomitant variation,[8] in
> which the analyst tries to establish causation by looking at the relationship between
> scores on an ordinally measured explanatory variable and scores on an ordinally
> measured outcome variable. (1999: 353)

This is what Tilly had in mind in talking about "textbooks and learned
essays" which hold that all valid comparison is variation-finding. It is also
the basic logic of those quantitative methods which talk of "dependent"
and "independent" variables.[9] (See appendix A)

Important here is the fact that causality is inferred *not* by identifying necessary or sufficient conditions, but in terms of correlations.[10]
Mahoney points to a host of problems in the attempt to combine this
method with nominal methods and the interested reader should turn to
his careful account. But the critical point to be made here is acknowledgement that while a correlation may be *evidence* for a causal relationship,
causality must be inferred. Thus, "the discovery that the explanatory variable is related to the outcome variable in an ordinal assessment does not
indicate how one should interpret the nature of the association" (1999:
354). This is familiar ground, but what is most remarkable is his idea
that "process tracing" is a critical part of the analysis.[11] This involves
"identifying the causal mechanisms that link explanatory variables with
the outcome variable." "Causal mechanisms," the text continues, "can
be defined as the processes and intervening variables through which
an explanatory variable exerts a causal effect on the outcome variable"
(1999: 363).

---

[8] In Mill's formulation: "Whatever phenomenon varies in any manner whenever another
phenomenon varies in some particular manner is either a cause or an effect of that
phenomenon, or is connected with it through one fact of causation."

[9] It is of more than historical note that Durkheim (1982) was very sensitive to the problems
of using Mill's versions of nominal strategies, and insisted that what Mahoney calls
"ordinal appraisal" was the most useful technique. Durkheim wrote before the invention
of linear regression models and followed what Mill called the Method of Concomitant
Variation. As Mahoney writes: "Ordinal analysis is in fact the strategy of inference that
comparative historical researchers turn to when they seek to identify linear correlations
across a small number of cases" (1999: 353).

[10] This is true also of more sophisticated linear regression models, discussed in appendix
A.

[11] See also "path analysis," appendix A.

This is a puzzling remark since it seems to reproduce the systematic ambiguity regarding causality between Humean and realist views. "Processes" suggest a realist conception of causality, but "intervening variables" suggest otherwise. Again, consider the example of the drunk driver. Assume a correlation between explanatory variable A, drunken driving, and outcome variable E, automobile accidents. This is non-spurious because we know that there is a mechanism which explains the correlation. It will be a complicated causal story, involving what alcohol does to the brain, how this affects motor control and perception, etc. But we know that drunkenness is causally related to accidents because we know that drunkenness is a cause in the realist sense: it is not merely "conjoined" to accidents nor is it an "intervening variable"; drunkenness can *produce* an accident (again, via well-known mechanisms).

Notice also that the correlation does no explaining. *After* the accident, we explain it *not* by appealing to the correlation, but by noting that in this *particular* case, the driver was drunk, carrying along in the background what we know about alcohol and our neurophysiology. Similarly, the probability of getting lung cancer is higher if you smoke, so it is very good policy not to smoke. But Sam who doesn't smoke wants to know why *he* got cancer, and Charlie, who does smoke, did not. The correlation is of no help. As above, smoking is neither a necessary nor sufficient condition for getting cancer, but here we remain in the dark regarding the mechanism which makes this probability what it is. Still, we believe strongly there is one. Indeed, identifying the mechanism or mechanisms is precisely the goal of inquiry. There is a strict analogy in historical sociology. But to be clear on this, we need first to look at Mahoney's ideas regarding "causal narrative."

Causal narrative

The idea has recently become fashionable, but as Skocpol (1994: 332) rightly remarks, since "narratives can be structured in many, many ways," "to advise people to write 'narratives' is really to advise nothing." Mahoney offers that the idea "has been extensively examined," and that "a consensus has emerged that narrative can be a useful tool for assessing causality in situations where temporal sequencing, particular events, and path dependence must be taken into account" (1999: 1164). But how narrative does this remains unclear.[12] There are, perhaps, two

---

[12] Mahoney provides a number of citations to the literature (1999: 1164). He hopes to remedy two fairly clear shortcomings: the absence of concrete illustrations, and the gap between narrative and "other" strategies of causal assessment. He is remarkably ingenuous with regard to his illustrations, but it seems to the present writer, at least, that the gap remains unfilled. See below.

very different conceptions of what is involved.[13] The following sums up Mahoney's view of the matter. With the technique of causal narrative, he writes:

the analyst attempts to validate aggregated cross-case associations by "breaking apart" variables into constituent sequences of disaggregated events and comparing these disaggregated sequences across time. The purpose of unpacking aggregated variables through narrative is not only to provide a contextualized description of cases; rather, the goal is to support a cross-case argument at a more disaggregated level.

This technique relies on historical narrative . . . However, the procedures through which analysts decide whether a narrative account lends support to a causal pattern have not been well specified . . . Event-structure analysis is the most developed statement on how narrative can be wedded to causal inference. (2003: 365f.)

Two problems may be noticed. First, disaggregation, a reductionist strategy, is intended to provide temporality, but as Sewell writes (following Burawoy), "by fracturing the congealed block of historical time into artificially interchangeable units," history is "frozen" (1996: 258); the temporality assumed, as Sewell says, is akin to the sort available in experimental contexts. This is not merely a matter of "grouping events" so as to compare slices of history, but a matter of eliminating time as process. As Burawoy insists, it fails to make sense of unique and sequentially unfolding processes within cases. Second, "causal patterns" established by nominal and ordinal methods are to be given "support" by means of narrative, but how "narrative" is to do this remains unclear, except to notice that there is a "complex trade-off" between "the clarity of informal narrative presentations and the rigor of explicitly diagrammed narrative accounts" (Mahoney, 2003: 367). Mahoney's efforts at "explicit diagrams" simply do not translate into causal narratives – except as chronologies, exactly because we have conjunctions and not causes, realistically understood. That is, instead of a causal story, we have "a series of connected events." One might note, as well, that common sense overcomes the most careful of writers. In moving to narrative, it is very easy to lapse, inconsistently, into hints of references to causal mechanisms, to promissory notes unfulfilled. Indeed, despite the "official" doctrine regarding causality, such

---

[13] Sewell helpfully identifies three ways that temporality is conceptualized: "teleological temporality" "experimental temporality" and "eventful temporality." We do not consider here "teleological temporality" which aims "to abstract transhistorical processes leading to some future historical state" (1996: 247). By now, it is hard to find anybody who would defend this idea although it may be in the background of some accounts. But "experimental temporality" conforms nicely to Mahoney's view of the matter, while the option defended here conforms to Sewell's "eventful temporality."

references are commonplace in both the social science literature and in ordinary thought and discourse.

A very different concept follows from rejection of the Humean notion of causality assumed in the foregoing. Briefly, explaining outcomes requires seeing how, through time, events and decisions were constrained and enabled by prevailing social mechanisms (processes). The only way to do this is with a historical narrative which integrates actions, events and mechanisms into an evidentially convincing "story."[14] On this view, comparative method is still employed, but it is not employed to find necessary and sufficient conditions, but rather, to identify the causal mechanisms at work in particular cases.

The difference in these conceptions of "causal narrative" is at the root of the debate between Sewell and Skocpol. As Mahoney says, Skocpol *did* employ nominal and ordinal methods, and she *did* employ narrative, but as argued here, Mill's methods did not and could not yield the outcomes that she had hoped for. On the other hand, her narrative fits very well into the description in the previous paragraph. Sewell rightly remarks that "the bulk of her book is composed not of a rigorous weighing of comparative evidence but of carefully constructed causal narratives specifying how social revolutions are brought about in her three cases" (1996: 260). And as he points out, the best statement of her narrative strategy is in a footnote, where she says: "social scientific analyses of revolutions are never . . . given sufficient analytic weight to the conjunctural, unfolding interactions of originally separately determined processes" (Skocpol, 1979: 320, quoted by Sewell, 1996: 260). Indeed, if we drop all talk of identifying the "sufficient distinctive causes" of social revolutions by means of Mill's methods, what remains of Skocpol's book is, as Sewell agrees, of considerable value.

One of the strengths of Skocpol's account is response to what she takes to be the existing social scientific theories of revolution. For her, "in contrast to modes of explanation used by currently prevalent theories, social revolutions should be analyzed from a structural perspective" (1979: 5). But this means that explanatory generalizations have been abandoned for a realist conception of explanation. She does not give a systematic analysis of her use of the concept of structure, but it is clearly influenced by Marx, and clearly, the "currently prevalent theories" to which her structuralism is opposed are the ones she refers to as "aggregate-psychological theories." Nevertheless, from what she does say about structure, and more

---

[14] Describing an account as a "story" identifies its rhetorical moves. Despite post-modernist appropriations, "stories" may be assessed for their truth-value, here a function of evidence, plausibility and coherence. But indeed, there may be several quite good, convincing, plausible accounts. See Hexter, 1971.

crucially, how it functions in her account, it is possible to make some important inferences about what she has in mind. For her, structures are determinate relations, objective and impersonal. They "condition," "shape" and "limit" situated actors, though they are not to be identified with the actual actions or transactions of acting agents. Structures also have a "dynamic" and a "logic" and these can be discovered (see especially pages 14ff.).

But indeed, if we think of "structure" in terms of the analysis of mechanisms as explored in chapter 4, we will have all the advantages of her structuralist perspective and none of the patent disadvantages. That is, we reject "voluntarism" because agents are always both enabled and constrained, whether they are the typical actors of "structures" ("financiers," members of the "dominant class," etc.) or the acts of monarchs and powerful others who, in C. Wright Mills's terms, make decisions of major social importance. We reject reified "structure" and do not give it causal status. Instead, social mechanisms are sustained (and transformed) by the actions of persons, represented typically. But while acts are both constrained and enabled, they are not "determined." This holds as regards the actions of typical actors and as regards the causally consequential acts of critical individuals or groups. Contingency remains a critical feature of the actual outcome.

Skocpol was not insensitive to this problem. It would be addressed in her narratives of each of the cases, both with promissory notes of mechanisms and by identifying critical decisions by critical actors.[15] For example, after noting that "most Bourbon kings had survived debt and bankruptcy," she wonders why "the troubles of Louis XVI developed into a major crisis" (1979: 63). The mechanism (in the way of a promissory note) is fairly straightforward: in the past the Chambers of Justice had been able to cancel debts to financiers. But when "high accountants" became "nobility" and merged with the traditional ruling class,

---

[15] Skocpol notes that Sewell was "correct to say that I should have devoted more space in 1979 to discussing the methodological connections between the comparative structural and the conjunctural-narrative aspects of the investigations and presentations that went into *States and Social Revolutions*" and notes also that "a very similar point was made years ago by Peter Manicas, 1981, in one of the best reviews originally written about my book" (1994: 333). Manicas appreciates her generosity but would now be clearer that the problem was trying to combine structural / conjunctural analysis – including the contingent acts of key identifiable agents – with "explanatory generalizations" aimed at providing "the sufficient causes of social revolution." On the other hand, if Sewell believes that "the narrative achievements of *States and Social Revolutions* exist – or could have been arrived at – apart from the macrocausal comparative analysis" (1994: 313) he is, as she insists, "dead wrong." The macro-causal analysis did not, as Sewell rightly sees, provide the necessary and sufficient conditions for social revolutions. But at least as I read him, he does not deny the importance of comparison properly conceived.

this was no longer possible. When the costs of war mounted, there was, accordingly, a financial crisis. But a financial crisis, too, might have been managed. In turn, in 1787, another mechanism comes into play: "news of the monarchy's financial peril precipitated a general crisis of confidence within the dominant class" (1979: 64). But the narrative is still radically incomplete. Thus, "as everyone knows, the summoning of the Estates-General [by the king] served not to solve the royal financial crisis but to launch the Revolution" (1979: 65). Her narrative is replete with instances of this sort. Indeed, no explanation of a social outcome can do entirely without reference to the causal mechanisms sustained and transformed by the actions of (typical) persons and the causal consequences of major actors. And the story will always be complex – and incomplete.

The role of comparison

As regards the uses of comparisons in historical sociology, we may conclude with a useful observation of Skocpol. She wrote that:

"comparative history" is commonly used rather loosely to refer to any and all studies in which two or more historical trajectories of nation-states, institutional complexes, or civilizations are juxtaposed. In this very broad sense, the term refers to studies with very different kinds of purposes. Some . . . are meant to show that a particular general sociological model holds across different national contexts. Other studies . . . use comparisons primarily to bring out contrast among nations and civilizations taken as synthetic wholes. But there is a third version . . . in which the overriding intent is to develop, test, and refine causal, explanatory hypotheses about events or structures integral to macro-units such as nation-states. (1979: 36)

We agree with Skocpol that the first purpose, to show that a general model holds, cannot be sustained (see chapter 5). The second purpose is too narrow. First, there is no reason to restrict comparisons to nations or civilizations understood as synthetic wholes. Of considerable importance is the effort to compare social mechanisms, paths and processes, both for their "resemblances" and for their differences. Second, one obvious goal is to explain these differences – as Weber and Moore insisted. The third version, then, is correct – if one abandons the covering law model and instead thinks of "causal explanatory hypotheses" as hypotheses about social causal mechanisms.

The comparative method, accordingly, serves a variety of roles, but it does not yield explanatory generalizations: it does suggest causal hypotheses (hypotheses about causal mechanisms) and, as Skocpol says, "comparative historical analysis does provide a valuable check, or anchor, for theoretical speculation" (1979: 39). She was correct in describing her effort as following the path set out by Barrington Moore, but as I have tried to show (chapter 5), Moore was fundamentally Weberian in his approach to historical explanation. His narratives gave causal accounts of three paths to modernization; Skocpol offered narratives of three paths to modern social revolution. As argued, in the different paths, there will always be "resemblances" and there will always be important differences.

Skocpol's conclusions were modest. She asked whether the "broad resemblances" she identified could be applied beyond the three cases of her focus, and answered, "unequivocally 'no'." She gives two reasons. Firstly, as Mills insisted, "the mechanisms of change . . . vary with the social structure we are examining" and second, "patterns of revolutionary causation and outcomes are necessarily affected by world-historical changes in the fundamental structures and bases of state power as such" (1979: 288). But why stop here? Why not assert that this is true of *all* history, *all* cases, *all* structures? "Resemblances" are just that: they are neither sufficient nor necessary conditions. They do not explain.

Sewell, in summarizing what he called, "eventful sociology," summarizes matters well enough:

Sociology's epic quest for social laws is illusory, whether the search is for timeless truth about all societies, ineluctable trends of more limited historical epochs, or inductively derived laws of certain classes of social phenomena. Social processes . . . are inherently contingent, discontinuous, and open-ended. Big and ponderous social processes are never entirely immune from being transformed by small alterations in volatile and local social processes. "Structures" are constructed by human action, and "societies" or "social formations" or "social systems" are continually shaped and reshaped by the creativity and stubbornness of their human creators. (1996: 272)

Appendix C   Rational choice theory and historical sociology

Rational choice theory (RCT) has become an important part of the debate not only in general sociology but in historical sociology in particular. This appendix picks up on several themes of previous chapters and in terms of them examines a very recent and lively debate, occurring both in the pages of *The American Journal of Sociology (AJS)* and in a recently edited volume.[1] This will, hopefully, both sharpen the issues and provide further evidence of the pervasive legacy of empiricist philosophy of science.

The *AJS* debate: realism and causality

Craig Calhoun (1998) notes correctly that a key point of difference between this debate and the earlier debates is agreement by the contending parties on the centrality of causal explanations in historical sociology, and, in particular, the acceptance of "the more recently fashionable label of 'realist' philosophy of science" (1998: 847). There are two critical questions here.

In this debate, in marked contrast to earlier ones, no one on the panel defends what Skocpol called "interpretative historical sociology." In their 1991 essay, Kiser and Hector had asserted that there is "wide agreement . . . across social science that causality is the first requirement of an adequate explanation" (1991: 4). This is a highly dubious empirical claim (as noticed by both Somers and Calhoun).[2] It rules out, by fiat,

---

[1] The symposium in *The American Journal of Sociology* (vol. 104, November 1998) had its genesis in a panel on history and theory at the 1989 meetings of the American Sociological Association. Drafts circulated among a number of important writers. The result was the *AJS* Symposium which has contributions by Margaret Somers, Edgar Kiser, Michael Hector, Craig Calhoun and Jack Goldstone. In what follows, unless otherwise noted, references to these writers are from the published symposium. See also Roger V. Gould (ed.), 2004.

[2] Calhoun (1998) is probably correct that even among those who think of explanation in terms of causes, there is little critical reflection of what this means – a point addressed in much of the present volume. Indeed, as he later writes, following Boudon, "most of what passes for causal analysis in the social sciences is in fact identification of more or less 'weak implication' between statistical variables" (1998: 866).

all interpretative sociology, a still important alternate conception of the human sciences.

As argued in chapter 3, interpretativists are not wrong in insisting on the importance of meaning and hence of ideas in their explanatory efforts: the question is whether, as Weber insisted, these need to be part of a larger causal argument. Interpretativists rightly rejected the dominating empiricist framework for explanation, including Humean causality and the covering law model, but seeing no alternative consistent with their understanding of human action, they threw the baby out with the bath water.

This is the second critical feature of the *AJS* argument. Both parties, Kiser and Hector, and Somers, say that they are "realists." This suggests that the once dominating empiricist philosophy of science is on the wane – at least among some sociologists. As with Kiser and Hector's claim regarding explanation, this too is doubtful – at least if realism includes some key theses regarding explanation. Realism, understood as an ontological position, holds that the real is not restricted to what is "in experience." Accordingly, as argued in chapter 1, causal mechanisms can be non-observable. This is a healthy step in the right direction, but will not, of itself, excite either most social scientists or most ordinary people. As a consequence of its ontological position, realism is also an epistemological position which can (and generally does) accept now-standard Kuhnian criticisms of empiricist epistemology. Both parties to the *AJS* debate suggest they have very different views on this – a point to which I return. But the most obvious problem with their realism is the idea of causality, and, in consequence, their "realist" views of explanation.

It is not clear whether the writers in the symposium have fully ingested a realist concept of causality, the burden of chapter 1 of this volume.[3] As argued in chapter 1, on a realist conception, causes are *productive* powers that *bring about* outcomes. They may be expressed in singular causal statements, e.g., "Sam crushed the cracker," or as promissory notes of mechanisms: "The iron rusted because it oxidized." The mechanism here, of course, is fully developed in molecular chemistry. In neither case are causal statements to be understood as law-like contingent regularities. It follows, accordingly, that explanation does not take the form of the covering law model. This is clearly seen by Somers. Kiser and Hector

---

[3] Calhoun notes that Kiser and Hector make no use of the work of Roy Bhaskar. Somers does, but rejects exactly what is at the heart of Bhaskar's account: "that causality is found in an entity's *essential properties* (1998: note 13, 743f.). See below. Neither party seems aware of the extensive development of realist causality in the work of Rom Harré (1970, 1975), and with special reference to social science, Varela and Harré (1996).

are less clear. Thus, Calhoun reads them as follows: "When Kiser and Hecter refer to explanation, they take it for granted that it means causal explanation in a covering law model" (1998: 856). There is a good deal of textual evidence for this in their 1991 paper, but little in their 1998 essay. In the 1991 essay, the problem would seem to result from their understanding of causality – which in the intervening years may have shifted. For example, in 1991, they wrote: "Causal uniformity implies the existence of law-like relationships that hold between events . . . In essence, causal explanation works by subsuming events under causal laws . . . and causal laws, in turn derive from general theories" (1991: 6).

Since realist causality is *not* understood in terms of law-like relations between events, and thus causal explanation is *not* subsumption of events under law-like statements, these remarks leave little room for doubt – at least as regards their posture in 1991. Somers, with considerable justification, insists that Kiser and Hector incoherently accept both the idea of scientific explanation by the covering law model *and* of explanation by means of "abstract models" of mechanisms – a distinctly realist move. Chapter 1 of the present volume offers arguments that indeed, these are inconsistent. The fundamental problem can be summarized here: the covering law model holds that the explanandum is a *logical consequence* of the explicans; the realist view defended in this volume insists that this is the wrong relationship: we explain when we know what *produced* the outcome.[4]

The problem is compounded by the fact that, despite their frequent use of the term, none of the writers in the symposium provides a clear idea of what they mean by "causal mechanism." Kiser and Hector note that, at least in the natural sciences, "mechanisms typically explain outcomes by invoking phenomena at a level of analysis lower than that of the outcome

[4] Calhoun says that "rational choice theory has played an important role in encouraging more emphasis on causal mechanisms alongside covering laws or causal relationships," suggesting that he accepts that the two ideas can cohere. But he also notes that "Kiser and Hector are actually somewhat vague about what is involved here" (1998: 5, 851). As Calhoun suggests, much is at stake here. The remainder of his note is helpful, but especially his observation that "their language shifts a bit between seeing the mechanisms as necessarily deduced from lawlike statements, and as simply being lawlike statements but of a different order from relationships of implication or correlation" (1998: note 5, 851). Seeing mechanisms as "necessarily deduced from lawlike statements" suggests fundamental misunderstanding. Law-like statements entail nothing about the nature of the mechanisms. What they are is the problem of theory and, as always, theory is underdetermined by "facts," including confirmed "law-like" statements. Nor is it helpful to say that mechanisms are "law-like" statements of "different order," even where *aspects* of mechanisms can be represented mathematically. See chapter 1 and references there. But it is correct to say that causal statements are of a different order from relationships of implication (as in the D-N model) or "correlations."

of concern" (1998: 790). But in part at least, because of their lingering commitments to the covering law model, there is no attention paid to how a realist understanding of causality and theory gives us understanding. Somers does better by providing an example. Thus, "since food has calories, and calories are energy, when we reduce our intake then the body has less energy to draw from external sources so it has to turn to internal sources, which are stores of fat, and the body uses up fat when it draws that energy, and so forth" (1998: 770). This is, as she says, a "causal narrative." It takes for granted a host of undetailed causal mechanisms represented by a host of theoretical ideas. Presumably, there will be an analog in social science.

General theory?

Kiser and Hector (1998) see themselves as following a more or less standard realist account of theory. Thus, they endorse the following two definitions: "[Theories] are causal explanations providing *intelligible* answers to why-questions about *empirical facts*"; and, "theory can be taken to mean a set of assumptions or postulates with which one approaches some part of the empirical world, and a set of propositions, emerging from the assumptions and relating the concepts, about the way this part of the world 'works,' which is checked against observations of that world" (1998: 793, note 20). These formulations smack somewhat of deductivism, but are sufficiently vague to be interpreted in realist terms. As above, we need to know more about how theory represents "mechanisms" and how they explain.

But there is a prior problem, regarding the question of "general theory" and exactly what Kiser and Hector mean by this. It is important to be clear about this since it may well be that while there are perfectly adequate theories of specific historically grounded mechanisms which produce specific historically bounded outcomes, there may be no useful or interesting *general* theories which apply willy-nilly to such outcomes. This is Somers's view of the matter, shared, as noted, by Skocpol (chapter 5, above) and the present writer. The position of Kiser and Hector is far from clear.

Compare here, molecular chemistry and Marx's *Capital*. Molecular chemistry is surely a general theory in the sense that it provides an account of mechanisms which apply to *all matter qua chemical, everywhere and anywhen*: the mechanisms are omnitemporal. But the theory articulated in Marx's *Capital* applies *only* to capitalist societies. Nor indeed can the mechanisms theorized there be "generalized" to offer an understanding of non-capitalist political economies.

Kiser and Hector write: "Although philosophers of science consider mechanisms to be abstract and omnitemporal (Bunge 1996), our critics [viz. Somers, etc.] prefer them to be historically specific" (1998: 796). But, contrary to Kiser and Hector, philosophers of science must surely consider whether the absence of omnitemporal mechanisms in social science may be the consequence of a key point of difference in the ontologies of the natural and the social world. A main goal of the present volume has been to show that explanation (and understanding) in both domains requires an account of mechanisms. But it has also been a major theme to note that there are important disanalogies which stem from ontological considerations.

Kiser and Hector want us to be clear that "the principal claim of [their] article was that general theory is useful in historical explanations since it is an important source of causal explanations. General theories provide both the omnitemporal laws [*sic*] that animate contextual models . . . and the guidelines necessary to attack particular substantive problems" (1998: 793). This is puzzling, but especially the idea that we need "omnitemporal law" and that these "animate contextual models." Kiser and Hector do not help their cause, partly at least because of confusion over whether or not they remain committed to the covering law model.

But a footnote follows the text just quoted. It opens new possibilities. They write, quoting Kuhn: " 'General theories' supply the group with preferred or permissible analogues and metaphors. By doing so they help to determine what will be accepted as an explanation and as a puzzle-solution; conversely, they assist in the determination of the roster of unsolved puzzles and the evaluation of the importance of each" (Kiser and Hector, 1998: note 21, quoting Kuhn, 1970: 184). The text quoted from Kuhn does not speak of "general theories." It speaks specifically of "models," "heuristic" and "ontological," and in the context Kuhn is plainly referring to what he was calling, following his abandonment of the fuzzy notion of a "paradigm," "the disciplinary matrix." This is an important Kuhnian point, now very much a part of current sociology of science and realist theory of science (Pickering, 1992).

If "general theories" are "disciplinary matrices," then the puzzlement can be overcome. Thus, within the Kuhnian frame, the social sciences are marked by the existence of *competing* disciplinary matrices. Kiser and Hector aim at offering what was termed in the present volume, a meta-theory for a human science: an effort to set out what *should* be accepted as an explanation and as a puzzle-solution in social science. Indeed, they are very clear in asserting that, for them, "all good sociological explanations must consist of separate arguments pertaining, first, to the *motives* of individual actors and, second, to *models* of the contexts within which their action takes place" (1998: 799–80). On this reading, their "general theory" tells us where to look for causes and what a *social* mechanism must include. And on this reading, RCT is but one of a family of possible "agent-as-mechanism" theories – including strong versions which effectively deny history. Of course, agents omnitemporally are motivated and have productive powers – indeed, this assumption is "essential" to our understanding of persons. But it allows for the generation of a number of alternative theories of mechanisms including, plainly, those which are historically grounded and limited in their application. It provides, as Kiser and Hector claim, a source which can "animate contextual models . . . and the guidelines necessary to attack particular substantive problems" (1998: 793). Similarly, ruled out are alternative "general theories" – disciplinary matrices, meta-theories – that look elsewhere for causes, for example, in social structures.[5]

Also puzzling is their idea that "the mechanisms derived from general theories are generalizable – they can be used in different substantive areas and historical periods" (1998: 706). Here they may be thinking of strong ahistorical versions of RCT. In any case, one wonders whether generalization is being confused with abstraction. That is, moving from the concrete to the abstract (abstraction) should not be confused with moving from a particular instance to a generalization about all such instances. Thus, it would be an error to argue that, for example, the mechanism identified which explains unemployment in Japan can be applied to understanding unemployment in the USA – or worse, the People's Republic of China. On the other hand, in the case of the USA and Japan – but not China – Marx's highly abstract account of the mechanism of capitalism is true of all and only capitalisms. It would be implicated in developing the mechanisms of unemployment in Japan and the USA – but again, not of China. That is, since for good historical reasons, Japanese and US capitalism are *concretely different* in critically relevant ways, the mechanism which explains Japanese unemployment will be different to the one which explains unemployment in the USA even if capitalist mechanisms are working in both. Similarly, assume that a principle of an abstract mechanism is the (Hobbesian) idea that people seek power. If this is not vacuous (as is often the case), then to give it explanatory bite, one must specify the particular conditions of persons, their specific motives and capacities. For example, even if at some high level of abstraction people seek power, the social mechanism which explains monarchic succession

---

[5] This reading may well be rejected by Kiser and Hector. If so, then perhaps there remains a lingering covering law view.

will be very different to the one explaining succession of the chief executive in a republic.

There are, as noted, alternative "general theories" ("disciplinary matrices"). Parsonian "general theory" is one obvious candidate.[6] It gives an omnitemporal conception of society as an ensemble of connected systems, each having distinct functions. It tells us the explanation proceeds by identifying the concrete instantiations of these and then showing how dysfunctions arise between, for example, the structure of the personality system and the social system. Indeed, while she might deny it, Somers inescapably also has a "general theory" – understood here as a metatheory which defines what a good sociological explanation must consist of. As noted, Kiser and Hector insist that "all good sociological explanations must consist of separate arguments pertaining, first, to the *motives* of individual actors and, second, to *models* of the contexts within which their action takes place" (1998: 799f.). This is precisely what is denied by Somers. Unfortunately, the debate got mis-couched as a debate over rational choice theory. We need to clarify this and then to set out her alternative. Finally, there is the question of what role, if any, narrative has to play in explanation in historical sociology.

Assessing the debate

We should notice, first, that the Kiser / Hector conception of what all good sociological explanations must consist of is perfectly consistent with the argument of chapter 4 (above); second, that it rejects alternative conceptions, e.g., functionalist theory; and that, third, as Somers argues, it inevitably includes a number of ontological commitments. One can reject these, to be sure, but if so, then some alternative set of commitments must be made.[7] Somers understands perfectly well the ontological commitments of the Kiser / Hector metatheory – even if they are sometimes expressed by her in a somewhat distorted fashion.

---

[6] No doubt the idea of "general theory" is a sociological invention spurred by Parsonian universalistic theorizing. Merton (1957) famously argued that sociology needed "theories of the middle range," theories which were suggested by "general theory," but were designed to address the historically concrete. And of course, Merton remained within structural functionalism.

[7] Somers writes: "the protestations of some social scientists notwithstanding, all theories of knowledge make a more or less explicit ontological choice between either the individual or the social structure as the basic unit of social analysis" (1998: 750). The argument of the present volume took the side of "the individual" as the sole causal power in society, but insisted also that a Giddens-type explication of social structure gave us all that we needed to avoid the pitfalls of "methodological individualism." But it would seem to follow that if Somers rejects agents as causes, then social structure does the explaining.

Thus, she writes that there is "a commitment to a causal ontology in which agential intentionality is posited the a priori causal force / mechanism at work in the social world" (1998: 750). Indeed, agential intentionality *is* posited as the causal force at work in the social world, but, we may ask why is this posit a priori? Surely, *everything* in experience says that agents are causes and that action is "intentional," even if it is not always self-conscious and even if its consequences were not intended?[8]

Some of her criticisms seem sound, but *not* versus the fundamental idea that agents are causes or that causal mechanisms must be models of the contexts within which action takes place. Her criticism is apt versus a version of rational choice theory – at least as she understands it. Thus, she attacks "essentialism" and a Hobbesian "pre-social" conception that posits "not only fixed solipsistic identities but ontological entities that are born preequipped to act through essential inherent causal mechanisms (reasons as causes) that drive action on their own autonomous momentum" (1998: 764). But there is nothing in an agent-centered ontology – including interesting versions of RCT – which *requires* that persons are "pre-social" or that they have fixed solipsistic identities. And, of course, people do act for reasons, and as argued in chapter 2, reasons are quite properly conceived as causes.

To be sure, a good deal of RCT is Hobbesian and does err in precisely the ways that Rousseau said that Hobbesian theory erred.[9] On the other hand, if sufficiently weakened, then while it sees that agents are causes, it is not clear whether it is any longer the theory that it claims to be.[10]

"Theoretical realism" and "relational realism"

These terms are Somers's and, as Kiser and Hector rightly see, "despite her claim that we share a commitment to epistemological realism, our philosophical differences with Somers are profound" (1998: 88). The main concern in this section is to examine the ontology which Somers offers as the alternative to the "agents as mechanism" ontology of Kiser

---

[8] Nor is it clear what could be meant by saying that the causal powers of agents is "exogenous" (1998: 750), except perhaps that she thinks of agent causality in mentalistic terms. Thus, "the explanatory work of the theory is carried out by this invariant causal mechanism of a dispositional agential intentionality that necessarily (in the absence of constraint) causes intents to convert to actions be they rational or irrational" (1998: 751). Again, actors have reasons for their actions and reasons are quite legitimately causes. But this does not require a Cartesian metaphysics. Indeed, it is inconsistent with one.

[9] In his too often unread "Discourse on the Origin of Inequality."

[10] Among examples are the writings on so-called "exchange theory," for example, Blau, 1964 and Coleman 1988, 1990. See also Chai, 2001.

and Hector. But to do this we need to say more about the two realisms as Somers sees them.

First, Somers seems to believe that a post-positivist, post-Kuhnian epistemology distinguishes "theoretical realism" from "relational realism." But this is hardly clear. On the one hand, despite her rejection of the idea that theory aims to represent reality as it is in-itself, she also holds that "relational realists believe in the importance of determining which theories more closely represent reality" (1998: 745).[11] So there is no argument between Somers and Kiser and Hector on this score. And she acknowledges that realists who hold to the view that theory aims to represent reality, for example, Bhaskar, are also "agnostic about the absolute truth of any given theory about the world" (1998: 744). So, despite occasional hyperbole in her attacks aimed at Kiser and Hector's "theoretical realism," this too is a non-issue. Finally, both parties can agree on by now standard criticisms of the empiricist epistemology, including the turn taken by post-Kuhnian sociologists and philosophers of scientific knowledge. They can, accordingly, reject Baconian conceptions of induction, Popperian notions of falsification and assent to the Kuhnian idea that "only certain types of mechanisms are deemed plausible by the relevant scientific community at any given time" (Kiser and Hector, 1991: 6).

Difference in the two views is most pronounced when Somers says, for example, that "there are no universally valid principles of logical reasoning; there are only problem-driven ones" (1998: 766), and in her denial of "essentialism," "a philosophy which looks to the 'essence' of things for information about their 'true' nature and behavior" (1998: 764). These are substantial differences, and indeed, Kiser and Hector infer, not unreasonably, that if logic is "culture bound," then Somers is committed to a radically relativist epistemological position – a position which in other places she would seem to disavow. More importantly, perhaps, given her views on these issues, it is not clear that her "relational realism" can sustain a plausible account of scientific practice as that is

---

[11] She also writes that the two realisms differ in that "while theoretical realism attributes an ontological truth to the *theoretical* phenomenon (e.g., the theory of electrons or the theory of market equilibrium), relational realism focuses on the relational effect of the phenomenon itself (e.g., the impact of the hypothesized electron on its environment or of the hypothesized market forces on an observable datum)" (1998: 745). This is puzzling. The remark smacks of an empiricist understanding of theoretical entities as "convenient fictions." But surely, if the electron is to have "impact," then it must exist. Mechanisms can explain empirical outcomes *only if* theorized entities and their powers are part of the ontology of the theory. On the other hand, Somers's criticism of explanations provided by neo-classical theory takes exactly this position. She writes that one cannot explain prices in terms of managerial decisions based on marginal costs, exactly because no manager "has the slightest idea of what the marginal cost of producing something really is." She rightly insists: "For a cause to explain, the cause really has to exist" (1998: 770).

currently understood by realist philosophy or sociology of scientific knowledge (Hacking, 1992, 2000). Otherwise, since they draw on now widely accepted criticisms of positivist philosophy of science, some of the attacks on Kiser and Hector's efforts to identify criteria for theory accept-ability are well-placed.[12] At the same time, much of the initial plausibility of Somers's alternative to the views of Kiser and Hector is stimulated by her effort to draw from the work of Kuhn, including, importantly, her main claims regarding "path dependency and causal narrativity in explanatory structure" (1998: 731).[13]

But before looking at this important line of thought, we need to exam-ine Somers's relational realist ontological alternative to the ontology of "agents-as-mechanisms." There is, unfortunately, very little to help us here. She writes:

> Beginning with the postulate that we are neither monads nor self-propelling enti-ties but "contingent, transitory connections among social constructed identities" (Tilly 1995: 1595), a relational pragmatist ontology takes the basic units of social analysis to be neither individual agents (agent, actor, person, firm) nor structural wholes (society, order, social structure) but the relational processes of interaction between and among identities. (1998: 767)

As already noted, there is nothing in the program of defenders of an agent-centered approach which requires that persons are "monads" (self-contained, complete and independent) and, consequently, there is nothing which requires denying either that identities are socially con-structed or that persons stand in relations that are themselves contingent and changing. Of course, if self-propelling means capable of acting, then persons surely are self-propelling. So it is not clear that her postulate counts as an argument – even the beginnings of an argument in favor of her alternative ontology.

It is clear that Somers wants to reject views that "solve" agent / structure dualism by eliminating either pole of the dichotomy; but for all her good intentions, she seems very much to generate a structuralist ontology which (following on her rejection of the ontology of Kiser and Hector) does eliminate agency.[14] Indeed, it is difficult to see what sort of mechanism she has in mind. She writes that "the basic mechanisms of causality are

---

[12] See Goldstone's helpful comments on these issues. Some of Somers's criticisms of "theoretical realism" depend on what are probably distortions of the views of Kiser and Hector, as they insist.

[13] Somers must be complimented for offering some novel insights here, but one can doubt very much her claims regarding much of Kuhn's legacy. For example, a good deal of anti-realist, even post-modernist anti-science thinking owes to readings of Kuhn. Some of the writings of Richard Rorty are good examples of this.

[14] Some of her remarks on this score are difficult to understand. Thus, her first "limiting principle" is that "belief in the causal power of a theoretical social dynamic (e.g., gender,

not within discrete agents, but in the *pathways of agential interaction . . .*"
(1998: 768). The key word here would seem to be "pathways" since
plainly the "agents-as-mechanisms" view focuses on "agential interaction."[15] What, then, is the force of "pathways"? Worse, she seems to step
into a very Hegelian sort of trap. She writes:

In place of a language of essences and inherent causal properties, a relational
realism substitutes a language of networks and relationships that are not pre-
determined but made the indeterminate objects of investigation. Relational
subjects are not related to one another in the weak sense of being only empirically contiguous; they are ontologically related such that an identity can only
be deciphered by virtue of its 'place' in relation to other identities in its web.
(1998: 767)

On its face, this seems inconsistent with the text quoted from Tilly
regarding "contingent, transitory connections among social constructed
identities." It would seem, at least, that if relations are "contingent and
transitory," they cannot be ontologically related. Indeed, her view seems
at least to takes us straight to the age-old ontological debate pressed by historical idealism: the pertinence of "internal" versus "external relations."[16]
Hegel (and Hegelian Marxists) hold that *all* relations are internal: the
truth is the whole. This is, accordingly, a profoundly relational conception of reality. Empiricists, by contrast, hold that all relations are external
and nothing is essential in the world. Realists hold that there are internal
relations, e.g., sister / brother, capitalist / wage worker, and these are a
critical part of understanding their "dynamics."[17] How all this bears on
questions of "identity," however, is quite another matter.

---

utility maximization, class struggle) is independent from belief in any *one* particular
theory" (1998: 766). This would seem to mean that her favored ontology is theory-
neutral – which, of course, it is not. If sexism and class struggle cannot be understood
in terms of the actions of agents working with materials at hand, then how are they to be
understood? Similarly, "a relational realist would use pragmatic reasoning to argue that
despite fate or fashion of any particular theoretical concept such as 'sex roles,' 'sexual
division of labor,' or 'gender' – each of which represents a different causal conception
of an unobservable postulated reality – we have reason to believe in the causal force of
that which terms variously attempt to signify largely for one reason: When we dress a
baby in blue, we can observe that people treat that baby differently than when we dress
that same baby in pink" (1998: 744). Fine, but which theory of mechanism gives us an
understanding of this?

[15] In a footnote, she observes that her relational realism "finds an analytic home in network
theory" (1998: note 29, 768), but one can still ask for the mechanisms, and one can still
offer an agent-as-mechanism account.

[16] A relation *aRb* is internal if both *a* and *b* are what they are by virtue of standing in
the relation *aRb*. By contrast, a relation *aRb* is external if *a* and *b* are what they are
independently of R.

[17] Similarly as regards "natural kinds." Something would not be salt unless it dissolved in
water. See Kripke, 1982.

The metaphysics of history

It seems clear enough that Somers wants very much to preserve contingency in history, but it is not clear how this is to be understood. The problem is the idea of *path dependence*. Goldstone points out, first, that the term is appropriated from contexts in which path dependence is a property of a system understood in a strict sense.[18] But unless Somers is assuming that society is a system in this sense, then we must assume that this is rather more a metaphor. But the main idea of path dependence as metaphor is not obvious: it cannot be, presumably, that once one has started on a path one is fated to continue on it. This makes "paths" freeways for which there are no exits![19] Something more like the following would seem appropriate: since "structure" is incarnate in action, and this is always the product of history, there will be both change and continuity in history. Path dependency then would seem to reduce to the near truism that even with change, there is continuity and that the past cannot be undone. Dramatic changes do occur, of course, and these do sometimes mark a new path in the sense that some important former possibilities are foreclosed and others become possible. Beginning a war is an obvious example. As regards the systems Goldstone refers to, we can speak of "another run." But this makes no sense in history. Nor is there any set of "initial conditions" from which history proceeds, not only because there is no Day One, but because *every* act and event contributes to the "making" of history. On the present view, since it draws on assumptions alien to historical analysis, "path dependence" is at best a misleading metaphor. "Paths" are historical legacies which enable and constrain current action; but since we are not "locked into paths," they are not determining of the future.

Somers also rightly sees that, in history, there are neither laws nor sets of conditions from which one makes deterministic calculations. Thus, Goldstone suggests that

[18] Goldstone summarizes: "Path dependence is a property of a system such that the outcome over a period of time is *not determined* by any particular set of initial conditions. Rather, a system that exhibits path dependency is one in which outcomes are related stochastically to initial conditions, and the particular outcome that obtains in any given 'run' of the system depends on the choices or outcomes of intermediate events between the initial conditions and the outcome" (1998: 834). But nothing in this involves the effort to explain the choices or outcomes of intermediate events.

[19] See also Lawson (1997: 251) who writes: "My worry is that, without due care to the way it is presented, the approach defended allows, even encourages, the inference that once an account is provided of how a form of social organization or a technology became established, this is more or less the end of serious inquiry . . . It facilitates the view that once a technology or social structure is in place then it can be treated as locked-in for good; that the past is not only ever present but also all determining."

what Somers and other critics of RCT are reacting to is the tendency of some practitioners of RCT to grossly simplify the actual complexity of initial conditions in order to make deterministic calculations of social outcomes . . . Many sets of initial conditions and interactions are indeterminate – like the path dependence of a Polya urn. For most RCT theorists, such problems are uninteresting . . . This difference in interests is precisely what causes the conflict or miscommunication between theoretical economists and economic historians. (1998: 840)

But the difference is here much more than a matter of "interests." The deeper reasons are differences in explanation and in the metaphysics of history. That is, RCT theorists, like mathematical economists, accept the D-N model, are ahistorical and fail to see the consequences of the absence of closure. One has a "determined" outcome by calculating an outcome from a premise set, but, as the historian insists, this is not how historical outcomes get produced or explained.

"General laws" and mechanisms

To explain some *actual* outcome, one needs to go back in time and identify sequentially the pertinent causes as they combined to produce the outcome. This will require a narrative which links critical actions and events with ongoing social processes grasped in terms of social mechanisms.

Goldstone argues that we need "laws" to do this. He offers illustratively the RCT "law" that "people seek to maximize their well-being, usually defined in terms of wealth, power, or status, through their interactions with other people" (1998: 833). First, there is a persistent temptation in this case (and others like it) to reduce laws to tautologies: anything counts as an instance of power-seeking.[20] Second, this "law-like" assertion is a generalization, not a law, since, if it is not a tautology, there is nothing "nomic" about it.[21] To be sure, it may still be a useful *generalization*: some acts do proceed from power-seeking motives. Goldstone insists that

---

[20] There is a section in Weber's *Roscher und Knies* (1975) where he has great fun with the idea of "laws" in historical explanation. He refers to a verse by the humorist Busch which goes as follows: "Whoever is pleased whenever he is distressed makes himself, on the whole, unpopular." Weber notes that Busch correctly sees that this is not "a necessary truth": it is a non-nomic generalization. And he notes also that *anybody* who has been properly socialized will have a battery of such generalizations – otherwise they could hardly carry on in society. "Would it," then, "make *scientific* sense for [the interpretative disciplines] to formulate special generalizations and so-called 'laws' that are intended to achieve abstraction? . . . Can this project be expected to produce new useful insights germane to their concrete problems? *In general* it is not in the least self-evident that this *must* be the case" (Weber, 1975: 107).

[21] No end of damage has been done with the term "law-like." Most are mere generalizations, which, even if true, can lay no claim to necessity – the critical attribute of nomicity. There are plenty of generalizations in history, but no historical "laws" exactly because agents always could have acted otherwise.

Somers is false to her assumptions since while she rejects "general laws," she nevertheless appeals to them. According to him, she *must* since "without the assertion of a necessary or probable connection, there is *no* causal account – it just happened that way" (1998: 833). But Goldstone here seems to be under the thrall of Humean causality in which true law-like sentences provide the causal connection. He says as regards the law of reflection that "positivists may state the general law, which accounts for all observations, and be content at that. Realists, however may wish to explain further what events or principles govern this result" (1998: 833). But even given a perfect observed correlation between the angle of incidence and the angle of exit, this does not "account for" the observations (even if it allows for prediction). Of course, once we have the mechanism, we can "account for" the observations. Indeed, given an understanding of the mechanism, the relation is shown to be nomic: it *had* to be what it is.

But even if we put this problem aside, Goldstone acknowledges that our Hobbesian "law" can "tell us very little about why particular national histories, e.g., turn out the way they do" (1998: 833). Thus, to explain why England surpassed Holland in the eighteenth century, "we must trace the action of this particular principle through the action of *particular historical actors in particular historical* settings" (1998: 834). Indeed. But we need no "laws" to say that their actions did not "just happen that way." We have a *causal explanation* of the particular decision of some particular actor, when we have knowledge of the particular motivations and expectations and particular conditions in terms of which the actor made choices. Roughly, if persons have reasons for their actions, since reasons are causes, actions need no covering laws. And while it may well be the case that in some particular case, the actor was motivated to seek power, there is no requirement that this "principle" is essential to the explanation, nor that the "principle" holds in every instance.

Similarly as regards Goldstone's observation that Somers assumes that "earlier institutions inevitably leave their impress on subsequent ones." This generalization, called by Goldstone "the law of historical sedimentation," like the Hobbesian "law," does not take us very far: again, we need specific social mechanisms. Thus, to explain both reproduction *and* change, one needs (as Goldstone would seem to agree) to understand the motives, expectations and conditions of action of typical groups and key actors in fourteenth-century England, France or Holland. While our narrative will no doubt contain references to the decisions of actors that were, as C. Wright Mills put it, "of major social importance," it was not only them who "made history." We cannot explain the French Revolution without reference to the acts of Louis XVI, but nor can we explain it